EDITH SÖDERGRAN

Contributions to the Study of World Literature

Benny Anderson: A Critical Study
Leonie Marx

Aksel Sandemose: Exile in Search of a Home
Randi Birn

EDITH SÖDERGRAN

Modernist Poet in Finland

GEORGE C. SCHOOLFIELD

Contributions to the Study of World Literature, Number 3

GREENWOOD PRESS
Westport, Connecticut • London, England

342465

PT 99 84.Z
SCH

Södergran (Edith)

Library of Congress Cataloging in Publication Data

Schoolfield, George C.
  Edith Södergran : modernist poet in Finland.

  (Contributions to the study of world literature,
ISSN 0738-9345 ; no. 3)
  Bibliography: p.
  Includes index.
  1. Södergran, Edith, 1892-1923.   2. Poets, Swedish—
Finland—Biography.   I. Title.   II. Series.
PT9875.S617Z83   1984   839.7'172   83-18527
ISBN 0-313-24166-X (lib. bdg.)

Library of Congress Catalog Card Number: 83-18527
ISBN: 0-313-24166-X
ISSN: 0738-9345

First published in 1984

Greenwood Press
A division of Congressional Information Service, Inc.
88 Post Road West, Westport, Connecticut 06881

Printed in the United States of America

10 9 8 7 6 5 4 3 2 1

86110097

Contents

Preface

In Finland, Edith Södergran--who wrote in Swedish--is seen as
a representative of the nation's bilingual literature quite worthy
of keeping company with the twentieth century's major innovators.
The poet Bo Carpelan has saluted her as a "precursor and portal-
figure" for the whole of Nordic modernism,[1] the critic Kai Laitinen
mentions her together with the young Ezra Pound, T. S. Eliot, Maya-
kovsky, and the Rilke of the Duino Elegies,[2] the essayist Mirjam
Tuominen detected a resemblance between Edith Södergran's "inexorable god" and Kafka's "inaccessible lord of the castle."[3] But
this "proud and violent member of the avantgarde," this "pioneer"
(in Laitinen's words), is strongly indebted to the ornamental style
variously termed Neo-Romanticism, or art nouveau, or Jugendstil,
as she is to the nineties' estheticism; and her middle collections
have elicited the not unwarranted charge that she was an "epigonic
Nietzschean."[4] The discerning poet-and-critic, Rabbe Enckell,
found in her work both a "baroque exuberance of the imagination
which recalls the pompous architecture of Czarist Russia" and "a
classical stamp."[5] P. O. Barck defined Edith Södergran (who lived
out her life beyond the crumbling edges of the Swedish-language
realm)[6] as one of the tongue's "most remarkable" figures in modern
times;[7] yet she has frequently been termed "un-Swedish."

Martin Allwood's translation has at last made her work accessible, à peu près in its totality, to an English-speaking public;[8]
the present book is meant to describe the life and works of the
poet for the same audience. The author has regarded it as his primary duty to sketch main outlines; he has not had the space to lin-
ger over the manifold problems of interpretation individual poems
contain. However, he hopes he will have made his readers aware of
the difficulties--of language and of content--which fill the work.
At first glance, Edith Södergran may seem simple, but she is not;
her apparent simplicity has led more than one translator down a

primrose path. The author is painfully aware, of course, that his discussions are scarcely exhaustive, and that many interesting pieces have been passed over. It is a mark of Edith Södergran's genius that none of her poems is insignificant.

Every attempt at Södergran-scholarship must depend on the studies of Olof Enckell and the biography by Gunnar Tideström; the present book's commentary will show the extent to which the author is in their debt. The author is also thankful to Professor Tideström for having introduced him, at Harvard, to the serious reading of Edith Södergran; and he holds the late Hans Ruin, at Lund, in grateful memory for having first taken him into the world of Finland-Swedish modernism. More practically, his thanks must go to Professor Leif Sjöberg for great patience and keen interest.

In addition, he must register his gratitude to Mrs. Rita Houde of the Yale Department of Germanic Languages and Literatures for her astute aid, and to Mr. Jay Lutz of the Yale Department of French for his skill, demonstrated in the final typing and in the making of the index. On another front, Gloria Schoolfield richly deserves praise for the forebearance she has shown toward Edith Södergran. Finally, a special debt must be mentioned, for stimulating comment and cheerful enthusiasm, to the members of a Södergran seminar, held at the Yale Graduate School during the autumn of 1977: Heidi Krueger, now of Amherst, James Parente, now of Princeton, and Ann-Marie Rasmussen, again of Yale.

All translations have been made by the author, unless otherwise noted; the intent has been to give a close rendering of the text, rather than a stylistically smooth one. Citations of single lines or portions of poems have been printed as a part of the text, in quotation marks and with virgules; whole poems are set off and indented. Swedish place-names, when they exist, have been used throughout (e.g. Helsingfors for Helsinki, Viborg for Viipuri), in the thought that Edith Södergran herself--whose contacts with Finnish-language culture were, regrettably, so tenuous--would have preferred them.

G. C. Schoolfield

Chronology

1892	April 4: Edith Södergran born in St. Petersburg.
1892	July: Family moves to Raivola in Karelia (Finland).
1902-09	Attends the "Höhere Tochterschule" (girls' division) of "Die deutsche Hauptschule zu St. Petri," St. Petersburg.
1907	October: Father dies of tuberculosis.
1907-09	Writes school-girl verse, principally in German.
1909-11	Five sojourns in Nummela Sanatorium, Nyland.
1911-12	October-January: Alt-Sanatorium, Arosa, Switzerland.
1912-13	Sanatorium Davos-Dorf, patient of Dr. Ludwig von Muralt.
1913	May-September: Residence in Raivola, brief treatments at Nummela.
1913-14	Second stay at Davos.
1914-15	Affair with Russian, name unknown ("the man from Terijoki").
1916	December: Dikter (Poems), published by Holger Schildt, Helsingfors.
1917	September: final visit to Helsingfors.
1918	January-April: Civil War in Finland, Raivola held by the Reds.

1918   December: Septemberlyran (The September Lyre), published.

1919   January-February: Debate on Septemberlyran in Helsing-
        fors' Swedish-language press.

1919   January: correspondence with Hagar Olsson begins.

1919   May: Rosenaltaret (The Rose Altar), published.

1919   Reads works of the anthroposophist, Rudolf Steiner.

1919   December: Brokiga iakttagelser (Motley Observations),
        aphorisms, published.

1920   December: Framtidens skugga (The Shadow of the Future),
        published.

1922   September-December: the journal Ultra appears.

1923   June 24: Edith Södergran dies at Raivola.

EDITH SÖDERGRAN

SÖDERGRAN

Star-catcher--
your net is glitter-full
with boom of gods
and dead flowers' rustle.
Unborn, you saw all;
sick, you healed the well.
No one begot poem-gnats as you did:
    life-living.
    blood-sucking.

Elmer Diktonius, Stenkol ('Coal,' 1927)

1.

A Life on the Edge

The family of Edith Södergran's father had lived in Närpes
parish (in Ostrobothnia, the Swedish-speaking coastal region of
western Finland) since at least the beginning of the 18th century.[1]
Its members had been peasants; Matts Mattsson Södergran (1846-1907)
was the first to leave the land, having received a "technical education" of sorts at Kristinestad and at Vasa, Ostrobothnia's main
city. His wanderlust took him first to southern Finland, then to
sea, and finally, in 1882, to St. Petersburg, where he was hired by
Alfred Nobel, in whose employ he traveled extensively; in Smolensk,
he married a Russian merchant's daughter, only to lose her to tuberculosis. Leaving Nobel for a wood-conversion firm, Södergran
removed to the village of Raivola, about twenty-five miles north-
west of St. Petersburg, on the railroad line to Viborg, the capital
of Karelia, Finland's easternmost province.

Now Matts Södergran's luck seemed to turn: he found a second
wife, Helena Lovisa Holmroos (1861-1939), the daughter of another
expatriate Finland-Swede, the ironmaster Gabriel Holmroos. Like
Södergran, Helena's father was of peasant origin (from Bjärnå in
southwest Finland) and had gone to the Russian capital in order to
put his practical skills to profitable use. Thanks to a steadiness
which Södergran lacked, however, Holmroos had acquired a considerable fortune; a prudent man, he married a girl with a background
even simpler than his own--the daughter of a cotter from the Åbo
skerries. Their sole child, Helena Lovisa, was given an education
in keeping with her father's new prosperity: she was sent to one
of St. Petersburg's most elegant girls' schools, the Annenschule
(where instruction was in German), and early developed a strong
interest in literature. When she was 23, she fell in love with a
cadet and eventually gave birth to his child, which died 18 days
later. It was probably with considerable relief that her parents

saw her wedded to Matts Södergran in June, 1890: she was pushing 30. A daughter, Edith Irene Södergran, was born on April 4, 1892; the little family lived at Raivola, in a villa Gabriel Holmroos had purchased for his daughter. Matts Södergran became the manager of a sawmill belonging to the lumber firm for which he had earlier worked; the undertaking had to be liquidated in 1895, after Södergran had once again demonstrated his lack of business sense. The next year Holmroos passed away, leaving half his fortune to his widow (with the stipulation that this portion would eventually go to Edith) and half to his daughter; but Matts Södergran wasted Helena's share directly. With the widow's consent, the will was changed, so that the interest from her portion could be put at Helena's disposal; the family was financially secure again, and, after grandmother Holmroos' death in 1902, the Södergrans lived quite handsomely on the family fortune until it disappeared in the collapse of Czarist Russia.

In 1902, Edith Södergran began to attend school in St. Petersburg: mother and daughter moved into the city for the term, while Matts Södergran stayed in Raivola; within a couple of years his health began to decline, and by May, 1906, his disease was diagnosed as tuberculosis. He was admitted to Nummela sanatorium, near Helsingfors, but was released as incurable; he spent a final summer at Raivola, dying there in October, 1907. It has been conjectured that Edith Södergran contracted her own tuberculosis from her father; she witnessed, of course, the terminal stage of his illness. Nor was this the only domestic tragedy; a foster child, "Singa," whom Helena Södergran had taken along to St. Petersburg as company for her daughter, ran away and was killed by a train as she walked along the track toward Raivola.

However, Edith Södergran's girlhood was not wholly unhappy; she found her school years pleasant enough—like her mother, she had a quick mind, and her school had an excellent teaching staff.[2] It was "Die deutsche Hauptschule zu St. Petri," which, by the way, Lou Salomé—destined to be the great and good friend of Nietzsche, Rilke, and Freud—had attended a generation earlier. No doubt it was the mother's decision that put Edith in a school where German was the language of instruction, although the Russian capital also had a Swedish school for girls. The German schools were fashionable, and Helena Södergran probably reasoned that her daughter, like herself, would have the advantage of learning a major language well. It was a decision of importance for Edith Södergran's literary development; she never wholly mastered Swedish orthography and grammar, and, in 1917, she astonished a colleague, Jarl Hemmer (1893-1944), by saying she had never read Gustaf Fröding, perhaps the greatest of Swedish lyricists.[3] Her own first verse was written in German, which, even near the end of her life, she called her "best language."[4]

Although Edith Södergran was frequently absent, she got a good education, acquiring not just German but French, Russian, and some English; and it may be worth noting that the school, officially Lutheran, provided religious instruction of a liberal sort. After

her death, her mother claimed that she had had few friends at school
(the majority of the pupils came from Baltic German or Russian
homes); nonetheless, she belonged to a coterie--its other members
being two Finns, an Armenian, and a Russian, Paula Orlovsky. Still
another girl, the passionately admired "Claudia," has never been
firmly identified: she visited the Södergrans at Raivola. Nor
were Edith Södergran's schoolgirl crushes limited to her comrades;
a sewing teacher, a French instructress, and the French master,
Henri Cottier, were all the objects of her affections.

     In the middle of what would have been her last year at the
Petri-Schule, 1908-1909, Edith Södergran came down with a bad cold;
on New Year's Day, 1909, she was diagnosed as being in the early
stages of tuberculosis. Dispatched to her father's old sanatorium,
Nummela, she began the first of her five longer stays there--a
series concluded in September, 1911. (Later, she had to return
frequently for brief treatments.) The sanatorium was new, founded
in 1903, and quite small; the journalist Gustaf Mattsson (1873-
1914), who spent the autumn of 1906 there, found that the place
was boring and, with its fresh-air treatment, cold: "Everything
is arranged so that the bugs and even one's own intelligence will
freeze to death."⁵ The reaction of Edith Södergran was more radical:
she neglected her appearance, refused to cooperate with the physi-
cians, tried to begin an affair with a junior staff-member--and was
thoroughly frightened by her disease. Yet she had a kind of linguistic profit from her sanatorium days in Finland: at Nummela,
where the staff (and most of the patients) were Finland-Swedes,
she came into a more extended contact with her mother tongue. Furthermore, she read some Swedish literature there, as a preparation
for the university entrance examination. No doubt she became
acquainted with the classics of Finland, Runeberg (1804-1877) and
Topelius (1818-1898); probably she also dipped into the verse of
living Finland-Swedish poets, Hjalmar Procopé (1868-1937), Arvid
Mörne (1876-1946) and Bertel Gripenberg (1878-1947)--the colorful
Gripenberg had a particular vogue in these years.⁶ The Swedish
Romantic Almqvist (1793-1866)--of whom her friend Elmer Diktonius
said, in 1933, that "without Almqvist there would be no Södergran"⁷
--may have crossed her horizon in the Nummela library as well; and
she could not have avoided making the acquaintance of Strindberg's
work. In addition, she improved her Finnish, a language she would
need for the university examination. It is improbable that she
read much Finnish poetry; but Jarl Hemmer reports that "only the
brilliant bohemian Eino Leino fully answered to her idea of a
poet"⁸--a remark which can be taken to mean that Leino (1878-1926),
with his slouch hat and cape, seemed particularly "poetic" to the
naive Edith.

     In the fall of 1911, Helena Södergran and her daughter set out
for the sanatoria of the Grisons. The director of Nummela, Dr.
von Bonsdorff, had some training at Davos and thought its climate
was especially salubrious: in 1910 he had sent Gustaf Mattsson
there. The ladies from Raivola spent a brief time at Arosa, then
moved on to Sanatorium Davos-Dorf. Here, inspired by an Australian
girl, Edith Södergran read Swinburne in the original, as well as

Shakespeare and Dickens; and, preparing for a trip to Italy (which the Södergrans undertook in the spring of 1913), she made her way through Dante's Inferno. As Tideström remarks, she had access to an extremely well-equipped reading room, with journals from the whole of Europe; she kept up with Finland by a subscription to Gustaf Mattsson's brilliant but short-lived Helsingfors paper, Dagens Tidning, which she and her mother liked for the sake of Mattsson's witty columns.

In Switzerland, she once again turned her affection to an inaccessible object, the sanatorium's director, Ludwig von Muralt. Dr. von Muralt had a happy hand with Edith; following his rules to the letter, she made the impression of being a "calm, distinguished, and reserved girl." When the news of Muralt's sudden death, in 1917, reached Edith Södergran, she mourned his passing in several poems. The Muralt episode demonstrates an interesting creative process: the passion takes belatedly adolescent forms (the young woman of 21 steals Muralt's gloves, to hide them under her pillow), but it also gives rise to some of her best elegiac poetry.

After the Italian trip, the mother-daughter pair spent another month at Davos and then returned to Finland for a summer at Raivola; the countryside's calm was interrupted by seven trips to Nummela for insufflation, which consisted of filling the patient's lungs with nitrogen gas. A second winter in Davos, under Muralt's care, apparently went less well than the first; by the spring of 1914 the travelers were home again; renewed treatments at Nummela were ended when she ran away. A letter to her physician, scribbled in pencil, has been preserved: "I have such a terrible, superstitious horror of Nummela. When I visited my father as he lay ill here, I felt this boundless terror, this terrible revulsion in the presence of death, a fear of this sickness, this long, conscious death."

According to the woman who was the Södergran's housekeeper in the summer of 1914, Edith told her a secret--that she had a sweetheart. The man in question, a physician, lived in the seaside resort of Terijoki; he was married, and sixteen years older than Edith Södergran. The romance lasted until the late winter of 1914-1915, when the doctor had to leave Finland for service in a military hospital. The anonymous lover, nota bene, had the same profession as the junior staffer at Nummela and Dr. von Muralt; a connection existed for Edith Södergran between illness and eroticism, and, indeed, it could not have been otherwise, considering the circumstances under which her life was spent. That Edith Södergran's health grew radically worse after the lover's departure is plainly a part of the same constellation. At the same time, she began to think seriously of collecting and publishing her poems.

Edith Södergran's existence at Raivola in these wartime years was not one of cruel isolation. The jaunt down to St. Petersburg was easily and frequently made, and the well-to-do Södergrans also undertook several trips to Helsingfors, thrice in 1915, for example, and at least once in 1916. In Finland's capital, Edith tried out her poems on Arvid Mörne, who was impressed by their quality and their resemblance to the lyrics of Almqvist, and on the university's acting professor of aesthetics and modern literature, Gunnar Castrén (1878-1959), who thought they were too much influenced by the German expressionists. She also looked up Hugo Bergroth (1866-1935), the philologist--Olof Enckell suggests that, on the occasion of an earlier Helsingfors visit of 1908, Bergroth advised Edith Södergran to abandon German verse.

By January of 1916, she was ready to take the literary plunge. A letter to the publishing house of Holger Schildt seems to have got no reply, or at least not a satisfactory one; in May, she tried again, this time directly addressing the house literary advisor, Runar Schildt (1888-1925), Holger Schildt's cousin, a novella-writer of distinction.[10] In this second letter, she says that "a critic in Helsingfors, who has recognized my talent" (probably Arvid Mörne), had advised her to approach the Schildt concern. A month later, she sent off the manuscript, with an accompanying letter altogether humble and painfully gauche in its tone: "...if you return my collection, I'd consider it an act of great friendliness on your part if you, in considerate language and using a sealed letter, would tell me (that publication is premature). I am neurotic and this step of mine entails a risk for my condition....One cannot deny that my poems have 'chic'. Some are short, to be sure, I hope that will not cause difficulties. I won't guarantee for the linguistic side of things."

There are indications that, at New Year's, 1916, she had sought a specialist's aid against a depression; and the simultaneous decision to turn to a publisher may have been a desperate gesture--seeing her work in print would somehow justify her continued existence. Runar Schildt sent the manuscript to his cousin:[11] "To be sure, she is obviously influenced by Sigbjørn Obstfelder, among others, but still I regard her (poetic) concept as completely original....For all (the poems') oddities, one gets a sense--it seems to me--of something absolutely genuine..." Holger Schildt agreed to publication if the author would eschew royalties; Edith Södergran requested only two free copies as her reward.

Dikter appeared for the Christmas market of 1916. The reviews were no worse than those accorded other debut collections. The provincial reviewers had cloaked their inability to understand the poems by making fun of them (one gave his review the title Dårdikter, which could be rendered as Lunatic Lines); the novelist and poet Ture Janson (1886-1954), writing in the major liberal paper Hufvud-stadsbladet, called these humorists to account, saying that, in Dikter, a sensitive and forthright artist's soul showed a "melancholy and bitterness" too large to be fitted into "traditional forms ...traditional cares...traditional forms of joy." The most favorable critic was Erik Grotenfelt (1891-1919): "This debut...gives cause for rejoicing. It not only introduces a new name into our poetry, it introduces a new direction which we have not seen before." The reviewers in literary journals were not prepared to go quite as far --the Runeberg scholar Ruth Hedvall (1886-1944) admired her "sharp intelligence" but found her to be a little morbid and "formless" in her free verse; a young docent at the university, Hans Ruin (1891-1980), thought her strength lay in her "original imagination," but said she was unaware that "great poetry is born of life's simple situations."[12]

Ignoring the praise, Edith Södergran took the blame to heart: on Christmas Night, 1916, she wrote a poem, "Jungfruns död," ("The Maiden's Death"), in the course of which the fragile and perceptive girl simply vanishes. The literary production of 1917 was small, and this falling-off in productivity can be attributed to several factors: the debutante's wounded vanity, a decline in her health (in April, she had begun to cough up blood), and, simply, a kind of restlessness: in March, she and her mother paid what was to be their last visit to St. Petersburg, just after the abdication of Nicholas II: she was terrified but exhilarated by what she saw in the streets. In September she made another last trip, to Helsing- fors, with the intention, as she told Professor Olaf Homén, of "mak- ing the acquaintance of literary personalities." She had recovered sufficiently from the reviews by Hedvall and Ruin to look up their authors; and the latter has left an account of her unannounced visit to him, at 9:30 on a Sunday morning: she had an autograph album with her, she constantly pressed her face into her muff, she spoke Swedish with an audible "accent," and her questions were both broad and direct: "Does life have a meaning? Is there a God? Is the soul immortal?"[13]

The highpoint of the September visit was a dinner at the fash- ionable restaurant Börs, with Grotenfelt and Hemmer. Grotenfelt left no record of the evening; Hemmer told the story twice.[14] The conversation was difficult: "she was too much the individual per- sonality, too filled with her lonely exaltation to be able to enter any sort of profitable exchange with the rest of us...." He recalled that Nietzsche was her supreme master, that she was familiar with the work of the German proto-expressionist Alfred Mombert, and that she admired the Russian futurists, particularly Severjanin--"her intellectual roots were different from ours."[15] As in her matutinal visit to Ruin, she startled her hosts with a question of enormous import: "Do you think that I shall be happy?" Hagar Olsson--shortly to be Edith's closest friend--would imply that Hemmer spread ugly hints concerning the girl's "thirst for life";[16] but Olsson's state- ments on Edith Södergran are often both possessive and hagiographic. As for Edith Södergran herself, she wrote to Hagar Olsson at the very outset of their correspondence (EB, p. 33) that the evening with Hemmer and Grotenfelt belonged "to the most beautiful memories of my life." On the other hand, she could be quite disdainful of the little literary world they represented; a poem from 1917 says: "I have nothing save my shining mantle, my red undauntedness. / My red undauntedness rides out, seeking adventures / in shabby lands."[17]

Within a few months, Edith Södergran and her mother were sub- stantially penniless: the Bolshevik Revolution had taken place. Then, in January, 1918, civil war began in Finland, and Raivola remained in the hands of the Reds until April 23, when elements of the White army captured the village. Some discussion has been devoted to the question of Edith Södergran's enthusiasm for the Revolution.[18] The evidence of her youthful German poems is clear enough: she looked forward to the fall of the Czarist regime. However, when Finland's Civil War brought the facts of the upheaval home to Raivola, her attitudes became ambiguous: there was the thrill of witnessing the creation of a new world, and at the same time the fear of what the agents of revolution might do; after all, the Södergrans were gentry, and native speakers neither of Russian nor Finnish. As for the ladies' impoverishment, she knew very well what had caused it; since the Södergran property was in Ukrainian and Russian stocks, "salvation depends upon Bolshevism's fall," she wrote to Hagar Olsson. It is foolish to enlist Södergran, posthumously, among the whole-hearted "poets of revolution"; practically, she could not belong to them, and, from an ideal point of view, her growing elitism--fed by her new-found passion for Nietzsche-- likewise disqualified her.

The Nietzschean exaltation made its first concentrated appearance in the eighteen poems dated September, 1918, from which she took the name of her next collection, Septemberlyran (The September Lyre). Adding other new verse, she copied the work into an old school notebook (no other paper was available) and sent the manuscript to Runar Schildt. In the first of her several letters on the matter (October 8, 1918), she betrayed a certain nervousness about the reception the book would receive. "I beg you, kindly omit weaker poems or those which could cause offence by their presumptuousness...." Schildt did not reply, and on October 18 she wrote again: "It is possible that the tendency in a number of the poems can cause displeasure...in such case it is best to exclude the 'worst'." Then, after the book had been accepted for publication, she asked, on November 29, if "there were any means of keeping the critics of the provincial press, and the broad public, away from the book." However, not altogether consistent in her demands, Edith Södergran was now more interested in royalties than before, and stipulated that she wished to retain the owner's rights to the new book (as well as to Dikter), "so that I perhaps could have a certain material advantage from it later....the war has placed me in economic difficulties." On the day before Christmas, 1918, Edith Södergran complained to Runar Schildt; he (or someone else) had left out several poems, as well as the dates of composition which she had wished to have included, eager to call attention to the development she had undergone: "May I be allowed to say that the book would not have appeared in this condition, in the event I had been able to participate in the final decision?"

It would have been wiser if Edith Södergran had left her regrets to the privacy of the correspondence with Schildt. Instead, she wrote an open letter, "Individual Art," to Dagens Press, which the paper printed on December 31:[19]

"This book is not intended for the public, scarcely even for the higher intellectual circles, only for those few individuals who stand closest to the boundary of the future. A circumstance has caused me not to be able to be involved in the final decision regarding the choice of the poems, and I did not read proof either. As a result, certain important poems are missing, and superfluous ones have been included. This gives a certain air of trumpery to the book, which already, in itself, stands under the sign of carelessness and is, in fact, nothing more than an intimate sketchbook. The dates have also disappeared, and poems are intermingled between which a chasm lies, as great a chasm as between my first collection and the present one. What makes many of these poems precious is that they come from an individual of a new sort ....A loftier flame streams from these poems, a mightier passion than not only (sic) from the art work of my past. I cannot help the person who fails to feel that the wild blood of the future courses through these poems...( )

I sacrifice every atom of my strength to my lofty goal, I live the life of a saint, I lose myself in the highest productions of the human spirit, I avoid all influences of a baser kind. I regard the old society as a mother cell which ought to be sustained until the individuals (sic) erect the new world. I admonish the individuals to work only for immortality (an erroneous expression), to make the highest thing possible out of themselves, to place themselves in the service of the future....I hope that I shall not be alone with that greatness which I have to bring."

This statement caused an unprecedented uproar in Finland-Swedish letters; experienced newspapermen could sense good copy here.[20] _Dagens Press_ carried a _causerie_, by a "Pale Youth," where the poems were called "thirty-one laughter-pills" and where "Tjuren" ("The Bull," a verse-attack by Edith Södergran on her critics) was parodied as "Kossan" ("Bossy"); in _Hufvudstadsbladet_, an article by "Jumbo" (Gustaf Johansson, a friend of the late Mattsson, whose lightly derisive style he tried to imitate) talked about "Nietzsche-crazed womanfolk." Indignant, the poet-and-artist Ragnar Ekelund (1892-1960) sent a letter to _Dagens Press_, praising Södergran's "ruthless honesty" but admitting that both the open letter and the introduction to the volume (see Chapter 4) betrayed an astounding naiveté; Johansson retorted with words that expressed what many readers of the open letter may have thought--that Edith Södergran had been "infected by the same intellectual disease which in the political field is called Bolshevism." His remark seemed by no means as farfetched in the Finland of 1918 as it does today.

The contribution of Ekelund had been preceded by the review which Erik Grotenfelt gave _Septemberlyran_ in _Svenska Tidningen_; it was one of Grotenfelt's last pieces of newspaper writing before he committed suicide, perhaps in remorse at the role he had played[21] in the summary execution of Red prisoners at the close of the war. Again, Grotenfelt distinguished himself by his perceptivity--he was peculiarly aware that the poetry was a spontaneous reaction to recent events: Edith Södergran herself had used the phrase, "an intimate sketchbook." Others joined Ekelund and Grotenfelt in Södergran's defence: in _Hufvudstadsbladet_, a paid public announce-

ment appeared: "openly and without hesitation, we wish to join
that band of lunatics who see in Edith Södergran's poetry an artist's
devoted striving." Among the signers were Mörne, Runar Schildt,
and Hjalmar Procopé, and the Swede Sven Lidman. The tenacious
Johansson hereupon tried to rummage up medical evidence that Edith
Södergran was indeed mentally disturbed. Asked for an expert opinion, the psychiatrist H. A. Fabritius, in an article called "Miss
Edith Södergran, Sibyl or Swindler?", cautiously stated that he
found her to be a poet with an unusual capacity for associative
thought and the owner of a special imaginative realm.

To an extent, Dagens Press made good the damage it had done
with the heavy witticisms of the "Pale Youth." On January 11, it
published a genuine review of Septemberlyran, made by a competent
and potentially sympathetic reviewer, Hagar Olsson (1893-1978).
(Extremely well-informed, Hagar Olsson would become one of Finland's
most pugnacious critics during the 1920's, and would contribute
both to the Finland-Swedish novel and the drama.) Presently, she
found that Edith Södergran had made a grave mistake with her open
letter. "Through writing of this sort, she has exposed herself on
the marketplace, to be gaped at by the mob, and thus has had to
receive the attention both of slanderers ('Jumbo') and noble
knights (Ekelund and the signers of the declaration in Hufvudstadsbladet)....Thus she has not behaved like someone filled by the
pathos of the cause—which, after all, makes some of her poems pure
and glowing—but rather like one of those cheap music-hall enter-
tainers who create advertisements for themselves. That same music-
hall urge is to be found in her poetry, together with a purity and
elevation of soul which belong to the mount of transfiguration."
With the last phrase, Hagar Olsson refers to the "high mountain
apart" (Matthew 17:1-2, Mark 9:2) where Jesus is transfigured in
the presence of Peter, James, and John; unwittingly, she presages
the reverence she would accord Edith Södergran after the latter's
death.

Edith Södergran was quick to reply to her reviewer, denying
that she had had "base motives," and putting all the blame for the
unsatisfactory aspects of Septemberlyran on the publisher. She
accompanied her letter with some unpublished poems and still another
communication for Dagens Press, which Hagar Olsson was asked to
pass along to the editors, "if it can be of great use for the cause"
(EB, p. 27). Almost half-a-century later, Hagar Olsson recalled
that she could not make heads or tails of the new public statement,
and advised Edith Södergran to send it in herself, hoping that she
would decide not to do so. Edith Södergran did not take the hint;
the "Open Letter to Critics and Champions" was published on January
29.[22] Its point of departure was the episode in Also sprach Zarathustra where the young herdsman, biting the head from a snake which
has crept into his mouth, is able to laugh about it. "With the support of Nietzsche's authority, I repeat that I am an individual of
a new kind." Rightly thinking that Edith Södergran had not rendered
her position completely clear, Hagar Olsson made a final contribution to the affair on February 8, in "Foolish Observations,"[23]
where she said that it was tasteless to imply that Edith Södergran

suffered from "some sort of individual megalomania"; instead, she had "consecrated" herself to "the role of a mere instrument and medium." In illustration of her point, Olsson quoted from Septemberlyran and from the unpublished "Where Do the Gods Dwell?" ("A ray of light fell on my poor way"), comparing their spirit to that of Angelus Silesius, the Silesian mystic of the Baroque. Hagar Olsson had just learned of Edith Södergran's physical condition; she went on: "this human being bears the earnestness of death with her...and (her) soul at least in blessed moments is as 'leer und rein' (empty and pure) as a Stradivarius waiting for the master's touch." (Edith Södergran had written to her that, in the September lyrics, she "suddenly felt with absolute certainty that a stronger hand had seized her pen.")

Edith Södergran was a possessive and a difficult friend. "I shall write love letters to you, Hagar, when I am in the mood. Now I have someone of my own, for my whole life" (EB, p. 33). In February, Hagar Olsson paid a command visit to Raivola, after an exchange which demonstrates how intense Edith Södergran was in her reactions: Hagar Olsson dared to take exception to statements in Edith's second open letter, and Edith, going from the informal "du" to the formal "Ni," issued an ultimatum, saying that she was prepared to receive her at Raivola "if you can tear yourself away for four days....If you refuse to do it, I shall break with you forever, for I am a person of irreversible decisions." Then, reverting to the informal pronoun: "I demand that you pay the price for your friendship with this trip--otherwise, I shall know how to be alone. Submit to my will, Hagar, you will come to something which is fairer than all love...." (EB, pp. 42-43).

Isolated, self-absorbed, the spoiled child, Edith Södergran refused to understand that her "sister" had a newspaper job, and that, from a medical standpoint, a stay at the Södergran villa meant the risk of tubercular infection. In addition, Edith had been offended by the comparisons with Angelus Silesius and with Sweden's Pär Lagerkvist (1891-1974); immediately upon the nervous Hagar Olsson's arrival, Edith let her know that she was not a mystic, but rather "a realist of the purest water and a heathen" (EB, p. 47). After the visit, Hagar Olsson sent her some works of Lagerkvist, and got the retort: "Why did you send me that polluted (material)? Such as he desecrate the temple of art. And so does the Star Child" (EB, p. 51). (The latter reference is to the quasi-fairy tale, "The Saga of the Star Child," in Hagar Olsson's Själarnas ansikten (The Souls' Countenances, 1917); it has a motto from Lagerkvist's Sista mänskan (The Last Human Being).) The upshot was that Edith Södergran returned the Lagerkvist items at Hagar Olsson's annoyed request, but kept Hagar's book, saying that she had cut out the fairy tale and burnt it. She had decided that her friend was, spiritually, in a bad way: "Hagar, you are a sick child. Come to my embrace as to a mother's...surrender yourself to my will, to the sun, to the life-force, to prana...." (The Sanskrit word, meaning 'life-breath,' had been borrowed from Nietzsche.)

While this battle of wills was being waged, Edith Södergran was putting together a new volume of verse, Rosenaltaret (The Rose Altar). The title was taken from a poem that had been excluded from Septemberlyran; but it may have seemed to Edith Södergran that it also resembled the name of the long prose poem by Ragnar Rudolf Eklund (1894-1946), presently Hagar Olsson's fiancé, Jordaltaret (The Earth Altar); Hagar Olsson had read aloud to Edith Södergran from Eklund's text, moving her to tears and making her flee to her room. By the end of February, Edith Södergran asked Hagar Olsson if she would edit Rosenaltaret, and a month later sent her the manuscript. The book was a tribute to their friendship: its climactic suite, "Fantastique," was "the sister-cycle," devoted entirely to Hagar and Edith's feelings for her.

Rosenaltaret appeared in the spring of 1919; and rather little attention was paid to it--the public had tired of the Södergran-sensation. Hagar Olsson decided that she could not review it for Dagens Press, because of her involvement in its genesis; Arvid Mörne discussed it there instead, placing it among "the strongest (poetry) written in Swedish during recent times." In Nya Argus, Karl Bruhn made a combined review of Själarnas ansikten and Rosenaltaret: they had in common "an almost ominously Romantic characteristic," reminiscent of Novalis and the Swedish Romantics Atterbom and Stagnelius. After considering the favorite words of both authors (among Hagar Olsson's are "great," "holy," "lonely," "deep," "soul," "star," "night," "infinity," "space," "spirit," "eternity," while Edith Södergran's, quite simply, is "god, spelled sometimes with a capital, sometimes not"), Bruhn calls the two authors "expressionists" who "measure the uttermost boundaries of woe and jubilation." Despite his fundamental aversion to his subjects, Bruhn is a pioneer in that he tries to analyze the style of the new poets, and gives them a collective name; later critics would replace "expressionist" with "modernist."[24]

Edith Södergran was already at work on another collection. In May she wrote to Hagar Olsson that she found her "latest poems... (to be) boring (sic) and with the color of action, they're almost all concerned with planets and stars"(EB, p. 74). The poems would comprise the first part, "The Planets Ascend," of her next book. As the summer wore on, Edith Södergran grew more and more uneasy. She knew that Hagar Olsson was visiting her parents in Räisälä Parish --as the crow flies, by no means a long way from Raivola. But the Karelian Isthmus teemed with soldiers; it was in June and July of 1919 that Mannerheim's plan for a Finnish intervention in the Russian Civil War was almost realized. Edith Södergran's letters are filled with proposals for getting Hagar Olsson past the sentries: "declare that you are a poet on the way to visit a poet" (EB, p. 82). At last, in August, Hagar Olsson did come, and was horrified by conditions in the Södergran household (there was simply no money), yet charmed by Raivola in the summertime; she gave a fictionalized portrait of its slovenly charms in the chapter, "Our Village," of her novel, Träsnidaren och döden (The Woodcarver and Death, 1940).[25] After Hagar Olsson's departure, the poet's letters became ever more exalted: "The whole time I have felt such an infernal electricity

within myself that it was almost impossible to endure it. As if I
lay in the very arms of Eros the whole time...Wound me, Hagar! If
I could create now, everything I've written before would be mere
chatter." She had found a title for her latest production: "At
Christmas I shall publish...Köttets mysterier (Mysteries of the
Flesh), which is the opposite to the mysteries of terror. Schildt
will gape with surprise and so will the other members of society"
(EB, p. 91-92).

Before the year was out, Edith Södergran sent her publisher a
manuscript comprising a series of aphorisms and the new set of
poems; she had thought better of the title she had mentioned to
Hagar Olsson, choosing Framtidens skugga (The Shadow of the Future)
instead. The aphorisms, unimaginatively dubbed Brokiga iakttagelser
(Manifold Observations) by Schildt's, made their appearance at
Christmas, 1919, almost unnoticed; after having sent off a reminder,
Edith Södergran got her sorely needed royalties, 500 marks, in January. Platitudinous on the whole, the pamphlet contains some material which, without question, bears directly on the situation in
which Edith Södergran found herself: "Life's three great gifts,
poverty, loneliness, and suffering, can only be given their true
and high value by the wise man", and "Ought not every great person
have a great fate all his own, beyond all the rest, a special focal
point in his life?" There is much Nietzschean admiration of "great
men," and, more telling, a revelation of a personal struggle against
despair: "Something distasteful lies in taking one's own life."[26]

When Edith Södergran told Hagar Olsson that she had burned the
Star Child episode in Själarnas ansikten, she had added the sentence,
underlined: "I do not wish to look through this gate" (EB, p. 54).
In the episode in question, the dying Star Child makes her lover,
Stig Henrik, feel that he is "face to face with that which is not."
For Edith Södergran, who had seen her father die and knew that she
was destined for an early death, such contemplation of ultimate
things was unbearable, all the more because she (unlike Hagar Olsson)
could not bring herself to believe in a life hereafter. Following
the letter of August 30 (EB, pp. 91-92), with its celebration of
Eros, there is a break in the correspondence; Olof Enckell argues
that Edith Södergran underwent a crisis in these months:[27] the manuscript sent to Schildt's in November closes with the "two most des-
pairing poems" from Edith Södergran's pen, "Materialism" ("I am a
chemical mass") and "Hamlet," with its allusion to the Hamlet passage
in Nietzsche's Die Geburt der Tragödie, "Knowledge slays action."
In November, too, Hagar Olsson sent Edith Södergran her new novel,
or long prose poem, Kvinnan och nåden (The Woman and Grace). The
narrative concerns a barren wife, "Elkana's woman," who, having
nothing else to sacrifice, offers God her "sufferings' and torments'
only precious fruit." In a "deep, primordial night," Elkana's woman
conceives, but Elkana himself dies. The widow wanders through a
war-ravaged landscape where she meets "the message bearer," who tells
her that she does not possess grace. Alone, she converses with the
child in her womb: "'But see,...I am persecuted, while the message
bearer's eyes speak of the peace of the rock (hälleberget), and while
his mouth bears witness to the strange sweetness of grace.'"[28] At

last, "feeling the surety of the rock beneath her uncertain foot, and with the most incorruptible peace in her heart,"[29] Elkana's woman dies in childbirth. In the epilogue, a "poor woman" is given a signal in a dream by a "tender angel"; she hastens to Elkana's hut, to find the dead mother "smiling blissfully" and beside her a newborn child. This legend, with its clearly Christian overtones, swept Edith Södergran off her feet: "I cannot tell you what your book means to me. There is such an aroma within me of hyacinths, lilies of the valley, and young birch leaves...Even terror is unimportant before the triumph of this holy greatness...I worship you now. To call you sister would be impudent" (EB, p. 95). Sometime early in 1920, she wrote the poems which comprise a new ending of Framtidens skugga; the first of these is called "The Hyacinth": "I am unbroken. A hyacinth cannot die."

Yet Hagar Olsson had not been very clear about the nature of grace, and how one gets it: "At times, I have such lovely dreams at night, like symbolic visions of another world. Oh, if you would only tell me about grace!" (EB, p. 104). Also, Edith Södergran wanted to cling to a natural process of death and revivification, as in the case of the hyacinth's annual bloom. "I realize that I have done mysticism an injustice. But I do not want that which is not but that which is...I wish a more boundless life, that which only mysticism can give, but--in that case--it shall be that which actually exists...I demand that nature shall answer my thoughts... Goethe as a mystic entrances me now." Goethe was "healthy," "your mysticism has the fault that it is sick" (EB, pp. 101-102). Simultaneously, Edith Södergran had acquired a spiritual advisor who could help, she believed, with these queries and demands of hers; his name--Rudolf Steiner (1861-1925), the anthroposophist--first appears in the letter where Edith Södergran celebrates Kvinnan och nåden. His works had been given to Edith by Dagmar von Schantz, a former teacher living in retirement at Raivola. Gunnar Tideström has made the wise observation that, although Edith Södergran devoured some of Steiner's very numerous works, such as Die Geheimwissenschaft im Umriss (Occult Science--An Outline), as well as the quite indigestible mystery plays, she was less interested in Steiner's "involved theories" than in one of his primary insights, "the experience of the divine nature of reality."[30] She had always possessed a sense of unity with nature, and now she learned that the objects of nature would reveal their spiritual meanings to the Steinerian adept. At the same time, the primer, Wie erlangt man Erkenntnis höherer Welten (Knowledge of the Higher World: How it is Achieved) instructed her that the pupil must try to have "an absolutely healthy spiritual life," to be obtained by achieving mastery over one's self --a course of self-discipline particularly difficult for Edith Södergran, with her associative mind and her quick (and frequently illogical) reactions to persons and events.

The misfortune of the next years is that so much of Edith Södergran's remaining strength went into the study of Steiner, and into efforts to persuade Hagar Olsson to embrace Steiner's teachings. "As I understand (it), you are a mystic who has only a part of the occult sense developed....But occultists such as Goethe and Christ

are real men of science, initiated into the fullest meaning, who
know everything and do not suspect or guess. You need only to come
into the hands of an initiate, and, with your mature, great occult
gifts, you'll soon be able to achieve everything" (EB, p. 107).
Something sadly comical lies in this epistolary lecturing; but it
is less amusing to discover with what contempt Edith Södergran now
views her work: "Since I became acquainted with Steiner, I have
done nothing save study him. Have put everything else aside,
regarding it as a waste of time" (EB, p. 136).

        It was not just the passion for Steiner which had driven Edith
Södergran away from her poetic calling. She devised plan after plan
to get money, by reviewing for Dagens Press, by translations, by
becoming Raivola's village photographer and making portraits of
"soldiers and their lady friends." One of the most heartrending
passages in the letters has to do with her efforts to sell a bottle
of perfume and a piece of lace, relics of happier days (EB, p. 119).
The situation was temporarily saved by the Norwegian author Barbro
Ring, who proposed to Schildt's that half the fee for a Swedish
translation of one of her books should be given to an "ill or aged
writer": the 1,000 marks were sent to Edith Södergran.

        All through the summer of 1920, Edith Södergran waited for a
third visit from the "enfant adoré," trying hard not to complain or
threaten, for such behavior would not become a pupil of Steiner:
"If I were the way I was before, I'd say I was terribly insulted by
your not wanting to see me, but I shan't say that, I have become a
different person" (EB, p. 143). (But she could not control her
dreams, which have a strongly erotic quality: "I dreamt tonight
that I drank the milk of a great black mare, and a black bear came
and sniffed in my lap" (EB, p. 142) and "I dreamt one night I kissed
you on the neck, we walked a perilous way together" (EB, p. 145).)
After a third, brief visit to Edith, Hagar Olsson in fact had the
chance to go to Steiner's Swiss headquarters, Dornach, together with
her dentist, an elderly Steiner enthusiast; still something of an
adolescent, Edith Södergran wanted to know what Hagar thought of the
second Mrs. Steiner: "Is Maria his equal, is the marriage inwardly
motivated?" (EB, p. 150). The reviews accorded Framtidens skugga,
which appeared at the end of November, 1920, meant nothing to Edith
now; they were generally cold, even those by the hitherto friendly
Arvid Mörne and the intelligent Agnes Langenskiöld. Once again,
Schildt's forgot to send the author's fee, until Runar Schildt's
elbow had been jogged by both Hagar Olsson and the poet herself.

        Next, the enthusiasm for Steiner seemed to cool; on November 9,
1920, Edith said that she suffered "terribly from the contrast
between Christ and Steiner...Steiner's explanation of the Gospels
is splendid and correct. But grace is found only in the Gospels.
I have no words for how I love Christ" (EB, p. 152). But by January
Steiner's stock had risen again: she felt she had been "as though
magnetized" (EB, p. 156) by a picture of him Miss von Schantz had
given her, and, in March, she said that: "Now my love for Steiner
begins--my gratitude. He is innocent and wise as the trees and
Råttikus" (EB, p. 158). (Råttikus was one of the Södergrans' cats;

another, Totti, had been shot the year before, probably--or so Edith Södergran thought--by their Russian neighbors, the Galkins, who owned the general store.) Life grew steadily emptier; Hagar Olsson spent the summer at Räisälä again, but, hampered by illness and an operation, she paid Raivola only the hastiest of visits. The economic situation of the Södergrans went from bad to worse; they had rented out the villa to the local defence corps, and lived in a small and drafty summer house. Still, Edith found the strength to worry about the refugees who had come across the Gulf of Finland, from Kronstadt, where the sailors had mutinied against the Soviet regime. It was a part of her Steinerian and Christian duty: "If I don't do something, I act against Christ" (EB, p. 164). Yet in the midst of all this, she yearned for the old, Nietzschean days. After reading Second Corinthians, she announced that "truth is found only in the New Testament and nowhere else in the world," only to follow this claim by a sigh: "I am quite broken by forcing myself to Christianity, (I am) hungry as a wolf for Dionysus" (EB, p. 166). More pathetically, she wrote in October: "Have had violent Dionysian attacks with the need of physically throwing myself into the air and dancing, dancing...May one dance with Christ, or is the dance the devil's sole property?" (EB, p. 172).

Suddenly, ideas about literature could not be repressed any longer. Edith Södergran imagined that she had good contacts with German publishers: the contacts consisted of one Herr Bogs, an acquaintance from Davos, who demonstrated his good will by sending the Södergrans small sums of money now and then; a manufacturer, Bogs had promised to serve as intermediary between the poet and the Rowohlt Verlag. Edith Södergran decided to make two translations into German, the one of Hagar Olsson's Kvinnan och nåden, the other of contemporary Finland-Swedish poetry, of which she meant to put together an anthology. The work on both projects fascinated her-- it was, after all, a kind of selfless literary creation and thus permissible; but she had great difficulties with the formal aspects of the poetry: "When it's a question of rhymed material, I'm really an idiot," (EB, p. 175). To make a long and painful story short: a preliminary manuscript of the anthology was sent to Germany in the summer or early fall of 1922; but Rowohlt replied that the times were unfavorable to young German poets, let alone Finland-Swedish ones. A pathetic interlude followed: Hagar Olsson had persuaded the Authors' Union to make a second gift of 5,000 marks to the Södergrans, and Edith wished to use this sum, which she needed for her own survival, as a subvention for the anthology. Practical-minded and humane, Bogs refused to submit the offer to Rowohlt; Edith Södergran then wrote directly to the publisher, but received no answer. Neither Hagar Olsson's tale (with which Edith Södergran took infinite pains) nor the anthology was ever printed; the latter manuscript was burned by Edith Södergran in the winter of 1922-23. Elmer Diktonius (1896-1961), whose work had been included, wrote to Helena Södergran, inquiring about the volume's fate, and got the reply: "She kissed the (notebooks) and placed them in the fire. She sacrificed them to God. 'I ought to have depended on Him and not on it (the anthology).' A year of her short life, her final strength."[31]

In January, 1922, Edith Södergran left Raivola for the last time, to meet Hagar Olsson at Viborg. The trip was a disaster; Edith Södergran wanted Hagar Olsson to share a room with her, and, for obvious reasons, her friend refused. A mild estrangement set in--Hagar Olsson had never seen Edith Södergran outside "her own kingdom" before, and the poet made a bizarre impression. Afterwards, Hagar Olsson was struck by pangs of conscience; she sent a new friend of hers, the above-mentioned Diktonius, as her emissary to Raivola. Diktonius had been the youthful violin teacher of Otto Wille Kuusinen, subsequently the intellectual leader of the Reds in the Civil War (in which Diktonius did not participate); after the conflict, and a spell as a draftee, he had gone to Paris and London to study music. Late in December, 1921, he returned to Finland, and the next month met Hagar Olsson, who was captivated by his "adventurous and continental air,"[32] and his book Min dikt (My Poem), which had just been published by a tiny Communist house in Stockholm. She gave it a sensational review in the rather conservative Nya Argus: "In Finland, we have no one save Edith Södergran herself with whom we could compare Elmer Diktonius....their imagination has an unmistakable sibling relationship."[33]   In March, Diktonius stayed two days with the Södergrans; he corresponded with Edith until her death, and with her mother thereafter. Edith Södergran was attracted by Diktonius' expansiveness, although she felt herself to be "an old lady" in comparison with him; she thought that the sixteen poems by Diktonius which she had taken into the manuscript of her "beloved madness" (the anthology) were too few. As for Diktonius, he described Edith Södergran in the first of his several tributes to her--the only one she lived to see: "In a little hovel beside a wooden Russian church in the Karelian borderland there lives a young woman. With a little, redcheeked lady who is her mother, and a black dog who is her friend."[34]

Hagar Olsson spent her vacation at Terijoki in 1922; on the way home to Helsingfors, she looked in at Raivola, arriving and leaving the same day. It was the friends' last meeting, and, according to Hagar Olsson, Edith Södergran's parting words to her were: "'You will still find Christ'" (EB, p. 195). However brief her stay (and she had been in the immediate vicinity for some time), Hagar Olsson had some encouraging words for Edith: she was to be the tutelary spirit of the "modernist" journal, Ultra,[35] a bilingual (Swedish and Finnish) undertaking meant to announce the message of "the new literature" in the North. Among the editors was Hagar Olsson; Diktonius made some of the most important contributions to the magazine and-- if the broad hints of Hagar Olsson are credible--obtained money for the project from his radical friends. The journal appeared only seven times, from September to December, 1922; in a sense, the funds from the left were misspent, if they existed at all--Ultra contained no political material, and its "literary and critical radicalism" seems very tame.

Hagar Olsson surmised, in retrospect, that Edith Södergran's failure to provide a contribution to the first issue stemmed from her concern about the political orientation of Diktonius. However, Södergran did appear in the second number, with a translation of

Severjanin's poem "Overture," to be followed in the third issue by
a new poem of her own, "My Childhood's Trees," and, in the fourth,
by three more ("The Gypsy Woman," "Home-coming," and "The Moon"),
together with Diktonius' accolade and a poem, "Edith Södergran," by
another emerging modernist, Gunnar Björling (1887-1960). Issue five
continued her aperçu on Severjanin, celebrating his "frivolity"
("such superior charm can only come from Russia, which has dancers
like Pavlova and singers like Chaliapin"[36]) and a translation of
verses by the French poetaster, Edmond Fleg; the final issue contained still another Severjanin translation, "Lake Ballad," and the
original poem, "November Morning," together with some new aphorisms
about nature. The demise of Ultra was no doubt a disappointment to
Edith Södergran ("Take as much of my work in Ultra as you possibly
can, so that I can exist this winter" (EB, p. 210)), but she had at
least been restored, briefly, to literary creation.

It would be pleasant to think that a great serenity came over
Edith Södergran in the last months of her life; having become a
devout Christian herself, Helena Södergran later dwelt on Edith's
final turn to the New Testament, and her wish to believe in reincar-
nation (which could have been supported by her studies in Steiner).
However, signs of hopelessness and of fear also appeared. Before
Christmas, 1922, she wrote to Hagar Olsson: "We were so young once,
we two, when we met four years ago...Now a great sobering has taken
place...Nothing shines, nothing glistens any more" (EB, p. 217).
She suspected that Hagar Olsson and her mother were planning to put
her in a sanatorium ("I already have too much to bear, and I'll
oppose (the plans) with all my strength" (EB, p. 221)), and she
thought that a proposed visit of Hagar Olsson, in March 1923, was
part of the plot; at the same time, she prepared with pathetic eager-
ness for Hagar's visit: "I have curled my hair and combed and
brushed Martti (the dog) almost every day, and Mother has made cook-
ies, and we have listened to every sound at train-time" (EB, p. 220).

Hagar Olsson left Finland in March, 1923, and was on the Riviera
when she got a letter from Helena Södergran with the news of Edith's
passing. In her own last communication to her friend abroad, Edith
Södergran had chatted as usual, recalling her own Swiss days, asking
Hagar Olsson to send her mother a postcard of Notre Dame ("she has
always dreamed of seeing it" (EB, p. 225)), telling about the illness
of Martti, and adding that her own health was better, but that she
was "so anemic that I have no menstruation." According to her
mother's letter to Hagar Olsson, the immediate cause of death was
heart failure; in the last weeks, she had suffered from sleepless-
ness, shortness of breath, extreme weakness, and neuralgia; "In her
torments, she wished that God would take her away" (EB, p. 226).
Just before she died, she wrote some lines to Hagar Olsson on the
inside of a notebook cover: "Have you forgotten me Hagar aren't we
bound together in life and death Out of my (heart) there ascends a
spring of reverence, in my moment of purity I call upon you Lord
(for) my dearest child in the loveliest of the pure moments I remember Hagar" (EB, p. 228). She was buried in the yard of the Russian
church.

Helena Södergran told Hagar Olsson, as she did Diktonius, that Edith had tried to destroy all her old papers: "'I don't want to leave anything for the corpse-worms,' she was accustomed to say" (EB, p. 227). Late in the summer of 1923, Runar Schildt suggested to his publisher-cousin that it might be a good idea to issue a "little, chosen selection" of the hitherto unpublished work of Edith Södergran; he recalled that they still had a large notebook, which she had submitted during the summer of 1916, with a "good many unpublished things which I excluded after an all too hasty examination.... A lyric expert ought to go through them..." Elmer Diktonius was entrusted with the task. When the book appeared in 1925, it was given the title of the penultimate poem of Edith Södergran, Landet som icke är (The Land Which Is Not), and included not only earlier work, but the poetry from Ultra and the deathbed verse.

In the 1930's, the Finland-Swedish Authors' Union decided to erect a monument on Edith Södergran's grave; the occasion was to be the tenth anniversary of her death. The text on the stone was from Edith Södergran's last poem, "Ankomst till Hades" ("Arrival in Hades"); Diktonius (as he reported) read "my old poem in her memory"[37] and, among others, Helena Södergran spoke, "a feeble, half-blind old woman," but "there was no lament in the words she cast out in bursts...it reminded one of scenes in some classic tragedy.". In the later 1930's, the water-side resort of Kuokkala, near Raivola, became a favorite vacation place of Finland-Swedish and Swedish poets, among them Rabbe Enckell, Diktonius, Gunnar Ekelöf, Johannes Edfelt, and Erik Lindegren; a pilgrimage to Raivola was obligatory, and the essays of Ekelöf and Edfelt bear witness to the magic the place had.[38]

One of the summer guests at Kuokkala was the récitatrice Ragna Ljungdell; she visited Helena Södergran again on the eve of the Winter War, and found her worried by the threat of a Russian invasion.[39] Helena died, as mentioned above, during the evacuation. When the Finnish army returned during the "Continuation War" of 1941-44, Sven Grönvall, one of the former habitués of Kuokkala, reported to Diktonius on what he found: "The church is gone, not a trace of it. Our (troops) set fire to it during the Winter War. Where it stood there is a large garage now....The gravestone no longer exists. Quite disappeared. Probably the Russians carried it away somewhere ....The Södergran garden is partly a horse-pasture, and partly a luxuriant thicket of blooming roses and bushes. Most of the big trees are burned or damaged. The house went up in flames at the same time as the church...."[40]

Much later, in 1960, the Soviet government gave the Finland-Swedish Authors' Union permission to erect a new monument. Raivola was now called Rodzino and had a completely Russian population; the stone was erected in a new Culture Park. Tito Colliander, who had visited the old grave, observed that it had lain several hundred yards from the new site. The theme of the ceremony was, according to accounts, less Södergran than Finnish-Soviet friendship.[41] Some thirteen years later, on the fiftieth anniversary of Edith Södergran's death, another ceremony was held in the Culture Park, this

time with somewhat more attention to literature. The principal
speaker from Finland was the poet and native of Ostrobothnia, Lars
Huldén. At the conclusion, her poems were read in four tongues,
Swedish, Finnish, Russian, and French, but not in German, the language in which she had begun her poetic career.[42]

2.

The Oilcloth Notebook:
Adolescent Poetry

The oilcloth notebook in which Södergran set down her poems
between January 29, 1907, and the summer of 1909, is very likely
only a part of her youthful work. Gunnar Tideström has guessed that
a few of the poems in Dikter were from Davos; the remainder of the
verse written between 1909 and, probably, the summer of 1914 (when
the affair with the man from Terijoki began) is lost, no doubt consumed in the auto-da-fé of the last years. Just how the notebook
survived, no one knows; Helena Södergran told a Finnish journalist
about it in the 1930's, and took it with her in the evacuation of
1939; it passed into the care of Elmer Diktonius and then, in 1957,
to the archives of the Finland-Swedish Literary Society, to be
edited, at last, by Olof Enckell in 1961.[1]

The number of poems in the notebook has been set by Tideström
at 225 and Enckell at 238--the discrepancy arises because Södergran
could make several stabs at the same theme, and because several of
the "poems" are in fact suites. More important than the number of
poems is the circumstance of the notebook's being a kind of diary,
in which a good many items are dated (according to the Old Style
calendar used in her school). It was not intended for publication;
her employment of Gothic script for the German poems, the frequent
use of pencil, and numerous references to quite obscure school events
and personalities--all these factors served to make the editor's
task more difficult.

An unusual aspect of the notebook is its polylingualism; there
is one Russian poem, five are in French, twenty-six in Swedish, the
rest in German. The first Swedish poem is from January, 1908 (ESD,
p. 108), and is altogether different in style from the German verse
in its vicinity; called "Sommarminnen" ("Summer Memories"), it is a
catalogue of twenty-three "summer things," a few with adjectives

attached, and can be dismissed as an attempt to show off a vocabulary of Swedish nouns—or, more significantly, as a first example
of the catalogue technique used so frequently in Dikter. She does
not write another poem in her home language until late March (a tribute, with many corrections, to the charms of Cottier), then a Heinesque poem a few days later, and, finally, a depiction of Midsummer
Day at Raivola (ESD, p. 131); the German verse ends abruptly on September 22, 1908, with a poem that speaks for itself (ESD, pp. 141-
142): "I do not know to whom I bring my songs, / I do not know whose
language I shall write." The next poem is in French, about Cottier
again; but Swedish holds the field from then on. Gunnar Tideström
calls No. 233 the first patently "Södergranian" poem (ESD, p. 152):[2]
"Happiness is a butterfly / Which flutters low over the field, / But
care is a bird / With great, strong, black wings, / They bear one
high above life, / Which flows along below in sunlight and greenness. / The bird of care flies high / To a place where the angels of
pain keep watch / Over the couch of death." His estimate is correct:
the juxtaposition of opposites, the division of the poem's realms
between "low" and "high," between "happiness" and "pain," will be
met again. It could also be noted that Edith Södergran—who,
schooled in Heine, rhymed easily in German—abandons rhyme here, as
she does in the majority of her youthful Swedish poems. Indeed, even
when Södergran sets out to write a rhymed poem in Swedish (as in No.
228 (ESD, p. 147): "My darling dwells in a dark lane there, / His
windows turned to the market square"), she abandons the uncomfortable
effort after two strophes. The poem, again addressed to Cottier, is
one of the few Swedish items with a city-setting. Swedish was the
language of nature and of Raivola, "our world" (ESD, pp. 148-149):
"Now our river lies under the ice / And the pine forest high up on
the edge / Smells as strong and as fresh / And as pure as in childhood's time," while German belongs primarily to St. Petersburg
(although Södergran, following the great German Romantic tradition,
of course, wrote some nature poetry in her school language as well).

The German poems are imitations of the style she had learned at
school (Heine) or from popular anthologies of "contemporary" verse,
such as Hans Benzmann's Moderne deutsche Lyrik (first published in
1903) and Hans Bethge's Deutsche Lyrik seit Liliencron (1905).
Appropriately, Heine is the only poet she names in the notebook, in
the poem "Geister" ("Spirits," ESD, pp. 102-103), where his spirit
appears to her on a warm spring night; and "Heinesque" verses comprise the majority of entries in the notebook: they have lines with
three or four feet, four lines to a strophe, one and three unrhymed,
two and four rhymed. As in Heine, the tone hovers between the sentimental, the satirical, and the conversational, a mixture appropri-
ate for the expression of schoolgirl crushes and aversions. It is
no wonder that almost all the verse devoted to Henri Cottier (some
fifty poems) follows the "Heinesque" style.

Evidently Cottier was a skillful and demanding teacher, not
unaware of the effect he had on his charges, who admired his elegance
and his good looks, but hunted eagerly for weaknesses in him. His
German was very bad, and Edith Södergran did not hesitate to record
the fact (ESD, pp. 9-10): "Yet sometimes you're so laughable—— / That

causes me awful woe; / I feel that my heart is blushing, / And my cheeks are bathed in snow." Poem No. 131, where she closely observes Cottier's insults to (and flirtation with) another pupil, is a particularly deft application of the Heinesque manner, with its intentional vulgarity (the nanny goat), its modish loan-word ("capricious"), and its cruel insights (ESD, p. 92): "He says that she's as capricious / As a nanny goat can be, / And, caught up in emotion, / He smiles so disgustingly."

Side by side with the poems to Cottier, there is a large semi-erotic group, expressions of affection for girls in her school. The poems to Claudia employ Heine's grammatical simplicity to express complex emotions (ESD, p. 42): "Her eyes come from a fairytale, / She's soft and cool and fair; / And she's the husband, I'm the wife, / We are a happy pair," and verse from later in the summer of 1907 may be taken as a considerably less naive statement of emotional upset. The glances of Paula's remarkable eyes make her turn cold, paralyzing her (no. 60); and, in No. 83, she has grown still more unsure of herself (ESD, p. 61): "And there was a painful quivering round your mouth, / And your hot eyes ran lightly over me ... / And since that day I have been well no more, / My glances must avoid you, anxiously." In order to have a more complete notion, however, of Edith Södergran's emotional confusion during this difficult summer (when a dying man lay in the "sunny house" at Raivola), it should be remembered that she had just written the longest, most passionate, and least ironic of her poems on Cottier, the opening of "Jugendträume" ("Youthful Dreams," ESD, pp. 53-59). Also, the observer must think of her later celebration of a general "Eros" as a sustaining life-source.

Edith Södergran's self-portraits take three forms at this time-- in poems about the illness or death of a young girl, in poems about the girl who becomes a princess in a fairy-tale world, and in poems where the girl becomes aware of her identity as a poet. A gruesome entry from January, 1908 (ESD, pp. 105-106) tells of a "beautiful maiden" who suffers from "incurable lethargy." Two students stand watch by her during a "gray springtime night", but the one leaves, unable to endure her "cold beauty"; when he returns, he finds his comrade "cold and dead," while the maiden sleeps on, a combination of la belle dame sans merci and Snow White in her glass coffin. A certain Frau Petrow lies on her bier, "white flowers in her black hair," while her husband seems "withered and old" at her side (ESD, p. 36); in "Dekadenz" ("Decadence," ESD, p. 43) the speaker of the poem imagines she is freezing in a field of snow as the moon trembles above her; in the untitled No. 175, a girl lies beneath the sea, entangled in algae, and is embraced by her beloved "at the midnight hour" (ESD, pp. 115-116); in the particularly macabre "Obduktion" ("Autopsy," ESD, pp. 124-125), the girl is dissected: "My lungs will be as black / As earth that's soaked with blood."

The girl becomes less moribund, and a princess, in such poems as "Märchenschloss," ("Fairytale Castle," ESD, pp. 24-25) where the mistress is a kind of Diana, with "cool" eyes and a "mocking smile," who rides, "her head held high," through the countryside. She herself is healthy--or at least her teeth are white, "shimmering and sound"--but black cats crouch on the walls of her manor, and the flowers in its garden have no aroma. In No. 87, the castle's mistress appears to have rejected a lover; night dwells in his heart, while she stands in the sunlight, "her head held high," having robbed him of happiness (ESD, pp. 62-63). A suite tells about a lover who wants to save an ailing queen with a kiss, or some more drastic means (ESD, p. 79)--"A thousand black and basely filthy thoughts, / Which can but desecrate her loveliness," but she recovers without his help; he is forced to leave, while she remains "flattered, insulted, and alone." Her ineffectual husband, who lurks in the background of the suite, gets his comeuppance in No. 185, "Im Schloss" ("In the Castle"), where she describes him (ESD, p. 122): "His ears are like a jug's, his legs are thin: / The people's slave, he's cashed his plumpness in." Like the dead or dying girl, the princess and the queen are a dangerous sort, all femmes fatales.

In December, 1907, the diary was asked why its author felt so sad (ESD, p. 89); after all, she possessed bliss itself: "The sweet and secret shudder which only a god bestows." The god was not Eros, as Enckell realized, but an even higher power, the "god of poetry" (ESD, p. 90), "The god of song, sweet and fair," (ESD, p. 99), who could make her forget the pangs of schoolgirl love and, even more significantly, the fear of death. By February, she has decided that the poet falls ill in the city, and can write "healthy poetry" only at home, in Raivola. Nonetheless, her "sick poet's heart" will suffer everywhere (ESD, p. 115); like Goethe's Tasso (she may well have read the play in school), she has been blessed with the ability to sing about her pain. As well, she has been given the marvelous gift of immortality itself. At the outset of the series of poems on poetry (ESD, p. 86) she placed the sententious quatrain: "And deep into the womb of time / Falls all for which we strive, / And, going into eternity, / Only our songs survive."

Bookishness and self-absorption are the hallmarks of much of Södergran's German verse; but the adolescent was also quite aware of the world in which she lived, St. Petersburg in the aftermath of the Great Strike of 1905. In the early summer of 1907 (following a recommendation by Cottier?), Edith Södergran devoured Les Misérables, and her imagination was captured by the radical students who went to the Paris barricades in the July Revolution (Part II, Book IV, Chapter I), and in particular by the androgynous figure of their leader, Enjolras. The result was a fragmentary address to him (ESD, p. 33), the "fair priest of the revolution," with "a pure and womanly face" and a "manly form." The fragment and its pendant (called "Barricades") lead again into the emotional labyrinth of the summer of 1907; in the first, the leader has a face that is "tender as a woman's, dreamingly fine and frail" (ESD, p. 35) and in the second, the revolutionaries, with their leader, await the attack (ESD, p. 36): "I love you, my commander, young and fair, / And I would gladly perish for your cause ..." At the same time, poems of flight appear; the person addressed in No. 44 rows across a lake, sweat runs from his (or her) forehead, "We journey into an unknown land" (ESD, p. 33). At the end of "Jugendträume" ("Youthful Dreams," ESD,

pp. 53-59), images of perilous escape return; the speaker would risk
her (or his) life for the beloved (ESD, p. 58): "Through autumn
tempests I have borne you true, / And I could risk my life itself
for you." The dreams were directed at their outset to the distinctly
masculine Cottier, "the hero of my poetry"; but a break occurs in
the middle of the cycle, after Section II: the admired figure
becomes, gradually, a kind of Enjolras, the fleeing androgyne, and
then patently feminine (ESD, p. 59):[4] "And though blood trickled
from your little feet, / Your laugh rang silver-bright and bravely
sweet." The laughter may recall the concluding lines, "Your silver
laugh resounds / Over the rocks to me," of "Im Reiche meiner Träume"
("In the Empire of My Dreams," ESD, pp. 72-73), about imagined love
beside a wild sea, a poem which Enckell has connected with the
Claudia-infatuation.

Just before "Youthful Dreams," using an orthography much clearer
than the pencilled scribble which makes the decipherment of "Enjolras" and the conclusion of the suite difficult, Edith Södergran had
addressed an unambiguously feminine allegorical figure. "Die
Zukunft" ("The Future," ESD, pp. 50-51) of July, 1907, begins: "The
future comes in rosy morning-light-- / It is a woman, young and bold
and fair ..." She strides through a "blood-drenched land" where
"thousands ask her for bread and for advice"; the victory will be
hers since she stands at the side of youth, and she neither trembles
nor "thinks of the past." Evidently, the apostle-to-be of Nietzsche
was ready to accept, and approve, the sacrifices, and even the injus-
tices, which revolution would entail. She is unsparing toward the
Czarist regime, saying in No. 12 (ESD, p. 15) that the throne still
stands, but "shakes and trembles," and, after a somewhat bewildering
beginning of No. 22 (where the Neva River hears the laments that
rise from the Peter-and-Paul Fortress), she gives the poem's second
half over to a caricature of a terrified Nicholas II in the Winter
Palace, a tyrant who cannot sleep (ESD, pp. 21-22): "Next day, he
puts his royal name / To death-decrees in reams, / But how his folk
will hang him is / The stuff of next night's dreams." The Czar's
Black Hundred--the orthodox priesthood--defends the regime's inter-
ests in an alliance with "alcohol and policemen" (ESD, p. 97); presumably, it is the Czar himself, speaking in the plural of majesty,
who builds houses for "gendarmes, / for detectives and for soldiers"
(ESD, p. 116). It must be added that, occasionally, not just hatred
for the Russian regime but a great distaste for Russians in general
can be detected--"the impudent Russians" invade Raivola, bringing
filth, bad odors, and even their priests with them (ESD, pp. 129-
130).

The attitude of the girl toward the Russian capital is somewhat
more complex. She was captivated by the river and the gardens ("I
love the greenish Neva", ESD, p. 62), but the city could also be
frightening (as in No. 109, where a creeping fog blankets terror),
or decaying, especially if contrasted to her home at Raivola (ESD,
p. 140): "The odor of decay here smothers me, / The narrow walls
set limits to my gaze, / My thoughts go backward to my homeland's
days ..." Of course, the terror-ridden and fog-shrouded city was
popular at the time (for example, James Thomson's and Conan Doyle's

London), as was the moribund city (Rodenbach's Bruges, d'Annunzio's
Venice, Meyrink's Prague)[5]; here Edith Södergran simultaneously followed a general literary mode, and dropped specific political hints.
Also, her equation of St. Petersburg with Cottier should not be forgotten. In a Swedish poem (No. 232), written in January, 1909, just
before the departure for Nummela, she confessed that, formerly, nour-
ishing "sickly thoughts," she felt herself caressed by the air in
St. Petersburg's dirty streets; this sensation arose, she says mys-
teriously, at a time when she thought she had found a "leading star
of the future." Whether the phrase has to do with Cottier, or with
her revolutionary dreams, it is impossible to say; the poem can
surely be taken, though, as a farewell to the city and to a period
in her life (ESD, p. 151).

Yet the more polished German poems of Södergran deal mainly
with sujets belonging to Raivola, not the capital. The poetic landscape has traits borrowed from the Jugendstil: against a stylized
forest background, one sees quiet (or even stagnant) waters, bor-
dered by or filled with somnolent reeds or water lilies. A skiff
floats on the water's surface; in it, the dreamy poet sits, vaguely
melancholy or permeated with a sense of unspecific piety (ESD,
p. 118):

> I lie in the skiff, gently rocked by the currents;
> Across the water to me, the wind blows
> The distant bells of the cattle at pasture,
> And all is quiet, and cool repose.
>
> Behind the water, the far forests tower,
> Darkling and lofty; a shudder of air
> Comes out of the woods to the stream and the meadows,
> And rests on my heart, like a pious prayer.
>
> Slumbering silently, the waterlilies
> Shine in their whiteness against the dark deep,
> And vapors of dampness emerge from the water,
> And all is dreaming and resting and sleep.

The somnolence can be disturbed at times, briefly by the wind from
the woods or more violently and lastingly by the autumn storms; but
the emphasis lies on a sad stillness--on the last roses of summer,
as it were, on the anticipation of beauty's death in its supreme
moment (ESD, pp. 135-136)[7]: "The flowers now are subject to pain's
sway, / They sense the advent of a fair and mighty time, / And sense
their own and terrifying death / Which comes, when autumn gales sweep
them away." Gunnar Tideström makes the argument that one of these
poems, "The night is dark and the night is warm,"[8] stands so close
to an item in the Bethge anthology, by the now forgotten Margareta
Bruns, that "a direct influence" could be assumed. Comparing Bruns
and the work of the fifteen-year-old Edith Södergran, we are tempted
to say that the latter comes off the better, since she avoids the
cloying sentimentality of Bruns' conclusion. And when she is less
dependent upon a source, she deftly uses the elements of the borrowed
style for creating a poetic Raivola--a southernized and "decadent"

Raivola, to be sure (ESD, p. 108): "Upon the moor, wild orchids
are abloom, / Where trembling feet within the green grow mired; /
The flower partakes of its poison breath until / It's dizzy with
drink and satiate and tired. // And when that flower comes into my
thoughts, / The moor, with awful dread, before me lies, / And to my
sight the forest and the stream, / The village, the garden, and the
house arise." The scenery is of home--the Raivola River leading
down to Lake Onkamo (the result of the river's being dammed), the
village, the Södergrans' garden and their villa. As for "the moor,"
it is at once a transformation of the lake into a favorite natural
phenomenon of contemporary verse, and a symbol for the seductive
perils existing even in Raivola. The poem has two more strophes,
one indicating that the place of composition is St. Petersburg ("outside, the great city roars"), the other a return to Raivola's safe
and sunny garden, where "the sky is infinitely blue and wide." Similar scenes will be found in Dikter and the collateral, uncollected
poems; there the dangerous town will have vanished, but the threats
to paradise--from that feverish moor--remain; indeed, the threats
will have grown in strength.

Did the adolescent girl dream for a while of becoming a German-
language poet? And was Bergroth's advice (see p. 12) the sole cause
for the switch to Swedish? It should not be assumed, though, that
Edith Södergran turned her back on German poetry, once she had decided to write no more in the language. The poets who meant the most
for her subsequent development--Max Dauthendey, Alfred Mombert,
Friedrich Nietzsche--are all represented in the two anthologies of
her youth, books which probably provided her introduction to them.

Although the Swedish verse of the notebook is "exceedingly weak
from an artistic standpoint,"[9] it has the great advantage of being
written in the language, of course, of her most intimate dialogues
with herself; here, she begins the construction of her peculiar imaginary world. Among the Swedish poems, there is one (ESD, pp. 145-
146), directed to "my darling," palpably Cottier, since he speaks a
line of French in the poem's course. It seems to be a development
out of "Youthful Dreams" but has a setting altogether different from
the melodramatic out-of-doors of that suite (with its golden firs,
wild storms, and swelling waves). Instead, the speaker of the poem
leads its object into "my dream's manifold chambers." (Edith Södergran must have been familiar with the "Intérieur" motif of decadence
--see the luxurious rooms of Huysmans, Jacobsen, and Bang, and the
Austrian Felix Dörmann's "interior of bright scarlet silk" in the
Benzmann anthology.[10]) The first room is filled with flowers, all
speaking the language of love, but the beloved says "'Je n'aime pas
les parfums'" and goes to the second room, where "emptiness, tired-
ness, and despair dwell." The third room has neither roof nor walls,
but rather "a constantly changing scenery": visions of evergreens
in a moonlit winter night, streets filled with traffic, sparrows
twittering, horses eating oats, "battles roaring from stone wall to
stone wall," happy children's voices, a sigh--but suddenly a gust of
wind catches "my darling's warlike form" and, comically, "his coat-

tails flap" (she uses the wrong plural of the noun). Next, the
"darling" stands alone in a fourth room, "as it were, the antechamber
to another. / There is a door, covered by white cloths." He tries
to force his way in, but something holds him back: "He knows that
someone is sitting behind it / And half embarrassed he goes away."
The blank-verse poem is altogether ambiguous in its intention,
despite the clarity of its layout. The dream-Cottier is apparently
offered love, which he rejects, is shown the despair in the dreamer's
heart and cannot endure it, is a passive witness to various aspects
of life (Enckell thinks that a coming revolution is hinted at here),
and at last vanishes. In every situation, he fails; confronted by
whatever lies within the fifth chamber (the white cloths, or sheets,
indicate illness or death), he slinks out of the poet's life. It
was not the only revenge Södergran would take upon a man.

3.

Poetic Debut: *Dikter*

Dikter, the first published collection from Edith Södergran's hand, contains 64 poems; Gunnar Tideström has shown that 16 poems from Landet som icke är are also "early": in the present chapter, they will be considered together with the texts issued in 1916. At first glance, Dikter may seem to be inchoate; after further readings, its structure will become apparent--a suite of landscapes, into which four sets of thematically related lyrics are woven: reflections on the enigma of the poet's self, a tale of unhappy love, variations on a central myth borrowed from antiquity, and a series of instructions for survival.

The landscape, naturally enough, is most apparent in the collection's earlier pages; the poet wants her audience to behold her world, a surprisingly lush and southern one, shot through with dreaminess and melancholy. Here, before the book's overriding theme of erotic disappointment is introduced, the melancholy arises from the encroachments of industrialization, or the metropolis, on old places, old houses, old beauties; it is a sadness familiar to the reader, say, of Herman Bang's Ludvigsbakke (1896)[1] or Tchekov's Cherry Orchard (1904)--Dikter repeatedly reflects literary concerns, and techniques, of the turn-of-the-century. In "Det gamla huset" ("The Old House" (SD, p. 45)), Edith Södergran says: "I live on in the dearness of old days, / amidst strangers who build their cities here / on bluish hillocks up to the heavens' rim / while I speak gently with the prisoner trees / and sometimes placate them." (For much of this mood-music, Edith Södergran uses the poetic devices of the German poetry of Jugendstil, regular rhythmic patterns and occasional rhyme, e.g., "himlens rand / ibland"[2].) The gentle melancholy of "Nocturne" comes from a different Neo-Romantic source, and is a response to the "Moon-lit evening, sheer with silver" (SD, p. 46): "Shadows fall across the pathway, / gently, at water's edge, the bushes weep, / black-

giants by the edge's silver keep / their watch. Deep silence in
summer's midst.". A similar sweet sadness clings to "Höstens dagar"
("The Autumn's Days" (SD, p. 48)): "It is so sweet without a wish
to dream / Sated with flowers and grown tired of green, / with the
vine's red wreath at pillow-side." Languor may be ruffled by longing ("Have you ever stood at the iron gate and yearned / and seen
how on dreaming pathways / the evening to blueness was turned?");
and there is a mild regret at passion untasted ("a blood-red sun
disappeared"), as in the poem, "Du som aldrig gått ut ur ditt träd-
gårdsland" ("You Who Never Have Left Your Garden-land" (SD, p. 49)),
or a mild anxiety at winter's coming, as in "Höstens dagar" or "Höst"
("Autumn" (SD, p. 66)): "A child still plays in the autumn's grey-
ish haze, / a girl walks forth with flowers in her hand, / and on
the horizon's band, / birds all silver-white ascend." Young Rilke's
poems with the same autumnal theme from Buch der Bilder (Book of
Pictures, 1902-1906) will come to mind; there, however, the mood is
variously more threatening or more pious ("And yet there is One, who
holds this falling, / with infinite gentleness in his hands"[3]),
while Edith Södergran studiously avoids the thought of a supreme
arranger of the seasons, and the universe. Life is what one beholds,
no more.

   Stock elements of the continental lyric of Neo-Romanticism are
adduced, again reminiscent of Rilke or Maurice Maeterlinck: the
haze, the solitary girl, the high-flying birds; and further poems--
for example, "Skogssjön" ("The Forest Lake" (SD, p. 72)) or "Irrande
moln" ("Wandering Clouds" (SD, p. 71))--have more elements of nature
as viewed by the lyricists of the preceding decades: "the clouds
wait for the wind which will carry them over the plain," the "sweetness of summer" drips slowly from the forest's trees by the lake;
vague anticipation--of a seasonal transformation, of an erotic adventure, of an end to the idyll--is the key signature of such poetry.
There is even a suggestion of a favorite deity of the late nineteenth
century's arts-and-letters, Pan: "The sick god lies in the shadows,
and dreams his malicious dreams" ("Skogsdunkel" ("Forest Darkness")
(SD, p. 77)).[4] (It should be noted that the fin-de-siècle's concern
with enervation or illness plays a significant role in Dikter; here,
literary custom went in tandem with Edith Södergran's own physical
condition.) Yet the world of these poems is by no means a literary
construction; Raivola is its source, with Lake Onkamo, the great
forest, and the Södergrans' garden--the magical place of "Tidig
gryning" ("Early Dawn" (SD, p. 83)): "Spread over the lake, a
silence rests, / There lies a whisper in wait among the trees, / my
old garden listens with half an ear / to the breathing of night, that
soughs across the path." As these whisperings become more audible,
their emotional burden becomes clear; the garden and the trees speak,
as they would again in the final poems of Edith Södergran. In consequence of her isolation, the objects around her must have voices;
and it is this almost childlike ability to bring her surroundings to
life that distinguishes her from the poets of the Bethge and Benzmann
anthologies she had studied and imitated. "Den sörjande trädgården"
("The Lamenting Garden") is a case in point, employing anthropomorphism to create sadness, a sadness deepened because the object's
questions are not answered (SD, p. 85):

> Oh, that windows see
> and walls remember,
> that a garden can stand and lament
> and a tree can turn around and ask:
> Who has not come, and what is not well,
> why is the emptiness heavy, saying nothing?
> The bitter pinks cluster along the way,
> where the fir-tree's darkness becomes inscrutable.

In fact, a reply is studiously avoided; in "Kväll" ("Evening"), the poet refuses at the outset to hear a tale that is implied by the sounds and shadows of nature, and leads the invisible conversational partner (herself?) to a path where no one comes (SD, p. 89):

> I do not wish to hear the sad story
> the forest tells.
> There is still a long whispering among the branches,
> there is still a long sighing in the leaves,
> still there is a long gliding of shadows between the
>   gloomy trunks.
> Come out onto the path. No one meets us there.
> The evening dreams pale-red around the ditches' silent
>   edge.
> The path runs slowly and the path climbs earnestly
> and long looks back to seek the shine of sun.

The forest and the path are the living entities in the poem, not the poet and her silent companion; these entities--the forest by its whisperings, the path by its strangely hesitating progress, as if looking over its shoulder--signify the yearning which is the central and unnamed emotion of the poem.

Had Edith Södergran produced still more pleasantly melancholy lyrics, and included them in Dikter, it could have increased the book's chances for wholehearted approval by Finland-Swedish criticism; the verse offered a home-grown form of a recent and altogether acceptable foreign fashion, and, in Finland, the way had been prepared by the popular collections of Hjalmar Procopé and Bertel Gripenberg--the title of the latter's book of 1905 is, significantly enough, Gallergrinden (The Grillwork Gate), where the poet stands before an enchanted garden, the would-be prisoner of vague yearnings, vague sorrows. The fatally original and upsetting element in Dikter was Edith Södergran's mythologizing of herself. The process had begun with the oil-cloth notebook (see Chapter 2), and was continued in the poetry from the continental episode at Davos and in Italy. On the scant evidence, it was a happy time: "Sommar i bergen" ("Summer in the Mountains" (SD, p. 131)) could not be more direct in what it says: "Simple is the mountains' summer: / the meadow blossoms, / the old farm smiles / and the brook's dark roar speaks of happiness found". "Det underliga havet" ("The Wondrous Sea")-- probably composed in consequence of the Södergrans' excursion to Venice--is a mixture of liberated rejoicing and childish naiveté (SD, p. 86):

> Strange fishes glide in the depths,
> unknown flowers shine on the beach;
> I have seen red and yellow and all the other colors--
> but the splendid, splendid billows are most dangerous
>   to see,
> it makes one thirsty and keen for adventures that await:
> What has happened in the fairy-tale will happen, too,
>   to me!

After Edith Södergran had returned to Finland, and to little Raivola, her enthusiasm vanished, to be replaced by desperation; yet the undersea image--first used by her in a German poem, "Tief unten am Meeresgrunde" ("Far down on the ocean's bottom" (ESD, p. 115))-- returns, now not as a sign of adventure, but as a metaphor of being trapped. In "Jag" ("I" (SD, p. 50)),[6] the poet--the title can be taken as a bald statement of autobiography--is held captive by the pressure of the sea. Its waters admit swirls of sunlight, and become, all of a sudden, air that "flows between my hands." The vague melancholy of the mood-poems turns to impatience, the garden and the forests become a prison, and the city, whose expansion was hateful to the poet in "The Old House," becomes a "homeland"--as in the "Fragment" of Septemberlyran (see p. 80), where St. Petersburg is called the place of her "childhood's enchanted banner," of her "youth's glow."

> I am a stranger in this land,
> which lies deep beneath the pressing sea,
> the sun looks in with swirling beams
> and the air flows between my hands.
> They told me that I was born in imprisonment--
> there is no face that would be known to me.
> Was I a stone that they cast to the bottom here?
> Was I a fruit, too heavy for its branch?
> I lie in wait here at the soughing tree's foot,
> How can I climb up the slippery trunks?
> Up there, the waving crowns meet,
> I shall sit there and look out
> for the smoke of my homeland's chimneys...

The thought of imprisonment in a strange, submarine world (where a human being cannot, in fact, survive) is followed by dreams of anti-cipation again ("I lie in wait"), and of yearning for escape--we may wonder if Edith Södergran had read the ambitious servant Jean's tree-climbing speech in Strindberg's Miss Julie. The poem is more vivid, certainly, thanks to its striking metamorphoses, than a thematic com-panion, "En fången fågel" ("A Captive Bird" (SD, p. 94)), where the sea-depths (or the forest) have been exchanged for an ideal land-scape, the almost feral ego for a captive bird, which sits "impri-soned in a gilded cage beside a deep-blue sea." The site of the imprisonment is altogether lovely; the castle is surrounded by "yearning roses which / promise pleasure and happiness"; but the bird sings of an Alpine world where "the sun is king and silence queen," and where "sparse little flowers in shining colors / bear witness

to life which offers defiance and persists." The Raivola world
softens and stultifies with its beauty, the harder Alpine world had
been life-giving. The poem's teaching--that hardship is better than
pleasure--will be offered again in the later pages of Dikter.

The imprisonment may take an erotic hue. Creating another legend (placed again in a quasi-medieval setting), Edith Södergran tells
of "Konungens sorg" ("The King's Sorrow" (SD, p. 114)), where the
monarch, fearing the lure of sex, bans the "little dancers" from his
sight and from his court. The imaginary royal world is familiar to
every reader of Maeterlinck; the philological manner in which Edith
Södergran describes the attempt to drive temptation away is altogether original: "The king had the word 'sorrow' forbidden at court, /
'misfortune,' 'love,' and 'happiness,' all words that hurt, / but
'she' and 'hers' were still left." Language cannot be de-eroticized,
nor can life. The theme of erotic imprisonment is continued in
"Prinsessan" ("The Princess" (SD. pp. 141-142)), not included in
Dikter. Unlike the king--who, a married man, evidently means to
repress adulterous desires for a "young woman with blond locks"--the
princess is surrounded by lovers, and accepts their advances: "every
evening the princess let herself be caressed." Just the same, she
is "the poorest being in the whole realm," for these caresses only
fill her heart "with sweet bitterness," while her longing for something better and deeper remains unstilled. Not surprisingly, the
princess of this fairy tale comes from "the south," a place of sensi-
tivity and emotional warmth: "The princess did not love the red
mouths, they were foreign, / the princess did not know the drunken
eyes with ice at the bottom. / They were all children of winter,
but the princess was from the uttermost south, and without whims, /
without hardness, without veils and without cunning." The last line
offers an accurate self-estimate of Edith Södergran.

In this hard northern world, then, Edith Södergran is what she
calls herself in one of the more sentimental poems of Dikter, a collection whose self-dramatizing component may not be overlooked:
"Höstens sista blomma" ("The Last Rose of Autumn" (SD, p. 62), the
poem's unabashed title), who has beheld "light from far-away hearths"
(a cozy equivalent, we may suspect, to the invigorating sun of Dr.
Muralt's Alpine village), and, as the final member of her line, has
discovered that "it is so easy...to die." When the poem subsequently
says "I shall close the gates of death," it means not that the flower
will somehow overcome death (after all, "my calix has no other seed
than death's"), but that, with her passing, death will have got the
last and special child of summer, the season of full-blown beauty.
Again, Edith Södergran uses a commonplace of the fin-de-siècle-- the
thought that the last, death-consecrated member of a great line is
its most fragile and most sensitive representative; see, for example,
the cases of Huysmans' Des Esseintes, of Mann's Hanno Buddenbrook.

The "south" (transformed now into the "orient") sends its emissary to the prisoner, in an effort to lure her out of her invisible
cage; notably, the messenger is not a human being but "the strange
tree" ("Det främmande trädet" (SD, pp. 107-108)): "The strange tree
stands with gaudy fruits, / the strange tree stands with purple

catkins / on a sunny slope, whispering gently..." The whispers are
a series of imperatives, telling the listener to take the path which
"no one can find alone," to a place far away, "where no one knows
you, there you shall meet oriental eyes..." The poem hints that the
tree wants the listener to go to the land of death; there may be an
echo here of Goethe's poem where a tempter, bearing a tree's name
("Der Erlkönig," "The Alder-king"), succeeds with blandishments that
lead to the listener's destruction. The tree promises a magical
transformation, if the listener will but put her hand on his bark:
"I shall conceal your limbs with the autumn's splendor," a thought
of death in beauty, amidst the leaves of autumn, to be taken up again
in "Jungfruns död" ("The Maiden's Death") in Septemberlyran (see
p. 64).

With her seductive tree, Edith Södergran skirts still another
popular erotic-artistic configuration of the late nineteenth and
early twentieth centuries: the representation of death as a desirable maiden or youth, as in Thomas Gotch's painting, Death the Bride,
or in the vision of "the pale and lovely Summoner" beheld by the
dying Aschenbach in Mann's Death in Venice. And she approaches the
topos more directly in "Livets syster" ("Life's Sister (SD, pp. 116-
117))], where death is not "greenish-white with its face on the
ground / or stretched out on a white bier"; instead, "death has soft
features and pious cheeks, she puts her soft hand on your heart."
But, having tricked her audience into thinking that death is a consolatory friend or lover, Edith Södergran directly reverses her
field, saying that awareness of death is a curse, a blight: "He who
has felt the soft hand on his heart, / is not warmed by the sun, /
he is cold as ice and loves no one." Just so, in "Den väntande
själen" ("The Waiting Soul" (SD, p. 124)), the speaker of the poem
is aware that love is everywhere in nature, in whose midst she apparently thrives--then, with a sudden reversal, to say that she feels
debased by this ubiquitous presence: "Great flowers look down
(italic added) on me from high stalks / bitter tendrils creep into
my lap."

At this stage in her poetic development, Edith Södergran could
write more frankly about the erotic drive than about the cessation
of existence; even so, she held back the poem "Till Eros" ("To Eros")
from publication. The poem is an outcry against what Edith Södergran
evidently saw as an expulsion from the sweet realm of childhood, and
the entrance into a humiliating slavery (SD, p. 140):

> Eros, you cruellest of all the gods,
> why did you lead me to the dark land?
> When little girls grow up
> they are closed out of the light
> and cast into a dark room.
> Did not my soul hover like a happy star
> before it was drawn into your red ring?
> See, I am bound, both hands and feet,
> feel, I am forced in all my thoughts.
> Eros, you cruellest of all the gods,
> I do not fly. I do not wait,
> I only suffer like an animal.

It should be added that, in the fourth line from the end, Edith
Södergran employs one of the popular catchwords of psychoanalysis,
the "Zwangsvorstellung" or "Zwangsgedanke": the Swedish runs:
"känn, jag är tvungen till alla mina tankar." Also, the last line
has the telltale verb, "lida" (suffer), which appears--explicitly
or implicitly--in the well-known mottoes of the Danish decadent Bang,
a persistent utterer of lamentations at man's enslavement to sex:
"we suffer and cause sufferings, more we do not know" and "there is
nothing save the sexual urge, and it alone is lord and master".[7]
Edith Södergran may have read both Freud (or, more likely, Mattsson's
journalistic resumés of Freud's work) and Bang; the concept of
sexual determinism lay in the air, and cannot fail to have caught
the attention of the lonely Edith, gifted or cursed with an over-
powering imagination.

Not surprisingly, she makes repeated efforts to re-establish
her spiritual virginity (a scholar of decadence, Hans Hinterhäuser,
has enumerated the "re-virginization attempts"[8] in the novels of the
period and their literary-historical forebears); frequently, Edith
Södergran's personae are free, young, and happy girls, the equivalents, let us say, of Charles Maturin's Immalee, alone on her Indian
island, or W. H. Hudson's Rima, the Bird-Girl in Green Mansions. The
being addressed by the tree in "The Strange Tree" is not only called
"you pale one, needful of blood" (a realistic look by Edith Södergran
at her own condition), but, in addition, "you golden daughter, you
wanderer of the autumn, / you listener to the woods" and "caressing"
and "happy" and "red" (i.e., vital).[9] (The mutually contradictory
aspects of the Södergranian heroine--for example, moribund and
athletic--are not usually placed within the same poem; the juxtaposition occurs in "The Strange Tree" because the persuasive tree
tries one appeal, then another.) The positive epithets applied by
the tree to the "golden daughter" have erotic implications, to be
sure; but it must be remembered that, in the poem's fiction, the
girl's eroticism is to be led toward a union with nature, not with
a (treacherous) human being. Similarly, in "Skogens ljusa dotter"
("The Forest's Bright Daughter" (SD, p. 80)), a marriage is prepared
--the phrase, "the forest's bright daughter celebrated her wedding,"
is the refrain of the poem, repeated thrice in what seems to be an
imitation of epithalamic-poetic practice. All nature, and mankind
with it, rejoices at the report: "When the forest's bright daughter
celebrated her wedding, / the firs stood all satisfied on the sandy
hill, / and the pines on the plunging slope so proud, / and the juni-
pers so glad on the sunny slopes." But, remarkably, the epithalamium
lacks a groom. In the description of the bride, we are told that
she was "shameless and laughed without measure" but never that she
loved a man (think of Immalee's nakedness and merriment), and that
she was "free from longing."

Edith Södergran's interest in C. J. L. Almqvist has been mentioned above (see p. 10); the novel which caught her special attention was Drottningens juvelsmycke (The Queen's Diadem). Its central
figure is the elusive and androgynous Tintomara, a musician like
Södergran's "bright daughter" (who had "borrowed the cuckoo's instrument, and wandered playing from lake to lake"), a creature, herself

without desire, who aroused the desires of men and women alike (even
as the forest's daughter is "pale and awakens all desires"). The
appeal of Tintomara to Edith Södergran, and the incorporation of the
fictional character into the Södergranian myth, rest on several factors: Tintomara's inassailable and prideful virginity, coupled with
her ability to arouse passion, her almost preternatural physical
adroitness and vigor, her curious blend of female and male components
(recall Edith Södergran's youthful identification with Enjolras),
and her sense of unity with nature, as demonstrated by the long episode of Almqvist's novel which takes place in the forest of Kol-
mården.

Descendants of Tintomara, and sisters of the "forest's bright
daughter," appear in some of the best-known of the Dikter. In
"Violetta skymningar" ("Violet Twilights") we are taken into the
poet's primal memory of an ideal landscape that seems borrowed from
a painting by Arnold Böcklin (1827-1901) or Böcklin's imitator Franz
Stuck (1862-1928), populated by the fantastic beings of antiquity
which Neo-Romanticism had revived, amazons and centaurs. [10] It is a
world without men (who are thoroughly denigrated in the poem's middle
section), and a world of female athleticism and energy, demonstrated
by beings which are at once innocent, war-like, and vital (SD,
p. 54):

> I bear violet twilights within me from my primeval time,
> naked maidens playing with galloping centaurs...
> Yellow sunshine days with splendid glances,
> only sunbeams can worthily celebrate a woman's body...
> The man has not come, has never been, shall never be...
> the man is a false mirror whom the sun's daughter, angered,
>   casts against the cliff's wall,
> the man is a lie, whom white children do not understand,
> the man is a rotten fruit, which proud lips scorn.
> Fair sisters, come high up onto the strongest cliffs,
> we are all warriors, heroines, riders,
> innocent-eyes, foreheads of heaven, rosy faces,
> heavy surfs and birds blown off course,
> we are the least expected and the most deeply red,
> tiger-spots, bows drawn tight, stars without dizziness.

The vision of the enormously healthy riders,[11] who crush unworthy
men, no doubt arises, like much else in Dikter, from Edith Södergran's peculiar situation--a woman ill and scorned: it is a wish-
dream, and a dream of revenge. Yet what is more important, though,
is her proposal that the proper "husband" of these women is the sun
itself--a statement of a conviction to which she will give a more
direct form elsewhere in Dikter: that women are in closer touch with
life's vital forces than are men. Subsequently, under Nietzsche's
tutelage, she would proclaim her own union, in glorious death, with
the sun; there, however, she would regard herself not as the member
of a better sex but as a unique individual, uniquely chosen.

Like "Violet Twilights," "Vierge moderne" must have been irritating to its early male readers--more irritating than the amazon-poem,

indeed, since the distressing thoughts there had at least been
expressed with classical images. In the thirteen bald and anaphoric
lines of "Vierge moderne," there is no such disguise; the rhetoric
is persistently and shockingly aggressive (SD, p. 57): "I am no
woman. I am a neuter. / I am a child, a page and a bold decision, /
I am a laughing strip of a scarlet sun... / I am a net for all greedy
fishes, / I am a toast to all women's honor." The existence of such
a "vierge moderne" is perilous but rewarding: "I am a step toward
accident and ruin, / I am a leap into freedom and the self..." No
wonder that recent feminist admirers of Edith Södergran in Scandina-
via have taken the poem, or lines from it, as a battle cry; see its
last line: "I am fire and water, honorably connected, on free conditions." Yet, however useful and apparently "modern" a program-
poem it may be, it has elements which are peculiarly Södergranian:
her Tintomara-like awareness of her androgyny, and her double desire
to use her sexuality for seduction ("I am the whispering of the
blood in the man's ear"),[12] and to maintain the spiritual virginity
she regarded as a special source of strength ("I am a fever of the
soul, the flesh's longing and denial").

A third poem about the virginal heroine, "Färgernas längtan,"
has caused complex efforts at analysis.[13] Its very title seems
ambiguous, for it means, literally, "The Colors' Longing"; however,
it becomes apparent from the text that it is the poem's speaker who
yearns, and thus Martin Allwood has offered the translation, "A
Longing for Colors".[14] (The misleading title arose, it may be
guessed, from the German substratum in Edith Södergran's language--
a construction such as "Farbensehnsucht.") The poem begins: "For
my own paleness' sake I love red, blue and yellow, / the great
whiteness of melancholy is the snowy twilight, / when Snow White's
mother sat by the window, wishing for black and red to be added."
Later on, Snow White appears as a central allusion in a long erotic
fantasy, "Älvdrottningens spira" (see p. 108); in the present
instance, the poet thinks of the wish of the queen in the Grimms'
fairy tale: "I wish I had a child as white as snow, as red as blood,
and as black as the ebony of the window frame." Like the mother,
putting together the varied beauty of her dream-child in the tale,
the speaker wants to add bright colors to the white melancholy of
her existence. The poem continues with a sentence of puzzling com-
pression, literally: "The colors' longing is the blood's," which
(again following Allwood's lead) may be taken to mean: "A longing
for colors lies in our blood," a reinforcement of the opening statement (as has been the allusion to Snow White's mother). Then, in one
of those pronominal shifts which indicate that the poems' speaker
addressed herself (or an imaginary partner/audience), the second-
person pronoun replaces the first, with an instruction: "If you
thirst for beauty, you will shut your eyes and look within your
heart." "Red" and "blue" are not expressly named again in the poem's
course, yet the reference to the heart--which is 'red', the color
of life and of the blood--explains the appearance of that color in
the opening color-catalogue: beauty lives in vitalism, in the well-
spring of the blood, of life itself. But, the argument continues,
beauty--albeit the very stuff of life--cannot bear public view; it
must be kept in the 'blue' concealment of the soul--in another poem,

Edith Södergran says that "My soul was a light-blue dress of heaven's
color" ("Kärlek," SD, p. 102); here, the formulation goes: "Yet
beauty fears the day and all too many glances, / yet beauty does not
endure noise and all too many movements--you shall not bring your
heart to your lips..." Changing the pronoun of address again,
expanding her audience, the poet continues the celebration of 'blue'
self-containment: "we ought not to disturb the noble rings of
silence and of loneliness,-- / what is greater than to meet an
unsolved riddle with strange features?" And, returning to her initial pronoun, the poet says what her future will be, in lines which
are both predictions and self-injunctions: "I shall be a silent
woman all my life, / a speaking woman is like a chattering brook
that betrays itself." Finally, refined into "golden," the third
color of the triad gets its due; it is the color not of vital beauty
or spiritualized reserve but of lonely strength--and strength grows
in loneliness: "I shall be a lonely tree on the plain, / the trees
in the forest perish from longing for the storm, / I shall be
healthy from top to toe with golden streams in my blood..." The
message is almost banal (even as "from top to toe" seems almost
childish in its would-be robustness): good health, physical strength
is literally "golden," that most precious thing. Possessing the
three colors--which, as every child knows, are the primary pigments,
red, blue, and yellow--the poet will be "pure and innocent as a flame
with licking lips," another version of the bright daughter of the
forest, the amazon, the "modern virgin" (who was also called "a
flame, seeking and bold").

    All these poems, of course, are attempts to ameliorate or to
wish away the miseries of a sick and solitary life, employing transformation and injunction: Edith Södergran tells herself again and
again either what she is, or what she must be. Although she insists
repeatedly that she does not seek pleasure, she is (however hard the
circumstances to which she submits herself in her poetic imagination)
a persistent searcher for happiness. (We may recall her naive question to Hemmer and his friends: "Do you think that one can be
happy?"). In "Vägen till lyckan" ("The Road to Happiness" (SD,
p. 75)), the quest is described quite sentimentally, and in stanzaic
verse of regular rhythm and rhyme. The poem's message--we are
tempted to say, its platitude--is that happiness cannot be found by
means of logic or plan; happiness comes unexpectedly, no "happy person" can remember the path which leads to "happiness' hidden door":
"Oh, seeking the bird-of-happiness' trail / Is like to traveling
without ways / Or grasping while our hands do fail. / Oh, becoming
king in happiness' tale / Is to stand stupid and amazed." At last,
in the third stanza, the brain grows tired of the search, "the day
withers and grows pale." A question ends it all, with the implication that some searchers are never vouchsafed happiness: "Is your
dream, your happiness' star / but fiction and fraud (sken och svek)?"
The phrase is worth remembering; in other and much better poems,
Edith Södergran will again be struck by the fact that the world in
whose natural phenomena she finds solace is but illusion and decep-
tion, indeed, is "nothing."

Yet the poetic search for happiness continued. One of the most frequently discussed poems in Dikter is "Den speglande brunnen" ("The Mirroring Well"). It has structural features we have seen in "Longing for Colors"--color symbolism, apparent pronominal confusion, repeated self-injunction--but, unlike that poem, it offers a picture; an artist, illustrating Dikter, would have no difficulty in making a vignette from it (SD, p. 164):

> Fate said: white you shall live, or red you shall die!
> But my heart said: red I shall live.
> Now I dwell in the land where all is yours,
> death never enters this realm.
> I sit the whole day long with my arm resting on the well's edge,
> when they ask me if happiness has been here,
> I shake my head and smile:
> happiness is far away, there a young woman sits, sewing a child's blanket,
> happiness is far away, there a man walks in the forest and builds himself a cabin.
> Here red roses grow around bottomless springs,
> here beautiful days mirror their smiling features
> and great flowers lose their fairest petals...

Several commentators have[15] seen in the poem a resemblance to Tizian's Sacred and Profane Love, where two women, one dressed, the other nude, sit beside a well surrounded by roses. (Edith Södergran had the habit of cutting out reproductions from journals, and the Tizian painting had become particularly popular, in the German-language realm, thanks to Paul Heyse's use of it in an erotic novella[16]). The suggestion may be of value for the interpretation of the poem, since the painting--as Heyse saw it--meant the presentation of a choice between two kinds of love, as "The Mirroring Well" does. As Gunnar Tideström has argued, the poet casts a backward glance at the Hobson's choice which fate--a kind of brutal physician--appeared to offer her, as a fragile tubercular: to live ascetically, or to die while partaking of the fullness of life; she decided to defy "fate," to attempt to live "red," fully, as long as she could. (In a later poem, "Eros hemlighet," she says: "I live red, I live my blood."[17]) But the decision, bravely taken, could not be put into effect; against her will, she was consigned to the contemplative and inactive realm of "the mirroring well." Olof Enckell, pointing to the great importance of Edith Södergran's poem-titles, has taken the apparently unreferential "yours" at the end of the third line as an allusion, in fact, to the well, of which the woman is now a captive. Gunnar Ekelöf's proposal is interesting: that the poem was written at Davos, with "the hothouse atmosphere of the sanatorium" and "enforced erotic resignation."[18] The watcher by the well is cut off from a vita activa: the images she used to describe happiness' location are strikingly reminiscent of the third act of Ibsen's Peer Gynt, where Peer comes closest to a genuine happiness, momentarily freed from the dreams which beset him; that world, we are twice told ("there / there"), lies far away, while "here" reflection becomes infinite, beauty is frozen in the mirroring well, and life is wasted.

The poem may be taken as an autobiographical comment again (as a comment variously upon sanatorium life, or that aestheticized and fairytale Raivola we have met elsewhere); or as a larger comment on the value, or inherent lack of value, of the aesthetic attitude. Later, particularly in Rosenaltaret, Edith Södergran tries to couple the aestheticism with active life, as the militant priestess of beauty. In "The Mirroring Well," her thoughts are less exalted and, ultimately, quite simple: constrained to a life of the contemplation of beauty, the smiling speaker realizes that, forever at rest and imprisoned by the surface of the well, she will never have the happiness of the woman who sews, the man who builds. Life is wasted in languidness; "great flowers lose their fairest petals."

    The best-known of Edith Södergran's efforts to break the magic ring was the affair with the man from Terijoki, the erotic misadventure which led eventually, it may be guessed, to the publication of Dikter, as a poetic proclamation of her human worth. The collection's striking overture, "Jag såg ett träd" ("I Saw a Tree") has been seen by Tideström as a retelling of the story, by means of carefully chosen detail (SD, p. 41):[19] "I saw a tree which was taller than all the others / and hung full of inaccessible cones; / I saw a great church with open doors / and all who came out were pale and strong / and ready to die; / I saw a woman who, smiling and painted, / cast dice for her happiness / and saw that she lost." In this, Tideström has detected the Raivola scene: the great trees, the community's Orthodox church, Edith Södergran herself as the woman who has lost; yet it may be asked if the poem, instead, is not a kind of preparatory life-review. The first of the anaphoric "I saw" constructions may be a reference to the experience with Muralt (the might tree of other poems, with its genuine inaccessibility); the second "I saw" may refer to her violent rejection of Christianity, the faith which gave strength and certainty with regard to death, but abhorred life's pleasures (near the end of Dikter, there is the parody on a hymn, "Kristen trosbekännelse" ("Christian Confession of Faith," SD, p. 111): "happiness is not in our longing's song"); and the third "I saw" arrives at the situation of the disappointed woman of Raivola—the audience, thus, is brought up to date. In the poem's conclusion: "A circle was drawn around these things / which no one crosses," the idea of the encircling and imprisoning ring is posited.[20] One of the themes in this overture to Dikter—the celebration of Muralt—is only sparsely represented in the book proper, another, the attack upon Christianity, is oblique here, and becomes patent only in Rosenaltaret; the other two themes, however, that of the woman who seeks happiness (and fails), and of the imprisoning ring, are repeatedly to be found. Throughout the collection, the poet presents her personae, again and again, as both the one and the other, the disappointed woman and the prisoner. Plainly, these are the thoughts that most obsess the poet, and about which she wishes to speak. Yet the overture's conclusion may have another sense, as well; these are secrets which the outsider may not approach: the ring may not be crossed from within or from without. The reader is warned, in effect, that he will confront hermetic structures—and so is lured into paying them close attention. "Longing for Colors" asks: "What is greater than meeting an unsolved

riddle with strange features?" Yet the teller of mysteries, even
as she warns against the solving of them, also wants them to be
solved.

Immediately upon the heels of the caveat, there follows "Dagen
svalnar" ("The Day Cools" (SD, pp. 42-45)), the four-part suite [21]
that is the most translated of all the poems of Edith Södergran.
Plainly, it is a little love-story, and not a happy one, for it
ends (by the poet's own concluding word) in the narrator's disappointment. In the first part of the suite, a multiple invitation
is extended: "Drink warmth from my hand... / Take my hand, take
my white arm, / take my slender shoulders' longing..." But we are
directly made aware of an incommensurability between the lovers:
we learn that his head is "heavy" while, as we have seen, she is
frail, and, as she speaks of the night of love ("a single night, a
night such as this"), she offers an example of what will be one of
her favorite rhetorical devices, the aprosdoketon, the unexpected
word: "It would be strange to feel...your heavy head against my
breast." Instead of "underligt," we might have looked for "under-
bart," "wonderful." In the pause between parts one and two, the
invitation to love has been accepted, and the female partner makes
a brief description of what has happened, of her loss of virginity
("red rose / white lap") and of the quick disappearance of his
passion (a double entendre--the "daughter of the forest" said she
was "shameless"): "You cast your love's red rose / into my white
lap-- / In my hot hands I hold tight / your love's red rose which
quickly withers... / Oh, you ruler with cold eyes, / I receive the
crown you hand me, / which bends my head down toward my heart." The
sexual allusions of the section's opening are clear enough; the
remainder is a little less transparent. He has become her ruler (an
ironic bow toward the operetta-song of the type of Robert Stolz's
"Du sollst der Kaiser meiner Seele sein" ("You shall be the emperor
of my soul")), but he is a ruler who directly shows his coldness;
he crowns her as his beloved (or, we might say, sentimentally "the
queen of his heart"), but his affection is a heavy crown[22] which,
quite literally, pulls her head, the seat of reason, down toward
her heart, the seat of emotion. She is not wholly overwhelmed,
however, for at the opening of the third part she is able to indulge
in cutting word-plays (at the same time putting the lover into the
third person, thus at a distance): "I saw my lord for the first
time today, / trembling I immediately recognized him, / Now I already
feel his heavy hand on my light arm..." For the first time, she has
seen him for what he really is; the term she applies to him, "min
herre," "my lord," has a second sense: it is the formally humble
and oblique way in which shopgirls once addressed male customers who
were patently "gentlemen." The gentleman's behavior is demanding or
peremptory, as though toward a prostitute, and the adjectives "heavy"
and "light" continue the comparison made in the suite's first part.
She reacts with amazement at her degradation: "Where is my ringing
maiden laughter, / my woman's freedom with high-borne head? / Now I
already feel his tight grasp around my quaking body, / now I hear
reality's hard sound / against my fragile, fragile dreams." Verbal
intensification shows what has become of her ("heavy" becomes
"tight") and describes her reaction ("trembling" becomes "quaking");

the full perception of the brutality of her lover (of the 'real'
state of things, unadorned) shatters her dreams, dreams as frail
(repeated for emphasis) as she is.

The poem's last section is an epilogue, a reflection, with
shorter lines than those in the body of the narration: the romance
is over, and the disappointment which she, in her heavy irony, attributes to him, is in fact hers. He sought a flower (or, we may say,
his rose sought a sexual respondent), he sought a source of refresh-
ment, he sought (literally) a woman, and, in each case, found something more mature, larger, more intangible: "You sought a flower /
and found a fruit. / You sought a spring / and found a sea, / You
sought a woman / and found a soul-- / you are disappointed." The
story is over, the man condemned. Edith Södergran has been a strikingly clever advocate of her own cause; the selfish male never has
the chance to speak in his defence. (We may wonder: did the "man
from Terijoki" ever see this poem, in which he achieved an anonymous
and unpleasant immortality? Could he have understood it, linguisti-
cally or emotionally, had he seen it?)

Sprinkled throughout Dikter, there are other poems which cast
sidelights on the broken romance. In eight lines, "Svart eller vitt"
("Black or White") tells of a shock, couched again in the undetailed
and faintly wistful manner of the German Jugendstil; the memorable
quality of the poem lies in the contrast between its muted quality
and the awful discovery (saved up to the last lines), rather than
in the threadbare topic. The phenomena of nature are unchanging,
but men are fickle (SD, p. 65):

> The rivers run beneath the bridges,
> the flowers shine beside the roads,
> the forest bends down soughing to the earth.
> For me, nothing is high or low any longer,
> black or white,
> since I have seen a white-clad woman
> in my beloved's arm.

There is an advance, structurally, over the mood-poems discussed
above; the underpinnings of rhyme and meter have been abandoned for
a concentration upon a diminishing number of verbal elements (three
aspects of nature, two possible divisions of thought (high/low,
black/white),[25] then the single and terrible sight)--climax is achieved
by reduction.[25] Telling of her by no means uncommon misfortune,
Edith Södergran becomes more and more the uncommon artist, finding
her own tone; with "I de stora skogarna" ("In the Great Forests"
(SD, p. 78)) she brings her gift for simple structural variations
to bear once again, dividing her life, and her misapprehensions about
it, into three distinct parts (as she has done in the overture to
Dikter), parallel to one another, yet different in their major words.
The divisions here are a childhood world (or an adolescent effort to
regain childhood), a period of intense dreaming in the "high mountains" (Davos again?), and what appears to be the discovery of happiness at last (the Karelian garden):

> In the great forests I went long astray,
> I sought the fairytales my childhood had heard.
> In the high mountains I went long astray,
> I sought the dream castles my youth had built.
> In my beloved's garden I do not go astray,
> there sat the glad cuckoo my longing had followed.

The happy ending deceives, however; the poem's principal verb, "to go astray," is emphatically negated, but the garden's longed-for resident is himself ambiguous. The cuckoo is notoriously a faithless bird (see Rilke's "Abschied" ("Departure") of 1907, where the woman, metaphorically, is a "plum tree, from which the cuckoo's flown away");[24] and "gök"--an etymological relative of German "Gauch" ("fool" or "fop")--can also mean, in Swedish not the happily singing bird but a frivolous male.[25] Not going astray this time after the vain hunts for fairytales and dream-castles, the wanderer has found her goal; but the goal itself has been unworthy of the search. A similar trick is played on the reader in "Lyckokatt" ("Lucky Cat" (SD, p. 79)), with its opening picture of what seems to be quiet happiness, and hopes of a still happier future. Purring in the speaker's lap, the magical cat is asked to get three things: "a golden ring, / which tells me I am happy, / ...a mirror, which tells me I am fair, / ...a fan, which brushes away my clinging thoughts." The doubts which gnaw at the speaker are readily detectible in each of the wishes.

Much of this "romantic" poetry is directly anti-romantic, prescribing a proud self-control, for example, the untitled "Låt ej din stolthet falla": "Do not let your pride fall"--as though it were clothing--"do not go naked, sweetly into his arms" (SD, p. 91). The erotic experience is denigrated, and Paul's injunction ("it is better to marry than to burn") is turned around: "For him who has seen the filth in joy's short spring / nothing remains save hotly freezing"--passion cannot be rooted out, but it must be controlled, at whatever emotional cost. The word "filth" ("smuts") comes back in "Två vägar" ("Two Ways" (SD, p. 109)), a poem of self-instruction, again with echoes of scriptural commonplace ("put off the old man, put on the new"). "You must abandon your old way, / your way is filthy / there men walk with lustful glances, / the word 'happiness' is heard on all lips, / and farther along the way a woman's body lies / and vultures tear it apart": the woman has succumbed to the seducers, has thought she found happiness, and has been destroyed. The new way, of the second strophe, is "pure"--but it leads again to a land of quieter unhappiness, where children's lives are stunted, and where they play with the flower of sleep and death, where women mourn, and where the dragon of sensuality is slain, but at what cost to the slayer! Purity prepares a place where "motherless children walk and play with poppies, / where women walk in black and speak of sorrow, / and farther along a pale saint stands with a foot on a dead dragon's neck." It is an insight which takes us back once more to Bang's remark on human sexuality, or to Södergran's "To Eros."

Sometimes, as in "Violet Twilights" and, by implication, in "Vierge moderne," the poems simply announce women's virtues and men's baseness. The title of "Vi kvinnor" ("We Women" (SD, p. 82)) has recently been used for the name of a selection intended to present Edith Södergran as a spokeswoman of feminism: "We women, we women are so near to the brown earth"--close to nature, asking the cuckoo what he expects of the spring, embracing the bald fir, exploring the sunset for signs and advice.[26] On the other hand, men are empty, lacking contact with nature, forgetful, unfaithful. "Once I loved a man, he believed in nothing... / He came one cold day with empty eyes / he went one heavy day with forgetfulness on his forehead." We might almost be tempted to think that Edith Södergran sees her romance as a Nordic production of Puccini's Madam Butterfly, and the lover--who comes not "un bel di" but "one cold day"--is another Pinkerton. But Södergran's abandoned girl has a talent for verbal revenge, and the wish to administer it, quite lacking in patient Cho-Cho-San. The poem's conclusion, its most memorable part, is a curse hurled at the lover, who kills whatever he touches, or begets: "If my child does not live, it will be his..."

The poet's desire for revenge can even become faintly comical. "Ett råd" ("A Piece of Advice" (SD, p. 98)), using the cast from Edith Södergran's imaginary castle once again, tells of a queen who complains to her "secret councillor" about her husband's unfaithfulness ("He loves all women who set his blood afire"), and is advised to combat her melancholy, and square the score, by letting the "emissary" (not otherwise described) kiss her "when the sun goes down." And sometime in 1915, Edith Södergran wrote the long poem, "Undret" ("The Miracle" (SD, pp. 150-157)), which she then described, in 1922, as "trash," all the while trying to get Hagar Olsson to have it published (EB, p. 213). The minature drama (it has one stage direction) is a conversation between a Catholic girl (Södergran characterized her as such) and a nun. The former dreams of murdering her faithless lover, who literally "has done (her) wrong," and the nun makes a longwinded effort to talk her out of her plan, but at length gives up: "Go, my child, I shall pray for you. / I cannot do anything else." In "Ur 'Liliputs saga'" ("From 'Liliput's Tale'" (SD, p. 118)), the lover is not only belittled by means of nomenclature; he fingers and fondles flowers ("he sank his hand into every flower's calix, / he felt under every leaf"), looking for a black worm; easily tired out, he falls asleep in the shadow of a blade of grass, and the worm eats his head. This is the grotesque little poem's first half; the second lists the women who mourned him: "Three women were present at his burial: / his sister wept; with her was a dancer in lilac veils, / she came in order to be seen. / A woman walked alone whom he had never loved." In each case the reader must draw his own conclusions: does the family member weep from a sense of obligation? Is the showy dancer, who comes in the sister's company, a favored mistress? There is no question about the solitary woman: her love has been wasted on the unworthy departed.

Edith Södergran was fond of the brief poem built around a triad of figures; it is assumed that she had found the model in the verse of Maeterlinck (see his "Les trois soeurs aveugles," "Ils ont tué

trois petites filles," and so forth.[27]). All these poems are early
(Edith Södergran abandoned the structure in her later collections),
and all have to do with the erotic experience in one way or another.
In "Sången om de tre gravarna" ("The Song About the Three Graves"
(SD, p. 106)), the preamble is not a satirical narrative, as in
"Liliput," but simply an introduction to the singer and, then, the
opening of her miniature ballad. "She sang in the twilight in the
dew-wet yard: / In summer three rosebushes grow over three graves."
The theme is a time-honored one, love and death, and the mood is
romantic, not acerbic; nevertheless, the word "heavy" is again
associated with the male partner, and "melancholy" with the female,
who--faithfully--holds love's flower, even in death. "In the first
grave lies a man-- / he sleeps heavily... / In the second lies a
woman with sorrowful features--she holds a rose in her hand." The
third grave reveals what has gone wrong: it is a "spirit grave and
it is unholy / there sits a dark angel every evening, singing: it
is unpardonable to fail to act!" A strikingly Ibsenian statement:
every reader will recall the unpardonable deeds (or non-deeds) of
Pastor Manders and John Gabriel Borkman, men who have gone against
the dictates of their own hearts in rejecting the proffered true
love of a woman.

The second triple-example poem, "Tre systrar" ("Three sisters"),
has men only off-stage, as it were; the preamble again sets a ballad-
esque tone, telling what sort of plant it was each of three girls
loved (SD, p. 116): "The one sister loved the sweet wild straw-
berries, / the second sister loved the red roses, / the third sister
loved the wreaths of the dead." The first sister, then, "got married: / they say that she is happy." The second sister gave passionate devotion, "with all her soul, / they say that she became
unhappy." The third sister, who loved grave-ornaments, "became a
saint, they say that she will win the eternal crown." It is a poem
manifold in its suggestions. In each instance, the reader is left
in doubt about the accuracy ("they say") of the reported fate; also,
in the first case, with its present tense, the possibility exists
that the sister's happiness will not last, or, indeed, is imaginary.
In Swedish, the phrase "wild strawberry patch" indicates a frail or
even dreamlike refuge from everyday life; Ingmar Bergman used it in
this poignant sense for the title of his classic film. In the second
case, the past tense suggests that the sister is dead, of love unre-
quited. In the third case, the sister--a saint, like the dragon-
slayer above--has cut herself off from life, to win (in the future
tense) the crown of heaven, whatever that may be worth.

The last example has two further implications for Edith Södergran's own work, quite apart from her ambiguous attitudes toward
human eroticism. The lines have a tinge of the anti-Christian senti-
ments to be perceived now and again in the collection; at the same
time, Edith Södergran is already interested by the concept of superhuman dedication to a cause, which she describes more positively in
"Min framtid" ("My Future," see p. 59), which she proclaims in the
open letter concerning Septemberlyran, and which informs her
Nietzschean lyric. In "Three Sisters," though, her sympathies lie,
naturally enough, with the second of the sisters, whose human, all

too human fate she presently imagined could be her own.

A third example of the triadic structure is "Ett möte" ("A Meeting"), less sentimental than the songs of the graves and the sisters,
and less sentimental, too, than the close of "From 'Liliput's Tale',"
while wittier and subtler than that poem's bizarre beginning. The
notion of revenge on men is changed into a comment on the reactions
of women to maleness. The poem, not included in Dikter, runs in its
entirety (SD, p. 135):

> Three maidens walked hand in hand over an open plain:
> They were met by a rider in thick coverings.
> The first maiden stretched out her arms: Come oh love!
> The second maiden fell to her knees: death, spare me!
> The third maiden turned around:
> the way to the city goes off to the right.

And so the impressive rider is rather snippily put in his place by
the maiden who refuses to be erotically overwhelmed or terrified.
The simplified legendary coloring and the tart humor will remind
the student of Finland's art that Edith Södergran was a contemporary
of Hugo Simberg (1873-1917)--indeed, Simberg would have been the
ideal illustrator for Dikter.

The awareness of woman's dignity (and of woman's betrayal of it)
gives rise to the several verses where the poet implores her "sisters" to forgive her own weakness; she has let herself be turned
into the slave of her own imaginings. (The uncollected "Sjuka dagar"
("Sick Days," SD, pp. 144-145) is particularly direct: "I have fever
like a swamp plant, / I sweat sweetness like a sticky leaf."[28])
Presented with the opportunity, the woman surrenders to the male
being who, she thinks, can turn her phantasies into reality. This
is the case of "Avsked" ("Departure"), an apopempticon where, at
some length, the speaker takes embarrassed farewell of her "sisters"
(SD, pp. 95-97): "My sisters, I do what I have never wished to, /
my sisters, hold me back-- / I do not wish to go away from you. /
When I close my eyes, he stands before me, / I have many thoughts
for him and none for all the others." It is revelatory that, as the
poem continues, she gives herself the serpentine attributes of the
femme fatale: she has already said that, in her new condition, her
heart is "capricious and cold"; "longing for (his) embraces," she is
in fact less the human being than she was before. She is reduced to
erotic symbols, like a Salome of Moreau or a Judith of Klimt: "When
I really think about it, / I have nothing left of myself but my black
hair, / my two long braids, which glide like snakes. / My lips have
become burning coal, / I no longer remember when they began to
burn..." "Sorger" ("Cares" (SD, pp. 99-100)) is addressed to a
single sister, to whom the familiar story is told once more, but with
a difference: the sister is urged not to do what the speaker has
done, not to go to "the mountains," which "betrayed" her, and "had
nothing to give to (her) longing." The imagery gives hints that
Edith Södergran has blended two disappointments into one; the allusion to "mountains" and to "the fir, which shadowed the pathway,
luxuriant as a plume" would point to the Muralt experience, to

"Elegi" (see p. 97) and "Älvdrottningens spira" (see p. 108): in
both instances, the dream-Muralt is characterized as a great tree.
(The same suspicion must arise in connection with "Sången på berget"
("The Song on the Mountain"): "someone stood up on the mountains
and sang... / I darkly divined that the song / was of something that
never returns" (SD, p. 22).)

An odd melange of attitudes lies behind such poems: a sense
that she has been protected by a sister or sisters whom she variously
betrays or feels she must warn, an overriding wish to surrender to
the lover (and we have seen the disgust which consummation brings),
and an awareness of her beauty and allure, which she nonetheless
profoundly doubts. (In "Cares," the speaker implies that her beauty
needs some aids: "in vain, I looked for an adornment to give my
beauty sheen.") All these elements appear in the short self-analysis
of "Min själ" ("My Soul" (SD, p. 101))--a soul which,altogether abandoned to its passions, has lost the ability to make logical decisions, or even to tell a story: "My soul cannot tell tales and
knows no truth, / my soul can only weep and laugh and wring its
hands..." The poem's second part is another tiny three-part auto-
biography, a stage-by-stage account of her life: "When I was a
child, I saw the sea: it was blue, / in my youth, I met a flower:
she was red, / now I sit by a stranger: he is without color." As
a child, she perceived the infinity of nature; as an adolescent, she
knew passion for the first time; now, however, her companion is a
stranger, and "I am no more afraid of him than the maiden was of
the dragon. / When the knight came the maiden was red and white, /
but I have dark rings underneath my eyes." Olof Enckell has suggested that the poem, "with its naive grace," is about death, the colorless stranger,[29] and that the dark rings are signs of the poet's
awareness of her physical deterioration. Surely, the poem becomes
a painful parody of the tale of a maiden in distress. In the "typical" legend, the maiden still waits, all blooming, for a worthy and
noble-hearted lover; the speaker, however, has found a "savior" (who
has turned out to be a representative of the dragon of lust), and
has bested him; he still sits beside her, a reminder of her mortal-
ity. (We remember the saint who slew the dragon in "Two Ways," in
the midst of a landscape of sadness and death.) Something bitterly
funny, enough to make one "weep and laugh and wring one's hands" (as
the opening of the poem says), lies in such a fate. (Later on,
according to Hagar Olsson, Edith Södergran went through a "Saint
George phase": eroticism was sublimated into dreams of crusade and
victory.[30]).

There are indications that Edith Södergran took some care in
arranging the parts of Dikter in an approximate sequence; "Kärlek"
("Love") follows directly after "Cares" and "My Soul" in a triptych
of uneasiness. It is one of the finest of her love poems, a confession of a loss of personal freedom, of betrayal of commitments, of
fears about sexual abnormality (or "incompleteness") and physical
disease (SD, pp. 102-103):

My soul was a bright blue dress of the sky's color;
I left it on a rock beside the sea
And naked I came unto you and resembled a woman.
And as a woman I sat at your table
and drank a toast with wine and breathed in the smell of
   some roses.
You found that I was beautiful and resembled something
   you had seen in a dream,
I forgot everything, I forgot my childhood and my homeland,
I only knew that your caresses held me prisoner.
And smiling you took a mirror and asked me to see myself.
I saw that my shoulders were made of dust and crumbled,
I saw that my beauty was sick and had no will than--to
   disappear.
Oh, hold me closed in your arms so tightly that I need
   nothing.

With what borders on satirical art, Edith Södergran suggests the
classical seduction scene of late nineteenth-century literature:
the chambre separée, wine, roses, the lover's flattering remarks,
his smiling efforts to get her to admit that she is beautiful; this
seducer's strain, composed of the expressions of practiced insincer-
ity, runs in contrast to her uncertainty, her surrender, and finally
her desperation. The concluding outcry is almost unbearably poignant; in her mortal terror at what her lover has shown her, albeit
half-realizing his unworthiness (was there a trace of cruelty in his
offer of the looking-glass?), she calls for the passing security of
his embrace.

     The lover as temporary savior (and possibly slayer) appears at
the climax of another poem about the love experience, "Våra systrar
gå i brokiga kläder" ("Our Sisters Walk in Many-colored Clothes").
The sisters have not yet known love, and anticipate it, caught up
in vague dreams (SD, p. 61): "Our sisters stand by the water and
sing, / our sisters sit on stones and wait, / they have water and
air in their baskets, / and call it flowers." Yet the speaker has
tasted love and its pain, a "cross" whose full (and non-Christian)
meaning becomes plain in the ensuing narrative: "But I cast my
arms around a cross / and weep. / Once I was as soft as a bright-
green leaf, / and hung high up in the blue air, / then two blades
were crossed within me / and a victor led me to his lips." If the
cross is a sign of suffering and loss (erected over the grave of
love), then the crossed blades are the conflicting urges within the
speaker: a desire to remain in the "soft greenness" of youth, hung
high against blue infinity (see the opening of "Love"), and a desire
to become the beloved of the victor. The latter seems to be more
generous and devoted than the heavy handed "lord" of "The Day Cools"
or the seducer, with his lethal mirror, of "Love"; in that poem, the
woman "crumbles" before her image, while this lover--although mascu-
linely strong--is gentler, and even gives a pledge of his devotion:
"His hardness was so gentle that I did not crumble, / he fastened a
shimmering star on my forehead..." Yet his concluding behavior
erases the favorable impression just made: "and left me trembling
with tears / on an island which is called winter."

Much of the poetry about love and abandonment in Dikter uses
scenic elements: the sea, the rocky shore, the desert island. Tideström's and Ekelöf's thesis--that the world of Dikter is based upon
the "most concrete reality" of Raivola--is a sturdy and serviceable
one; it does not hold, however, in the present case--Raivola simply
did not offer the topographical features just listed, and the bathing
resort of Terijoki, thirty kilometers away, on "Finland's Riviera,"
had sandy beaches and a crowded casino. Yet the speaker of "Oroliga
drömmar" ("Restless Dreams") is a castaway, or an exile (SD, p. 56):
"Far from happiness I lie on an island in the sea and slumber. / The
mists rise and disperse and the winds shift, / I dream restless
dreams about wars and great festivals, / and my beloved stands on a
ship and sees / how the swallows fly and knows no longing!" The
beloved resembles the man of "The Day Cools" in his lack of emotion
and (as we shall see) his heaviness; perhaps he is exculpated,
though, by the fact that he is controlled by fate: "There is something heavy within him that cannot move, / he sees his ship glide
into the unwilling future, / the sharp prow cut into recalcitrant
fate." These lines could be taken, to be sure, as transparent allusions to the call to the colors which (according to the scanty
reports) took the Russian lover away from Terijoki, just as the
island ("called winter," "far from happiness") could be the simplest
of metaphors for the woman's state. Nonetheless, the island returns
with startling persistence in the poetry of disappointed love, so
often that the reference would become threadbare, were it not for
Edith Södergran's gifts at variation. In "Sick Days" the castaway
is reduced to the organ of emotion, the heart, a heart imprisoned
and living on a cruel diet of deprivation: "Narrowly my heart is
preserved in a small crevice, / far away my heart is placed on a
distant island. / White birds fly back and forth / and bring the
message that my heart is living. / I know how it lives, / from coal
and sand / and sharp stones." Or, in "Mot alla fyra vindar" ("Toward
All Four Winds"), the speaker herself is wholly cut off from the
world, and lives in fear, like an animal (SD, p. 60):

> No bird is blown off course to my hidden corner...
> In the rock's shadow my wildness keeps watch,
> ready to flee at the slightest rustle, and an approaching
>   step...

Her only companion is the sky itself, with its blue infinity:

> Silent and blueing is my world, the blessed one...
> I have a portal toward all four winds.
> I have a golden portal toward the east...for love which
>   never comes,
> I have a portal for the day and another for sadness,
> I have a portal for death--it stands forever open.

Days pass, sadness comes, love does not come, death would be welcome.
In "Två stranddikter" ("Two Beach Poems" (SD, pp. 68-69)), the woman
lies prone as she waits; in the one poem, she is in the first-person
past tense ("I lay naked the long day through on the gray rocks"),
and in the other, in the second-person present. (We have seen before

how easily, in her eternal conversation with herself, Edith Södergran
changes from the one pronoun to the other.) "Between gray stones /
your white body lies lamenting / over the days that come and go... /
Silence without echo, / loneliness without mirror." The same empty
world surrounds the prostrate figure in "Den låga stranden" ("The
Low Beach" (SD, p. 87)): "Here I lie on my belly and look straight
before me: / here all is foreign and wakes no memories, / my thoughts
were not born in this place; / here the air is raw and the stones
are slippery, / here all is dead and wakes no merriment, / save for
the broken flute the spring left on the beach." We are back again
at "the island which is called winter"; a detail has been added,
the broken instrument left behind by the springtime of love--the
poet does not play pastoral tunes any more, but tells of her despair.
She laments, and the cause of her lament is what we have come to
expect: the poem has opened with a statement of her exclusion from
the world ("The light birds high in the air / do not fly for me, /
but the heavy stones on the low beach rest for me").

What might be called an open secret in the mythology of Dikter
lies at the root of this repetition; Edith Södergran has turned herself into Ariadne, deserted by Theseus on the wintry beach of Naxos.
No one would claim that Edith Södergran was a learned poet, but it
did not take particular learnedness, in the early twentieth century,
to be aware of the Ariadne tale. We can be sure that Edith Södergran
had read Nietzsche's poem, "Klage der Ariadne" ("Ariadne's Lament"),
and that she knew the Ariadne passage in Ecce homo, which she appears
to have come upon at Davos. [31] (The Ariadne theme was very much on
the mind of contemporary poets and musicians: in his Venetian novel,
Il fuoco (The Flame, 1900), D'Annunzio's singer, whose voice enchants
the book's hero, achieves her greatest triumph in her performance of
"The Lament of Ariadne," the great surviving aria from Monteverdi's
opera, and Richard Strauss' Ariadne auf Naxos had its premiere in
1912. [32]) Not only is the central configuration the same (the woman
left alone on the island, the man who sails away); the poems contain
evidence of still closer knowledge. The speaker of "Love" has "forgotten her childhood and her homeland"; Ariadne betrayed and deserted
her father, in order to sail away with Theseus. The penultimate
line of "Restless Dreams" predicts the lover's subsequent misadven-
tures: "wings bear him away to the land where all he does is in
vain"; returning to Athens, Theseus inadvertently causes the death
of his father, and is driven out, in time, by a rebellious populace.
And "Our Sisters" ends with the line: "he fastened a shimmering
star to my forehead, and left me trembling in tears"; before leaving
Ariadne on Naxos, Theseus gives her a crown he has fetched from the
sea or, variously, from the sky. [33] It is odd, of course, that Edith
Södergran does not once name Ariadne [34] in her poetry; she approaches
a revelation only in the "Dionysus" poem of Rosenaltaret (see p. 98),
where the speaker--like Ariadne on Naxos--is carried aloft by the
god. What her reasons were for this concealment, we shall never
know; perhaps she felt that the specific intrusion of classical myth
into her collection would have destroyed its extremely personal and
naive air, and its air of novelty. In some of her aspects, Edith
Södergran was very much the traditionalist (a child of a poetic world
that loved classical allusion) but she was a traditionalist concealed, even as she was a hidden Ariadne.

She is also a traditionalist as she fills her collection out
with specimens of the catalogue poem (which, in Edith Södergran's
practice, is customarily a catalogue of definitions, the stating of
various and sometimes mutually contradictory meanings for a word or
concept), a structure to which she often gives, by implication, a
didactic content. (Tideström suggests that Edith Södergran learned
to write catalogue poems from Whitman, Enckell suggests Stefan
George.[35]) "Vierge moderne," mentioned above, is an example of her
practice, defining and instructing;[36] in its thirteen anaphoric lines
(or fourteen: the first line is comprised of two sentences), it
tells the "modern virgin" how to use her manifold strengths. Still
another example is "Livet" ("Life" (SD, pp. 121-122)): "Life is the
narrow ring which holds us prisoner /...Life is scorning one's self
/ and lying unmovable on the bottom of a well"--existence must be
perceived as imprisonment; here, the anaphoric structure is less
faithfully observed but still discernible. "Gud" ("God") has twelve
lines, again anaphoric; only the second line breaks the pattern (SD,
pp. 52-53): "God is a couch of rest, on which we lie stretched out
in the cosmos, / pure as angels, with saintly blue eyes answering
the greeting of the stars; / god is a pillow against which we lean
our head, god is a prop for our feet; / god is a storehouse of force
and a virginal darkness..." It is not a poem careful of the feelings
of churchgoers: the implication of the second line may be that,
using the word "god" as a cushion and prop, we can take the spiritual
life easy, deeming ourselves "pure as angels." In at least one
instance, it becomes pugnaciously anti-religious ("god is a prison
for all free souls"); but (again mixing definition and instruction),
it concludes by saying that "god" is what we make of him, and the
best use to which the concept can be put is as a sense of the infinite, an object of our longing, whose "coming contours" we ourselves
construct.[37] Edith Södergran equips her final definition with an
exclamation point, as though to fasten the last and best use of "god"
within our minds: "god is what longing can persuade to descend to
earth!"

"Helvetet" ("Hell") takes another word often on the lips of
the clergy, and gives definitions as witty as those at the opening
of "God," but infinitely grimmer. It begins with a derisive praise,
"Oh, how splendid hell is," meant to have antithetical effect. The
word "hell" appears eight times in the eleven lines of the poem; as
in "Livet," the anaphoric pattern is not strictly maintained (SD,
p. 123): "In hell no one speaks of death. / Hell is walled into
the earth's innards / and adorned with glowing flowers." Defining
hell, Edith Södergran gives a perverse twist to some fundamental
concepts of Christianity: like heaven, hell defeats death because
its inmates have eternal life in their eternal torments; as in
heaven, everything is meaningful ("no one says an empty word")
because its inhabitants suffer unceasing pain, even as the blest
enjoy unceasing happiness; as in heaven, "no one grows sick and no
one tires." These displays of terrifying paradox are intermingled
with statements that sound almost parodistically primitive, as if
taken from a hellfire-and-brimstone sermon: "hell is walled into
the innards of the earth...," "In hell, no one has drunk and no one
has slept / and no one rests and no one sits still," and, in the

abrupt conclusion, "hell is unchangeable and eternal." Yet, reading
them, we realize that Edith Södergran writes, in fact, not about a
medieval inferno, "adorned with glowing flowers," but about the
walled-up quality of earthly life.[38] As in "Life" (which directly
precedes "Hell" in Dikter), we are prisoners, as long as our perception lasts.

    "Skönhet" ("Beauty" (SD, pp. 112-113)) is a more diffuse and
less effective poem than "Hell." After its opening query ("What is
beauty? Ask all souls--"), it gives a series of eleven anaphoric
lines, constructed precisely like those in "Vierge moderne" or "God."
Again, it mixes the homely with the sublime, or, at any rate, the
small with the large ("Beauty is the parrot's feathers or the sunset
that forebodes a storm"), and in one instance (the most quotable line
in the poem, and the line where the pattern of statement is broken
by an emphatic negative) it succeeds in a piece of mordant wit,
putting poser-poets in their place: "beauty is not the thin sauce
in which poets serve themselves up." But irony is kept at a minimum
in "Beauty"; beauty is too serious a matter for jokes, and, in fact,
becomes synonymous with the intensity which--Edith Södergran liked
to argue--alone makes life worth living. Thus she can be led to
apparently dangerous statements: "beauty is making war and seeking
happiness, / beauty is serving higher powers"; in Septemberlyran,
and the subsequent collections, written under Nietzsche's aegis,
her urge toward the vita activa, at all costs, grows stronger still.

    Having railed against imprisonment in an inactive existence,
having rejected a flight into dreams, the poet finds it necessary
to instruct herself, repeatedly, on the value of pain, the price to
be paid for participation in life. One of the most tantalizing
questions about Edith Södergran concerns her knowledge of and reaction to the Russian cultural ambiance; was she aware of the strong
emphasis the Orthodox Church puts on the redemptive quality of suffering? Or does she draw directly upon the moralistic western teaching of ruinous pleasure and painfully stern virtue, as represented,
for example, in the most famous of Sweden's baroque poems, Georg
Stiernhielm's (1598-1672) about Hercules' choice between "Lady Pleasure" and "Lady Virtue"? Edith Södergran's "Två gudinnor" ("Two
Goddesses" (SD, pp. 92-93)) are similarly called "happiness" and
"pain": "When you saw the countenance of happiness, you were disappointed, / this slumberer with flaccid features / ...and you
resolved never to serve her." Instead, the speaker takes "pain with
deepness in her eyes, the (goddess) never appealed to / she who rules
over the strong seas and the sinking ships, / over those imprisoned
for life." The poem "Smärtan" ("Pain" (SD, pp. 125-127)), which
concludes Dikter, tells what pain will do for her votaries. "Happiness is impotent, she sleeps and breathes and is aware of nothing";
pain makes her followers aware of life--and thus a return is made to
the credo of intensity, of living life, even as a prisoner, for all
it is worth, despite its manifold treacheries and disappointments.
Pain, the active forerunner of motionless death, is the greatest of
inspiratory forces; the last of Dikter's catalogues is in her praise:
"She gives pearls and flowers, she gives songs and dreams, / she
gives us a thousand kisses which all are empty, / she gives the only

kiss which is real. / She gives us our strange souls and special moods, / she gives us all life's highest profits: / love, loneliness, and death's face." Pain should be cherished, happiness destroyed: "Strike your happiness so that she crumbles, for happiness is evil."

How seriously Edith Södergran took her own instructions can be seen in the uncollected "Min framtid" ("My Future" (SD, p. 143)), which begins with a brief backward glance: "A caprice-filled moment / stole my future from me / a future accidentally improvised." (For the phrase "tillfälligt hoptimrade," we are tempted to say "jerrybuilt"; she had planned poorly, and a whim--her own or someone else's --has destroyed the poor structure.) Now she means to construct a new future, carefully laid out; it is important to note that the noun "will," not used before in her work, is the credo's foundation-- it has a central function in the Nietzschean poems to come: "I shall build it up more beautifully by far / as I had thought of it from the start. / I shall build it up on the solid ground / which is called my will. / I shall raise it up on high pillars / which are called my ideals. / I shall build it up with a secret passage / which is called my soul. / I shall build it with a high tower / which is called loneliness." The poem is full of admirable determination; had Edith Södergran included it in Dikter, her audience might have been pleased with it, for at first glance it seems to continue the idealism which marked Finland-Swedish verse of the Age of Runeberg. Still, the audience would have been made uncomfortable by the emphasis on the will, on the preservation of a special personality ("my soul"), and on a lonely superiority not only accepted but nurtured. It is an individual's program she outlines here; note the repetition of the first-person pronoun, five times, as a sentence opener.

In another uncollected poem, though, Edith Södergran provided a lesson which--although couched in terms incontrovertibly her own-- could have general validity: "Ingenting" ("Nothing" (SD, pp. 146-147)) has deservedly become one of the best-known of her poems. The poem has been taken by some critics as a conversation between mother and child; one account has it that the poem was written in consequence of a scene Edith Södergran had witnessed at the Raivola railroad station. The suggestion has also been made that the passage about the "bluer sky" is like a forlorn travel poster on a station wall, and Gunnar Ekelöf (who saw Södergran's homeland with the keen eyes of the gifted tourist in 1938) has found the poem's landscape to be peculiarly Karelian--the monotony of the evergreen woods, cut through by the railroad tracks, which seem to run off into infinity. Once again, the present world is a prison, but the poster's world, albeit gaudier, would be a prison too:

> Be calm, my child, for there is nothing,
> and all is as you see: the forest, the smoke, and the
>   flight of rails.
> Somewhere far away in a distant land
> there is a bluer sky and a wall with roses
> or a palm and a milder wind--

and that is all.
There is nothing more than snow on the fir tree's branch.
There is nothing to kiss with warm lips,
and all lips grow cool with time.
But you say, my child, that your heart is mighty,
and that to live in vain is less than to die.
What did you want of death? Do you know the repugnance
    his clothes spread
and nothing is more loathsome than to die by one's own
    hand.
We should love life's hours of sickness
and narrow years of longing
as the brief moments when the desert blooms.

Helena Södergran told a Danish interviewer that her daughter had
read "both Kant and Schopenhauer";[40] and it would be quite possible
to see the poem as a gloss on one of Schopenhauer's central concepts
--that the world is an illusion, "Schein," in which we may refuse to
believe or participate, thus destroying our will to live. An interpretation of the poem in Schopenhauer's spirit could be made: as we
know, Edith Södergran had a penchant for word-plays, and, when she
wrote "the flight of rails" ("skenornas flykt"), she could also have
thought of the like-sounding Swedish noun for "illusion," sken, and
its German cognate. (She had already used the word in "Vägen till
lyckan" (see p. 44), in its concluding query; she would adduce the
word again at the climax of "Materialism" (see p. 112), her outcry
of despair at the thought that a human being is but corruptible
flesh.) The poem's opening would also seem to say that the phenomena
of the world--the North's sparseness and tedium, the South's bright-
ness and exoticism--are all nothing, or illusion, and thus not worthy
of concern: everything will pass away, our passions too. ("Smoke"
and "snow," of course, are time-honored symbols of life's transitoriness and vanity.)

    The other, unheard "speaker"--"my child"--appears to counter
with the lament that its heart is nonetheless filled with passions,
which in its isolation it cannot bring to bear; the "child" would
rather die by its own hand than to live "in vain." (Strange senti-
ments for a child: is not the poem in fact another of Edith Södergran's many arguments with herself, a wiser and older persona chiding
a more foolish and younger one?) The wise voice replies that death
is horrible, death by suicide still worse (Edith Södergran had con-
templated suicide several times in her life), and that we should love
whatever life gives us, however poverty-stricken or hasty the gift
may be. If anything, then, "Nothing" is directed against an abandonment of the world, and is one of the greatest of Edith Södergran's
lyric lessons in how to endure life, surpassing the more abstract
"Two Goddesses" and "Pain" by wonderfully clear and simple images.
Elmer Diktonius saw the poem in this "anti-Schopenhauerian" light;
the "nothing" of the title and the first line is not an absolute,
but a concept to be taken relatively, an indication of a world of
radical limitation where happiness is to be found in the smallest
and apparently most insignificant sensations. In 1928, Diktonius
dedicated a book of idylls, called Ingenting (Nothing), to Edith

Södergran's memory. It opens with the author reduced (like the dead Orpheus) to a head, lying on a stall-ramp in the sun, and singing of the wonderful poverty of things around him: "The smoke, coming up from the wash tub, is nothing, but perhaps beautiful, just as the forest and the flight of rails. And all is as you see, and my huge head's right eye sees something in nothing, and is satisfied. With the essential."[41]

Edith Södergran essayed the theme of the perceived "nothingness" of life in one more poem, again from the time of Dikter but not included in the collection--"Ett liv" ("A Life" (SD, pp. 148-149)): "If happiness never comes? What is life? / A little water lily withers in the sand." Existence passes quickly and vainly, leaving only a grotesque remnant behind--a remnant that can well be taken as a comment upon Edith Södergran's own physical condition: "What has the dragonfly done with its single day? / There is no answer save two lifeless wings / over a sunken breast." At this point, more didactically than in "Nothing" (yet with the typical Södergranian surprise, the paradoxical images), the message of self-maintenance against hopeless odds, and hopeless prospects, is stated once more: "Black will never become white-- / yet the sweetness of the struggle remains for all, / and everyday fresh flowers come from hell." As the desert blossomed briefly, so flowers spring from torment, equivalents of the gifts that pain bestows. But the poem does not end on this indomitable note. Beyond the struggle, there lies the true nothingness, the void--Edith Södergran's besetting terror, so awful that she can seldom bring herself to write of it: "But a day will come when hell is empty and heaven is closed / and all stands still." The poet returns to the dragon fly, the metaphor of her own brief existence:[42] "Then nothing remains save a dragonfly's body in the fold of a leaf. / But no one will know of it any longer." The poet's intelligence has been extinguished, her voice silenced forever.

4.

Nietzsche and Civil War:
Septemberlyran

In the version of Septemberlyran which appeared at Schildt's in
1918 there are 31 poems, in Gunnar Tideström's edition there are 45.
Of the 14 poems making up the difference, seven had been printed in
Landet som icke är, seven were given to the world for the first time
by Tideström. There had been, however, 51 poems in the fair copy
which Edith Södergran sent to Runar Schildt; of these four were held
over until Rosenaltaret (among them, that collection's title poem)
and two were not even admitted by Tideström to his augmented Septemberlyran of 1949, but were rather consigned to the commentary (SD,
pp. 409-411). These are "Jägarens lycka" ("The Huntsman's Happiness"), which Tideström believes is influenced by Kipling's Jungle
Book, and "Dianas körer" ("Diana's Choruses"), which Edith Södergran
herself had asked to have withdrawn from the manuscript. Probably
she had realized that its regular meter and its rhymes set it off
quite clearly from the rest of the poems; it would have clashed both
with Nietzsche's condescending remarks on rhyme in Die Geburt der
Tragödie and her own statement on rhythm in the introduction to the
new volume: "That my poetry is poesy, no one can deny, I will not
assert that it is verse. I have tried to put certain recalcitrant
poems into a rhythm, and in the process discovered that I possess a
strength of word and image only in full freedom, that is to say, at
the cost of rhythm. My poems are to be taken as careless sketches.
As far as the content is concerned, I let my instinct build up what
my intellect, in an expectant attitude, observes. My self-assurance
rests on the fact that I have discovered my dimensions. It is not
proper for me to make myself less than I am" (SD, p. 160).

There is a contradiction both in the open letter to Dagens Press
(see p. 14) and in this introduction; on the one hand she calls her
poems an "intimate sketchbook" and "careless sketches," on the other,
with her proclamation that she had consecrated herself to the "high-

est things," and her insistence upon the discovery of her "dimensions," she caused even the friendly Jarl Hemmer to say that Septemberlyran was "the introduction to the most measureless self-assertion
which had ever taken place in the Swedish lyric."² Similarly, as we
have seen, Edith Södergran gave Runar Schildt free rein, yet complained bitterly to Hagar Olsson that he had taken advantage of it:
"Runar Schildt has probably been confused by the poems and didn't
understand them a whit. He's naive, after all" (ED, p. 33). These
ambiguities in her attitude toward her work arose, probably, from
the experience she had in the September of 1918: "I was reborn in
September, therefore Septemberlyran. I suddenly felt with unfailing
certainty that a stronger hand had seized my pen" (EB, p. 32)--an
experience which might have been suggested to her by Nietzsche's
"holy January." She then dismissed the poems written before the
experience as being of little value (the reason for her dismay at
Schildt's omission of the dates of composition), but, at the same
time, she was afraid that the public would not accept the full-blown
products of her new ecstasy. Despite her haughtiness toward her
possible readership, she wanted badly to be read. Nor did she help
her readers by her reference, in the open letter, to the "scrappi-
ness" of the book, and her opinion that "O mina solbrandsfärgade
toppar" ("Oh My Sun-flame-colored Tops"), "Vanvettets virvel" ("The
Whirlpool of Madness"), and "Världen badar i blod" ("The World Bathes
in Blood"), belong to a "transitional stage"; privately, to Hagar
Olsson, she named some poems where "the spirit is banal . . . this
rests on the fact that they come from the time to which I ascribe
my debut book" (EB, p. 22). These are "Jungfruns död" ("The Maiden's
Death"), "Till en ung kvinna" ("To a Young Woman"), "Vad är i morgon?" ("What is Tomorrow?), "Triumf att finnas till" ("Triumph of
Existing"), "Starka hyacinter" ("Strong Hyacinths"), and "Trädet i
skogen" ("The Tree in the Forest").

Without agreeing with all Edith Södergran's value judgments, we
may use her divisions of the poetry to construct an outline of the
book's contents. The poems from 1916-1917 would indeed be quite at
home in Dikter--"Skymning" ("Twilight," (SD, p. 165)) is a mood-poem
with an attractively childlike touch ("The night comes large in his
woolly beard"), and the unhappy love-affair can be discerned behind
several of the poems. "Upptäckt" ("Discovery," (SD, p. 166)) has
the often quoted lines: "Your hand is lust--my hand is longing";
the "Young Woman" is told that, after listening to the man's many
promises and clinging to him as "a flower does to its stalk," she
will discover that ". . . he lives only from your purity's white
bread / and that his blood merely streams in your motherly tender-
ness' basin" (SD, p. 164), the last formulation particularly bold if
one remembers that "bäcken" also means "pelvis."³ Otherwise, the
story not of woman's submission but of her superiority reappears,
quite plainly, in the discarded "Diana's Choruses" and more crypti-
cally in "Strong Hyacinths," contemporaneous, it should be remembered, to the lost prose-tale, "Princess Hyacintha," whose heroine
(or so Hagar Olsson recalled) lived in a shining castle surrounded
by four islands, among them an "isle of maidens."⁴ The "disgusting
flies" of the poem are human triviality in general (Olof Enckell saw
a resemblance to "Concerning the Flies of the Market Place" in Also

sprach Zarathustra)[5]; but the triumphant and pure flowers of the poem, the hyacinth and the lily, can be associated with Diana's aggressive purity (SD, p. 167): "They won't get me to believe in disgusting flies / --revenge and small desires. / I believe in strong hyacinths which drip primal juice. / Lilies are healing and pure as my own sharpness." The speaker of these poems of chastisement and rebuke would seem to threaten the addressee of the poem "What is Tomorrow?" with a kind of haunting; the reader will recognize the familiar anaphoric style of Dikter, as well as the intention of revenge on the man (SD, p. 168): "I shall go from you with a certainty which is like no other: / I shall come again as a piece of your own pain . . ." The speaker gives herself animal attributes; she will turn the recipient's former "barren" passion into the scene of something new, wild, and (for him) frightening: "I shall come to you strange, angry and faithful / with a wild animal's step from your heart's desert homeland." But then a final degradation of the man is threatened, using especially 'feminine' imagery (threads, yarn, dress) to humiliate him: "I shall smile and twist silken threads around my finger / And I'll hide your fate's little ball in a fold of my dress." In the German poetry of the notebook, Edith Södergran twice mentioned the approach, feared and desired, of "male footsteps" (ESD, p. 94, p. 114); now, the predatory beast's footsteps will draw near, with the faithfulness of hate, the threads will be wrapped around the woman's finger (Swedish shares the idiom with English: to twist someone around one's finger), the skein popped into a fold of her skirt. But still more important than the speaker's quick metamorphoses is the poem's hint of what is to come--its minatory tone, its sense of certainty and mission, while a word such as ond ('angry' or 'wicked') calls to mind that Zarathustra was "ein Freund des Bösen," "a friend of that which is angry (or wicked)."

Beyond erotic disappointment, another wound dealt Edith Södergran also got a poetic response, the critical reception accorded Dikter. "The Maiden's Death" was written, as Tideström says, directly after the somewhat chilly review of the debut book by Holger Nohrström (SD, pp. 170-171):

> The tender maiden's soul never made a mistake,
> she knew everything about herself,
> she knew still more: about others and the sea.
> Her eyes were blueberries, her lips raspberries, her hand
>   wax.
> She danced for the autumn on yellowed carpets,
> She shrank and whirled and sank--and was extinguished.
> When she was gone, no one knew that her corpse was left in
>   the forest . . .
> Long she was sought among the maidens on the beach,
> they sang of small mussels in red shells.
> She was sought among the men who were drinking,
> they fought for shining knives from the duke's kitchen.
> She was sought in the field of lilies of the valley,
> where her shoe was left since last night.

Tideström calls the poem a death-fantasy, and Finn Stein Larsen a "documentation for the fact that (she) actually entertained thoughts of suicide."[6] But the poem is not just an imaginary and graceful departure from the stage, in response to criticism's and life's cruelties, although the first three lines could be taken as a mildly ironic resumé of the contents of Dikter. It continues, Larsen says, with a catalogue of the means she had employed to "overcome . . . her own hopeless situation." The girl seems to be a relative of the "Princess" in Landet som icke är (SD, p. 141), whose longing was a "shy mimosa," and who knew that her heart must die and be "wholly crumbled, for truth gnaws." ("'Crumble'--'söndersmula'--is a favorite verb of Edith Södergran to describe the destruction of the loving woman; recall the "crumbling" shoulders of the speaker of "Love" in Dikter.) Here, the parts of the maiden, as she is described, suggest fragility--berries grow quickly stale, unless eaten; wax, the substance pale as death, breaks easily. At least two of the parts suggest eroticism as well: see the Swedish folksong about longing, "Out in our pasture there blueberries grow," and J. L. Runeberg's imitation folk-ballad, where the girl, coming from a tryst, tells her mother that her lips are red because she has eaten raspberries.[7] In addition, all three items of the description come from nature, and it is to nature that the girl will return. She is plainly a counterpart of the "Forest's Bright Daughter," and of the listener to the blandishments of "The Strange Tree," who is promised that her limbs will be concealed "in the splendor of the autumn" (see p. 40). The places where she is sought all indicate, to Larsen, that the means of her possible succor have been insufficient, or have failed: "love, a feeling for nature." Certainly, he is right on the first score; he makes the interesting argument that the mussels in the red shells of which the girls sing are those creatures "whose sensitive helplessness forces them to surround themselves with an impenetrable shell . . ." and that they "have strong qualities in common with the heart . . ." But the girls on the beach, who are expressly called "tärnor" (a word either old-fashioned, from the folksong, or, simply, a terminus technicus, 'bridesmaids'), sing a song which could be more banally erotic: the mussel shell (concha, vulva) is commonly used as a symbol of sexual love (cf. Alfred Mombert's "You wash bright colored shells upon the beach . . . And resting hand in hand with you / I feel something immortal within me"[8]), and "red," as has been pointed out, is the color of eroticism for Edith Södergran. The bridesmaids are singing an epithalamium for a marriage that will not take place, and, indeed, that the maiden would not want to take place, if the groom is from among those pugnacious and greedy men in the (implied) castle, who fight, in that odd construction, "for the shining knives"--"shining" because they are polished, or shining with grease from the kitchen?[9] One might see a further reason, in this web of associations, for the use of edibles earlier in the poem: the berries and the mussels. The maiden does not wish to be devoured (above, the "young woman" gave the white bread of her purity to the man); instead, she prefers vanishing into nature--and it would seem that nature, Larsen to the contrary, has given her a kind of succor after all, a resting place in the forest. The poem may very well be suicidal, and certainly it is filled with contempt for its other humans, the drinking (and drunken?) men, the bumbling searchers, perhaps even for the bridesmaids and their song; but it is also filled with exaltation: the shoe was lost while running through the field of purity, beauty, and the spring, and the maiden herself was extinguished ('slocknade') like a star. (Larsen senses this aspect of the verb: he speaks of an "autumnal star-death.")

One of the ironies attaching to the reception of Septemberlyran was that "The Maiden's Death," written in response to what Edith Södergran took as unfavorable criticism of Dikter, was the object of puzzlement in the reviews of the new book. However, the criticism of Septemberlyran thus called attention to a poem--ranked by Edith Södergran herself as "banal"--which was a milestone in her verse, a culmination in her use of the fairy-tale allusion, and an apparent farewell to that intimacy with nature which is characteristic of her first collection. Having pretended to vanish into nature with the feigned suicide note, the poet may now give herself over to what Larsen calls her "heroic aestheticism or poetic clairvoyance."

Other poems in Septemberlyran also respond to the critical reception which Edith Södergran had been accorded. "Tjuren" ("The Bull") was regarded by Elmer Diktonius (who used a quotation from the poem as a motto for his newspaper article of 1924, "Tjuren och vi" ("The Bull and We"), about criticism's inability to deal with modern poetry) and by Hagar Olsson as a statement on the indifference of Swedish Finland's reviewers to the splendid novelty of Dikter.[10] Critics themselves missed this point, the infamous "Jumbo" implying that the poem was an erotic wish-dream on the poet's part (SD, p. 175): "Why does the bull hesitate? / My character is a red cloth," and even Sten Selander, a Swedish poet and critic of considerable stature, took the poem to be an erotic statement, saying that it "only apparently" deals with the indifference which met her "proclamation," while its "unconscious and thereby primary content is surely disappointment that men have not conquered her."[11] The proposal of "Jumbo" seems vulgar, and Selander's extravagant; yet so cautious a scholar as Tideström was not willing to reject these thoughts out of hand, knowing about the sexual dreams, with animal figures, which Edith Södergran recounted to Hagar Olsson: how a "splendid black horse" plunged at her (EB, p. 45) and again--after mentioning that "Hagar kissed me once"--how, in a dream, "a horse rushed after me." (EB, p. 54). Even when she spoke consciously about criticism, her erotic urges revealed themselves: "Lillgubben" ("Little Old Man" (SD, p. 172)) in Septemberlyran is incontestibly an epigram aimed at those pedantic critics who "count eggs" and thereby reduce the value of a poet's work. But, in its manner and its main figure, it resembles "Ur 'Liliputs saga'," one of the poems on erotic revenge in Dikter. Later on, Edith Södergran became quite aware, as we know, of the erotic force's permeation of the whole of life.

Yet in the more self-conscious "Grimace d'artiste" from September, 1917, there is very little, save the word "red" itself, which could lead the mind back to the erotic world of Dikter. Here, Edith Södergran is already quite aware of having been 'chosen,' even though the marvelous Nietzschean month lay just one year away. Erik Therman observed that the poem was particularly direct,[12] for it stated what, to Edith Södergran, was obvious. The speaker (or, indeed, the proclaimer) of the poem has nothing save her "shining cloak," her "red undauntedness," armed with which she goes out in search of adventure --the knightly quest again--into "shabby lands." The progress of the poem, though, is made not from place to place, but from poetic apparatus to poetic apparatus: from the mantle of strophe one to the "hard lyre" of strophe two, to the "highborn crown, / my rising pride" of strophe three. At the poem's end the speaker takes farewell with a theatrical gesture, rather less subtly than when the maiden vanishes in the forest (SD, p. 174): "My rising pride takes the lyre beneath its arm / and bows farewell."

The title, "Grimace d'artiste," has an air of wryly smiling at the poem's melodrama; and Hagar Olsson attested frequently to her friend's fluctuation between good-humored common sense and quite unreasoning exaltation; there is plenty of evidence in the poetry written before the marvelous September that the one side of her personality viewed the other with considerable skepticism. The opening poem of Septemberlyran is the jubilant "Triumph of Existing," the title of which has become a motto for Södergran enthusiasts, since it captures that affirmation of existence which is basic to her poetic world; two selections from her poetry bear the poem's name.[13] Its principle theme is a Zarathustran celebration of the sun ("Truly, like unto the sun, I love life"):[14] "I walk on sun, I stand on sun, / I know of naught else than sun" (SD, pp. 161-162). The quiet hint in "The Maiden's Death"--the girl is like a leaf (or a star) that is extinguished--turns, here, into a full and victorious metaphor: "What do I fear? I am a part of infinity. / I am a part of the cosmos' great strength, / a lonely world among millions of worlds, / like unto a star of the first power which is extinguished last . . ." This star (or existence), fed on that special Zarathustran food, honey ("The sun fills my breast with sweet honey to its very brim"), at the end is persuaded by the sun that "all stars disappear at last, yet they always shine without terror," thus giving an oblique answer to the opening question, "What do I fear?" The speaker of the poem, while she lives, will not merely find triumph in survival, but will live bravely and splendidly, like a star, without fear of the eventual disappearance which (again a Zarathustran thought) is in the order of things.

However, this "hymn to the sun" and "these triumphal lines"[15] have grown uneasy even in the first strophe, for the poem also contains an awareness of time's passage; the speaker simultaneously knows the "triumph of feeling time run icecold through one's veins / and hearing the night's silent river." And persistent time returns in the second strophe, her name three times repeated, with her attributes: "Time--transformer, time--destroyer, time--enchanter"; she offers lures ("new tricks, a thousand subterfuges") to the effect that the speaker's existence may indeed continue, as a "little seed, a snake, a cliff in the sea"; but these blandishments of time (now called a murderer, or rather, murderess, "mörderska") are shoved aside with a variation upon Christ's words to Satan, "Vik ifrån mig," "Get hence." The speaker rejects, or suppresses, the thought of an

ordinary death, at time's hands, and the thought of a continued
existence, in transformation; for she has learned, she insists,
heroic acceptance of the end, becoming, as in Nietzsche, "a sun one's
self and an inexorable sun-will, ready for destruction in victory."[16]
An element of understandable self-hypnosis, or arrogant illogicality,
lies in the poem. Her end will not be like that of others, mere
mortals.

The Zarathustran spirit also informs "Oh My Sun-flame-colored
Tops": the straining for the heights, the sense of being chosen and,
so, isolated, the sense of contempt for those below, the sense of a
return to a lost homeland, the ecstasy of direct contact with the
pure blue sky, the sea of light (SD, pp. 177-178): "Oh my sun-flame-
colored tops, / will you take me back?!!! / I will live forever in
your lonely garden of paradise, / There alone is my home, / there
fire-eyed angels / kiss away all the dew of longing from the earth. /
O my undarkened tops! / Far from you I do not live for a day, /
Wretched, I should perish. / The earth died for me on the third day,
/ her forests murmur out of a dream for me. / What are bridges,
fields and villages to me? / Spots on your pure blue sky, / shadows
on your bright eye, day, / howl of wolves from an abyss." The language, however, has strong echoes from Scripture as well: the "lust-
gård" of the third line recalls the Garden of Paradise, the fire-
eyed angels recall the repeated description of the Son of Man in
Revelations ("And his eyes were as a flame of fire"), and the line,
"The earth died for me on the third day," is a reference to the central Christian text, "that he hath been raised on the third day
according to the scriptures," its use here made more blasphemous
still (to pious eyes) by the suggestion that the poem's speaker,
reborn, has ascended to the mountain tops, if not into heaven. She
has reached, indeed, a very special salvation of her own, which, in
its turn, may save the world: "If I heal myself, / this drop is
enough for all that breathes," and therefore her "longing" and her
"will" are instructed to fly ever higher, away from the ground:
"Rise up, bold warriors, / light and happy as armed devils." To
Edith Södergran's consternation, the second of these lines was
printed with wide-spaced letters, giving too much emphasis to what
was in fact a detail of borrowed Nietzschean language in the poem
(one thinks of the demand, in Jenseits von Gut und Böse, that "we
last Stoics" should take "whatever we may have of devilishness in
us," in order to undertake a house-cleaning of the world[17]). The
printer's mistake, together with the faun, or imp, which had been
chosen as an illustration for the book ("They crowned it with a
devil," Edith Södergran wrote to Hagar Olsson), could divert the
audience from Edith Södergran's intention--the poem was placed first
in the original printing of the book, and this fact, together with
the vignette Schildt's had chosen, gave the book an air of turn-of-
the-century naughtiness, while Edith Södergran meant, of course, to
proclaim something new and daring, so daring, in fact, that she was
assailed by doubts about it in mid-poem, something that Carl-Erik af
Geijerstam noted.[18] The third statement of the poem's central line,
after the brusque farewell to earth, is followed by a nervous question: "--could I exchange a world for my strength?" The poem, as
we know, was from the "transitional" stage; the conviction was not
yet absolute.

The quasi-biblical and liturgical language does not abate: in "Bön" ("Prayer," (SD, p. 176)), God is enjoined to "have mercy on us," an imitation of the formulation of the kyrie; "Seven months and three years" (thus, reckoning from August, 1914, one arrives at February, 1918, in the midst of Finland's Civil War) "at the same spot, / we pray for your grace, / give us entrance to the still chamber where you ponder things." The ways of God are equally mysterious in "The World Bathes in Blood" (SD, pp. 179-180); an attempt is made to regard the events of the war as a necessary preparation for a new world, a proposal which leads to Nietzsche again (as does the ease with which Edith Södergran slips from "God" to "the gods", and back again): "What do we know of how the eternal one languishes, / and what the gods drink in order to nourish their strength. / God will create anew. He will transform the world to a clearer sign." This creator-God is described, then, in language redolent of Scripture without having a specific text as its basis; "Therefore he girds himself about with a belt of lightning" and "Therefore he bears a crown of flaming barbs." (A third element, beyond Nietzsche and the Bible, may be apparent in the language here: both "bälte" ('belt') and "tagg" ('barb') have a military air to them, the one suggesting "patronbälte" ('cartridge belt'), the other "taggtråd" ('barbed wire').) The poem ends with the "trembling of senses half-awake," "dizziness as upon looking into an abyss, / a silence as in the forest before the sun rises, / before jubilating choruses burst out in a hymn of praise." We cannot help thinking of the Goddess of the Future in the adolescent verse, who brings the storm, but "in the rosy morning light" (ESD, p. 50).

The storm came; the poems from the spring of 1918--"Stormen" ("The Storm"), "Aftonvandring" ("Evening Promenade"), "Månens hemlighet" ("The Moon's Secret"), "Visan från molnet" ("The Song from the Cloud")--bear the marks of Finland's own chaos. Long before Raivola was taken by the Whites, there had been fighting in its vicinity; on March 10, the Reds, who held Viborg, had advanced on the White position at Antrea, and, later in the month, Russian forces from St. Petersburg had gone up the second of Karelia's railroad lines to a station called Rauta, where bloody fighting took place at the end of March and the beginning of April. Tideström suggests that "The Storm" contains an allusion to the approach of the White army, whose general, Mannerheim, had suddenly taken the destiny of Finland into his hands (SD, p. 181): "Where will he strike, / the one come from the heights, unconquered, future-winged," and he precedes his suggestion with the thought (in which he is seconded by Enckell) that there is a strong echo of Nietzsche here, of the salute to those beings for whom Zarathustra waits in the mountains: "I wait for others here in these mountains--for higher, stronger, more victorious, happier-hearted ones";[19] it is a message Zarathustra gives his strange company of guests, themselves "higher men" but not lofty and strong enough for the task. The poem ends with: "Guests seat themselves again at toppled tables / Unknown ones steer the world . . . / Higher, fairer, like unto gods." Certainly, Edith Södergran and her mother looked forward to the coming of the Whites; but it was the mythical aura of the victorious general (who, as it were, had come out of nowhere) which charmed her--a year later, she dreamed that

Mannerheim embraced her.[20]   The storm, "carried up to imperishable heights by eagles," is clearly masculine, called "han" ('he'); and there is an army with him: "Do you not hear voices in the storm? / Mars-helmets in the mist . . ."

"Evening Promenade" and "The Moon's Secret" are written on paper of an identical kind, paper which Edith Södergran otherwise does not use, and probably stem from about the same time. The first (SD, p. 180) stammers with excitement:

> All the time's golden stars upon my dark velvet dress.
> I am the triumphant one . . . tonight . . . I shudder.
> Fate's iron bars hammer from my breast,
> Does the wind whirl the sand from the sidewalk?
> ---
> Is there death for me, annihilation--No.
> Death is in Helsingfors--
> he captures sparks on the roofs.
> I go across the square with my future in my hand.

The poet, aware of the importance of the historical moment and the danger to herself, takes an evening walk in Raivola, even as the house-to-house fighting goes on: sand spurts up from the richocheting of bullets, yet she proceeds, secure in her sense of mission. But why is death in Helsingfors, and what is he doing there? An answer may lie in the simple lag of news in these hectic weeks: when newspapers describing the capture of the capital (by a German expeditionary force, on April 12-14) reached Raivola, Edith Södergran combined this information, or the impression it made on her, with her memories (or imaginings) of the perilous walk she, the chosen one, had taken in her little village. As for death, catching sparks ("han fångar gnistorna på taken"), it should be remembered that a "gnistfångare" is literally a spark-catcher, attached either to a chimney or, for that matter, a locomotive funnel, and that 'spark' often appears in the compound noun, "livsgnista," 'spark of life.' The extinguished sparks are many, the triumphant promenader is one-- adorned with the signs of distinction (it is impossible not to think of medals on the breast of this military-heroic figure), and given the splendid appellation, "triumfator," an exotic word in Swedish, and one which should have been familiar to Edith Södergran from the liturgy of the Russian church, with its emphasis upon Christos Triumphator, Christ the Victor. Like Christ after the harrowing of hell, the speaker of the poem has conquered death, or, at any rate, has conquered her fear of it--the struggle which is fought out in Edith Södergran again and again.

Death--someone else's--is given a kind of picturesque beauty in "The Moon's Secret"; later on (EB, p. 22), Edith Södergran wrote that the poem had "a sneaking desire for the smell of corpses which ought to gain the favor of the public." Evidently, she was not particularly proud of what she had wrought; elsewhere, in her aphorisms (SD, p. 298), she expressed her revulsion at the summary executions of Red prisoners as they came back to her in a dream: "I saw executions everywhere on beaches and hills, human hands and tree branches

smeared with blood and brains . . ." The poem, to be sure, avoids
a detailed presentation of the horror (SD, p. 183):

> The moon knows . . . that blood will be shed here tonight.
> On copper paths across the lake a certainty goes forth:
> corpses shall lie among the alders on a wondrously
>   beautiful beach.
> The moon shall cast its most beautiful light on the strange
>   beach.
> The wind shall go forth as a reveille-horn through the
>   firs.
> How beautiful the earth is in this lonely hour.

In fact, its central word is 'beauty' or 'beautiful' ("underskön
strand," "skönaste ljus," "Vad jorden är skön"), which, combined with
its 'certainty' of violent death, made Enckell put it in the tradition of European decadence.[21] And its aestheticism is thrown into
high relief by the unobtrusive 'military' words in its vocabulary:
"banor" are not merely '(copper) paths' but 'trajectories', and car-
tridges have copper casings; the odd form, "väckarehorn", as a comparison for the wind (which supplies the sound effect for the scene,
as the moon does the illumination), is more memorable by far than
the normal 'signalhorn' would have been: it will not be able to
awaken the dead who will lie upon the beach.

Edith Södergran's remark about the "odjur", the 'monsters',
which infest the woods in "Visan från molnet" ("The Song from the
Cloud") has been taken as an expression of repugnance at the Red
stragglers who waged guerrilla warfare after the major fighting had
ended; the hunting-down of these "bandits" was the substance of Jarl
Hemmer's novella from 1928, "Ett budskap från ödemarken" ("A Message
from the Wilderness").[22] Yet, as in the foregoing poems, the real
event becomes the seed of the personal reaction,[23] here, the proud
escape from an unbearable world (SD, p. 184):

> Up on the clouds there dwells all I need:
> my presentiments sure as daylight, my certainties quick as
>   lightning-light,
> and on the clouds I myself dwell,--
> white, in sun that blinds,
> inaccessibly happy, waving farewell.
> Farewell, green forests of my youth.
> Monsters infest them--
> I shall never put my foot on the earth again.
> An eagle took me up on its wings--
> far from the world
> I have peace.
> Upon the clouds I sit and sing--
> down onto the earth there drips quicksilver-mocking-
>   laughter--
> out of it grow crater-grass and explosion-flowers.

The pattern is a familiar one: the taking of a farewell, the soaring
aloft into Zarathustran realms of sun. The trip on the eagle's back

has prompted Kjell Espmark[24] to call attention to two poems by Alfred
Mombert in Der himmlische Zecher ((The Heavenly Toper), nos. 67, 68).
It is hard to decide what may be Mombert's here and what Nietzsche's;
Mombert has an eagle which hangs "like a dark cloud of late autumn
over a withering world," a cloud from which drops fall to earth,
Nietzsche has Zarathustra himself, "See, I am a proclaimer of the
lightning and a heavy drop from the cloud."[25] The version of Edith
Södergran is more playfully inventive than that of either of her
putative predecessors, as she piles coinage upon coinage, "kvick-
silverhånskratt" (quicksilver-mocking-laughter), "kittelgräs"
(crater-grass), "flyg-i-luften-blommor" (explosion flowers). Only
the third is transparent: Tideström says that the poet wants to
"explode everything" from her heavenly vantage point and adds that
the second of the unusual words suggests potshaped craters--"kittel"
is the equivalent of German 'Kessel,' English 'kettle'.[26] His explo-
sion-argument can be extended: "quicksilver-mocking-laughter" is an
ironic play upon the traditional phrase, "silver laughter," but the
joke is more complex still. Edith Södergran was the daughter of a
technician, who had been employed by Nobel: 'detonating quicksilver'
('knallkvicksilver') was commonly used in the early twentieth century
for the production of explosives. And, as for the mysterious
"kittelgräs," may it refer not to the crater itself, but to the
instrument that produces it--the German "Kesselbombe" (Swedish
"kittelbomb"), the mortar bomb? The poet's laughter rains, literally, verbal bombs upon the earth. (These are not the only technical
references in the poem; the "blixt-ljus" or "lightning-light" of the
second line--literally, the photographer's flash-bulb--calls to mind
the fact that Edith Södergran was herself an amateur photographer;
she has wedded the name of the instrument of her would-be trade to
a common Swedish adjective, "blixtsnabb," "quick as lightning," to
make the extended compound "blixtljussnabb.")

     After speaking of a "hallucinatory condition" and calling atten-
tion to Edith Södergran's affection for "splendid Words," Walter
Dickson concludes[27] that the poem "Landskap i solnedgång" ("Landscape
in the Sunset")--the only landscape poem in the new collection, by
the way--is another description of the triumph of the Nietzschean
will, of the "above" over the "below" (SD, pp. 187-188): "See in
the sunset / swimming fire-islands proceeding / imperially over
cream-green seas. / Islands in flame! Islands like torches! /
Islands in victory procession! / Up from the depths flashes black a
forest, / crafty, envious--enraptured, forming lines, triumph upon
triumph . . . / Poor strips of forest in pale mists / are seized,
lifted up--unite themselves to majesty." The fire-islands are
related to Södergran's sun-touched mountaintops and clouds: indeed,
they are the latter--clouds in sunset proceeding over the "cream-
green seas" of the sky. The dark and hostile forests below prepare
an ambush, but are quickly overcome, taken up, as it were, into the
procession of burning clouds. (The poem is based upon a lighting
effect: as the sun sinks, its rays strike first the clouds and then
the forest, appearing briefly to set first the one, then the other
ablaze.) Edith Södergran has offered street-to-street fighting,
executions, bombings; now she has a naval encounter--the fire-islands
sail in line of battle, and the hidden squadron attacks them. The

language, too, has its warlike overtones: in "blixtra" ('flash'),
which is what cannons do in boys' adventure books, in "radande sig,"
("falling into line"), and in its elements of bombast, at which
Dickson smiled: "tåga" ("to march or sail in procession"), "imperi-
alt" ("imperially"), "segertåg" ("victory procession"), "triumf,"
"majestät." It is the victorious world of the "triumfator" in
"Evening Promenade." The poem is ended with still more outcries
("Gloria! Victory!"), and an address to the dark powers which have
been overthrown: "Kneel, lion-monsters, / in the world's dark corners," reinforcing the triumph and recalling the mythological beasts
to be seen at the four corners of old maps or prints. Then there
is an abrupt coda: "The day goes throning to its end . . . Invisible hands clip off the threads of light." The editor of 1918, or
typesetter, who put in "öden" ('fates') for "töcken" ('mists') in
the penultimate line of the middle section, may have been misled
by the suggested appearance of the Fates ('ödesgudinnor') in the
last line, snipping the threads of man's life.[28] The triumph will
be cancelled, the light annihilated, night will come as soon as the
sun goes down. A hint of theatricality has attached to the whole
poem; now the spectacle is over.

One more poem from those which prepare for the outburst of
September should be discussed, "The Whirlpool of Madness," where
the doubts about the validity of the higher calling are clearly
expressed, not least in the very title (SD, p. 185):

> Guard your boat from superhuman rapids,
> madness' whirling tumble,
> guard your boat from the jubilating waves of the falls,
> they have the power to smash.
> Guard yourself--you are no longer valuable here--
> to strength's frenetic joy life and death are as one,
> here there is no 'slow,' 'careful,' 'try.'
> Stronger hands seize your oar in the flight.

The first line reads, in Swedish: "Akta din båt för övermänskliga
strömdrag": the pun on Nietzsche's "Übermensch" is transparent, as
is the central image, a boat in the rapids, out of the rower's control; the threefold injunction makes the structure of the poem's
first part quite clear; the penultimate line (with the threefold
listing of "careful" words) serves as a retardation before the victory of the "stronger hands" at the section's end. However, as
soon as their triumph is apparent (another of the several victories
in these "banal" or "transitional" lyrics), the poem's language
becomes less lucid--even as the rower becomes immortal:

> There you stand yourself, a hero with blood reborn,
> enraptured in the calm, a bonfire of joy on mirroring ice,
> as if death's message were not written for you:
> blessed waves lead your keel forward.

Why suddenly a hero with blood reborn? The description (which cor-
responds to the "triumfator" of "Evening Promenade") may be a hapax
legomenon in Edith Södergran, the single allusion she makes to

Finnish literature. In one of the best-known episodes of the
Kalevala (XIV-XV), the hero Lemminkäinen is slain by the "old man
with the watery hat," and his body hurled into "the most terrible
whirlpool," where it is cut to pieces. Learning by magical means
of his death, his mother puts the pieces of his body together, saying, in her incantations, that: "Where too much of blood was
wasted / There must other blood be poured in," and Lemminkäinen
awakes, reborn. The second line of the hero-section begins with
"Hänryckt" ('Enraptured'), the word which began the description of
the transformed forest in the sunset poem; it is the state which
the lower being must enter as he or she surrenders to the power
surpassing reason. As for the "bonfire of joy," on the ice, the
hero is now metamorphosed into a pyre on the water (he is standing
in the boat) which appears as smooth as ice to his exalted vision:
like the clouds and the forest in the sunset poem, he has caught
fire.

The poem has led into a wilderness world, where, incidentally,
the bonfire on the ice--a common practice of fishermen and sealers--
is by no means unusual. Trying to remember what her daughter liked
to read, Helena Södergran came up with a surprise, "The Jungle Book
was our delight."[29]   One of the two poems omitted "for linguistic
reasons" from Septemberlyran, "The Huntsman's Happiness," has lines
which refer to Mowgli's trip through the trees with the monkeys:
"Cast me in feeling's trees / from branch to branch / I can do it,
I can do it" (SD, pp. 409-410). Södergran's speaker can bear great
stress but is not ready (as yet) for supreme intellectual daring:
"If I could do one more thing / throwing off my clothes / diving
head first into the cold pool of thought / If I could do this /
I would not be unsure in the forest / not a prey / but everywhere
I would be the sole huntsman . . ." Kipling's Mowgli, saved from
the monkeys, grows up to be a mighty huntsman; he is amalgamated,
in Edith Södergran's mind, with the huntsman Zarathustra, who dares
all (see "I am the huntsman" in Zarathustra's "Second Dance-
Song").[30]   In fact, "The Huntsman's Happiness" is a preparatory
exercise for the lament, "Vid Nietzsches grav" ("At Nietzsche's
Grave," (SD, p. 201))--itself a series of glosses on Nietzschean
texts. It opens with a paraphrase of a line from Die Geburt der
Tragödie, "The great Pan is dead,"[31] here "The great huntsman is
dead," describes the mourner seated on Nietzsche's grave, mocking
the old world her mentor has taught her to despise (Zarathustra
calls himself "Courageous, carefree, mocking, violent"), and alludes
to the prophecy which Zarathustra makes to the guests at his banquet
(" . . . 'Did you hear naught of my children? And that they are
underway to me'")[32]: "Strange father! / Your children will not fail
you, / They come over the earth with the stride of gods, / rubbing
their eyes: where indeed am I?" These children, like the hero in
the boat, have been reborn; they will form, in time, the company of
"higher beings" in Rosenaltaret.

Sometimes, the September poems enjoin the whole of humanity to
follow Zarathustra's way, as in "Samlen icke guld och ädelstenar"
(SD, p. 204): "Mankind, / do not collect gold or jewels . . . /
give your children a beauty / which human eyes have not seen, / give

your child the strength / to break open the gates of heaven," but
more frequently they are self-harangues, demands the poet directs
to herself for superhuman efforts, to break open heaven's gates, to
test her strength against the new "horizons of light." However, it
is essential that these efforts be carried out with grace, with
lightness, a key concept in the world which Södergran improvises out
of Nietzschean concepts. The goddess in "Gryningen" ("The Dawn",
(SD, p. 203)), for all her air of hard militarism ("I am the day's
merciless goddess / in mistgrey veils / with a little early morning-
helmet-glint") says that her winds must run "lightly, lightly . . .
over the sea";   the inhabitant of "Feens slott" ("The Fairy's
Castle", (SD, p. 189)), a "being never more than fifteen years old,"
wants to give her "light heart to those who meet her"; the speaker
of "Den skönaste guden" ("The Fairest God", (SD, p. 202)) has a heart
as "light as a bird / a more delicately formed thing is not to be
found upon this earth," and is borne upward by her wings to "an
unknown god." Her heart (which itself, we have been told in the
first line, is "fairest in all the world") will be presented to this
god as a sacrifice; then she will return, "a shimmer around her
forehead." Edith Södergran's cult of the maiden continues; only the
lightfooted and lightbodied girl is fit to ascend to the realm of
the god, and to return with his sign.

The "fairest god" of the poem just quoted gets his name written
with a small initial; in "Sorglöshet" ("Lightheartedness"), he is
capitalized, perhaps because the poem draws upon Scripture, albeit
Scripture used to Edith Södergran's special end. As so often in the
September verse, the speaker is proud, lonely, contemptuous of the
very human beings whom she means, elsewhere, to save, and, of course,
she is "light," of foot and of heart (SD, p. 198):

> I do not believe in human beings.
> I would have destroyed my lyre,
> if I did not believe in God.
> God shows me the way
> out of the mist to the sun's shining disk.
> He loves the lightfooted wanderers,
> Therefore he gives me this lightness of heart.
> I depend firmly as on a rock (hälleberg).
> If I am his true child--naught can befall me.

These lines will readily call to mind Christ's charge to Peter ("upon
this rock (hälleberg) I shall build my church"), and the opening of
the 23d Psalm ("The Lord is my shepherd, I shall not want"), familiar
biblical echoes which made Agnes Langenskiöld perceive "a childish
faith in God" here. But the emphasis lies, really, not with God but
with the lightfooted wanderer, whose deity is, if anything, her own
belief in her calling--a scholar has called the "God" of Jugendstil
poetry "a game whose purpose is: being stirred."[33]

The other cardinal property of the chosen girl in the September
poems is not a physical-spiritual characteristic (so easily connected
with Nietzsche's admiration for the dance and for gaiety of spirit),
but a musical instrument, the lyre. It appears five times in the

September series--in "Sorglöshet," in "Gudarnas lyra" ("The Lyre of the Gods"), "Villkoret" ("The Condition"), "Är jag en lögnare?" ("Am I a Liar?"), and "Min lyra" ("My Lyre"); two other poems from the collection use it as well ("Revanche" and "Orpheus"), and it is a part, obviously, of the book's very title. The observation of Johannes Salminen--that Edith Södergran, for all her vaunted 'modern-ism', actually paid homage to an "older aesthetics of idealism"[34]--is correct; her dependence upon the instrument of the bard, of Apollo, as a symbol of her poetic gift, harks back to the beginnings of the oedic tradition, with which, it may be assumed, Edith Södergran had become acquainted in school, through reading such German heirs of that tradition as Klopstock and Schiller. She has a strong sense of responsibility to her lyre and she cultivates the attitude of the vates: that the poetic gift must be used for the education and edi-fication of the mass. In the case of Klopstock, Schiller, Hölderlin, Stefan George, the poet regards himself as leader, chastizer, and savior of a nation; in Edith Södergran's, she takes the whole of humanity (vaguely discerned, to be sure) for her charge.

"The Lyre of the Gods" and "The Condition" were not printed until the collected works appeared in 1949. The first poem is com-posed in a readily discernible pattern of amphibrachs and dactyls (SD, p. 192): "Where then is the lyre / of silver and ivory / which the gods once lent / to the mortals' race?" The lyre is not lost, of course, for such divine gifts are eternal; if a singer comes, chosen by fate, he will find the lyre in "forgotten vaults"; after the bard has restrung it, the world will know that the gods still live "on undivined heights." Is there not an echo here of Klopstock's "Der Hügel und der Hain" ("The Hill and the Grove"), where the song of the lyre is lost for centuries in the "night of oblivion," to be redis-covered by the German poet?[35] And is there not a palpable imitation of Klopstock's intentionally lofty and artificial syntax in "The Con-dition" (SD, p. 193), where Edith Södergran argues that the poet must not only have a calling but a cause: "Though for me the lyre is the earth's loftiest thing / if I stayed true to it / I should not set a soul aflame." (The Swedish is remarkably stilted: "Är dock mig lyran . . . / bleve jag den trogen . . . / vore jag . . .") The task which the bard assigns herself in "The Condition" is an assault, per-haps vain, "with bloody nails," upon "the wall of ordinary life"; in "Revanche" (SD, p. 188) (the French loan word implies an attempt for victory after a first defeat), the possibility is conceded that "the tower in the city of reality" perhaps will not fall as a result of her efforts, but she will still "sing down the stars from the sky," sing so that even her "enormous longing" will be exhausted. Then she will put the lyre aside. She will have succeeded in showing "every-day life" how banal it is, as the singer does in "The Song of the Troubadour" (SD, p. 208): in that poem, where Nietzsche's "The Drunken Song" and the lyrics of Maeterlinck are joined in a happy union,[36] the troubadour, singing in a courtyard before his princess's tower, is showered by her with stars. After the rain of beauty, he measures the bricks of the wall with his hand, laughing mockingly: "'Day, what do you have to offer / after the night of song?'" As Enckell has pointed out, the troubadour paraphrases the charge that Zarathustra, praising midnight, makes against the day in Nietzsche: "Day and world, you are too coarse."[37]

The transformations of the poet, with his lyre, are many: the vates, the troubadour, the singer of battle (as in the fragmentary "Apokalypsens genius" ("The Genius of the Apocalypse," SD, pp. 194-195), where Edith Södergran says that "profusest (sic) red warrior's blood" flowed in the veins of the singers of old), and, of course, Orpheus himself, an Orpheus who can tame savage beasts ("Tiger, panther, and puma follow my steps"), but who also has the utter freedom of Dionysus (or a Zarathustra or a Mowgli: "All is pardonable for me"), and whose song can change the world, giving beauty the gift of life (SD, p. 218): "I touch the lyre. A wind goes over the earth / slowly, solemnly, in tears / kissing beauty's white lifeless statues on the mouth, / that they open their eyes." Or the singer may be a Lucifer-figure, the "boldest angel," whom "god" nonetheless did not cast out of heaven; instead, the angel-singer received a gift of "honey and wormwood," from which, in turn, literary creation was made, and transferred to mankind: "I cast the foaming mixture out over the earth. The form held" (in "Särtecknet," "The Special Mark"). The mark itself, in this poem from the Nietzschean September of 1918, betrays the identity of the angel-singer; it is Edith Södergran, with her tubercular infection (SD, p. 207): "(God) gave me a black-red rose-- / the smallest in the world. / It gives me a distinction before others, / from far away, one sees it on my white dress." According to the family legend told by Helena Södergran, the physician who diagnosed Edith Södergran's illness said, with considerable ambiguity, "Du hast das grosse Los gezogen"--"You have won the main prize."

The probability of the poet's imminent death comes up several times amidst the ecstasies of the September-poems, in every case in lyrics dealing principally with poetic creation; much of this verse offers special problems of interpretation, probably because of its mixture of bliss, willingly proclaimed, and fear, severely repressed. "My Lyre" begins in medias res (SD, p. 209): "I abhor (the) thought . . . / Where is my beloved giant lyre? / Sunshine-stringed, fairy-tale-like, hanging from the clouds. / O my giant lyre, / you hang above the world like a question mark." Olof Enckell argues that the mysterious first line should be taken as an attack on "dry intellectualism," rational thought in general, to be contrasted with the mighty lyre of poetry, which has never paid heed to logic, and which appears to the world as a question mark, variously baffling or challenging.[38] The strophe is followed by a string of dashes, a device which Edith Södergran often uses to indicate work of a fragmentary nature. The second strophe begins as abruptly as the first, with a vision of the poet's death: "When I die, / I shall cast myself unconcernedly into your strings . . .". Two spirits, "arising from the unknown," will carry the singer and her instrument out over the seas of the world, stopping in the midst of the Atlantic. There, after a second line of dashes, they disappear: "And we are both vanished from the world, / my beloved lyre!" Is the surprising adverb, "unconcernedly," a sign that the singer (like the girl of the cloud, dropping her bombs) no longer cares about the world, and goes willingly into death? And is the final pair of lines to be read as a somehow contemptuous valedictory to the world, which does not know what it has lost (or what it may unwittingly have gained: in "The

Dawn," the Atlantic is the "birthplace of the future"). Or is the conclusion to be read as an outcry of despair, at ceasing to exist? In such case, the poem's opening line, "I abhor (the) thought," might be a specific statement, of abhorrence of a specific thought, that of her personal annihilation, and with her, the lyre's. Thus the poem, made up of three clearly delineated fragments, is the record of an inner argument, the voice of terror, followed by the voice of lofty unconcern, followed again by fear: "And we are both vanished from the world."

    In its construction, "My Lyre" apparently is built on a statement/rejoinder/statement construction; the equally thorny "Är jag en lögnare" ("Am I A Liar?"), is a long crescendo of if-and-then clauses, each protasis followed by an apodosis which does not give a firm answer to the painful query, building a tension which is not released until the "may"-verb preceeding the penalties for the poet's false claims is replaced by the "shall" of the charge to the angels (SD, pp. 205-206):

> If I am a criminal, my sin is immeasurable . . .
> If I am a trickster, I play my tricks with holy
>   things . . .
> If I am a liar, may I plunge from the skies
> crushed upon your market places.
>
> If I am a liar--
> may damned spirits bury my lyre
> in rotting pools of sulphur,
> may it stretch out its arms in beseechment on moonlit
>   nights
> when no living being passes by.
>
> If I am a liar--
> may my wondrous signature be erased from heaven's wall,
> may the letters of pearl be crushed against the rocks of
>   the sea,
> may the waters be silent about my origin,
> may the world never hear my tale.
>
> If I am a liar--
> then fair angels shall love me all the same
> as a fair and a damned brother:
> she[39] told tales to the moon and the arch of heaven,
> without them they could not exist,
> their fragile beauty would crumble.

There is an amelioration of the poem's extremism at the end; even though the poet's claims may be false, she has still helped to preserve the "imaginary" or beautiful realm which makes life endurable, Nietzsche's realm of the Olympians. The poem's main question is, in effect, left unanswered; an apologia, nonetheless, is made for the poet's calling, a reason is given to the life now seen as ended. (The reader will have noticed that the apologia was in fact begun at the poem's outset: the criminal has at least attempted "immea-

surable" sins--we think of Luther's injunction, <u>pecca</u> <u>fortiter!</u>
("sin strongly!")--and the trickster has not given his attention to
profane objects, but holy ones.)

A homely pendant to the poems on the lyre remains; did Schildt
decide not to include the little poem, "Förhoppning" ("Hope" (<u>SD</u>,
p. 219)), in the original <u>Septemberlyran</u>, thinking it was of a less
dignified tenor than its fellows from the September group?

> I wish to be unconstrained--
> therefore I scorn noble styles.
> I roll up my sleeves.
> The poem's dough is fermenting . . .
> Oh, one worry--
> not to be able to bake cathedrals . . .
> Loftiness of the forms--
> persistent longing's goal.
> Child of the present--
> does your spirit not have its proper crust?
> Before I die,
> I shall bake a cathedral.

Staffan Björck has offered the practical thought that Edith Södergran's fondness for food-imagery had a basis in reality:[40]   she was
often hungry; further, he points out that the idea of "baking a
cathedral" was by no means fanciful: the making of architectural
wonders in cake-form was a world-famous specialty of the <u>confiseries</u>
of Saint Petersburg, longingly recalled here. Also, on another
plane, he says that the line, "The poem's dough is fermenting,"
provides an illustration of the statement in <u>Septemberlyran</u>'s introduction: "I let my instinct build up what my intellect, in an expectant attitude, observes." Relaxation, working with sleeves rolled
up, lack of constraint, have been necessary factors in Edith Södergran's process of creation; she is concerned (and the rhetorical top-
loftiness of some of the September-poems shows that her concern was
not unfounded) with her ability, or inability, to mix her verbal-
associative technique with the complexity of structure and elevation
of tone which she thinks are necessary for making (or baking) the
cathedral's edifice (Södergran's word "höghet," is ambiguous, connot-
ing both "tall" and "sublime"). The argument is carried out, to be
sure, with humor--as is the case in so much of Edith Södergran's
most memorable poetry; the reference to the "child of the present"
offers a reminder that a cathedral of pastry is an object of "persistent longing" for children in particular, or for those who can be
childlike; in "The Genius of the Apocalypse," Edith Södergran said
that "Life is divine and for children." "Hope" is playful, but it
is also didactic, for the poet herself (as a technician of verse and
a human being) and for her readers. And it contains again, as so
often, the awareness of the end: "Before I die, / I shall bake a
cathedral."

As it first was printed, <u>Septemberlyran</u> closed with two poems
which (in contrast to the pastry-poem) are a solemn probing of the
poet's self. One is the three-strophed question, "Varför gavs mig

livet?" ("Why Was I Given Life?", (SD, p. 210)), in which she asks
whether she was intended to be a victor ("to flash past all the
people in a triumphal chariot"), or a priestess ("to seize the glim-
mering bowl in ring-adorned hands") or a magic book ("to pass from
hand to hand, / burning through all souls")--roles all indicated by
the September poems; but the key to the poem lies not in the catalogue (which can be reduced to the question: has she in fact been
born to dazzle, to lead, to inspire?), but in the refrain about her
driving force, "longing for more" and, twice, "thirsting for more."
It is that measureless urge for something higher and beyond human
power which is the main urge of the September poetry and, in fact,
of the whole of Edith Södergran's works. The second "autobiographical" reflection, however, begins with a disgusting shock. After
two lines of dashes, once again indicative of the visionary nature
of the work, the "Fragment" (SD, pp. 211-218) which is the longest
of Edith Södergran's extant works begins as follows: "Life's bac-
teria flourish on your mucous membrane." (The line was deleted from
the original printing by Schildt, and restored only by Tideström.)
Forced to observe her own body's functions and malfunctions closely,
she felt no embarrassment at putting such observations into her work
--it was an old practice of hers: the adolescent verse (ESD, p. 87)
says: "Today, the cosmos is menstruating." However, it is possible
that another of her habits--that of seizing a striking image from
another writer, and putting it to her own ends--may be in play here
as well; Andrej Biely's novel of 1913, Petersborg, has the "flourish-
ing bacillae" of the Neva as its leitmotif, "green waters seething
with bacillae," that are also the germs of revolution.[41] Södergran's
description of St. Petersburg, which follows, likewise bears traces
of her enthusiasm for Dostojevsky, but blended with the personal
imagery we have seen in Dikter and in Septemberlyran, the visions of
depths (beneath the water) and heights (the battlement), and of the
fairytale childhood: "...you have depths / where we deep-sea fish
breathe. / Petersburg, Petersburg, / from your battlements the
enchanted banner of my childhood flies," and "Petersburg, Petersburg,
/ arise from golden visions, / I shall sum up what I love in discon-
nected words. / I strew the violets of memory on the golden sidewalks
of dreams." In the manuscript, "gratitude" was crossed out in favor
of "memory"; yet Edith Södergran was patently grateful to the city
of her youthful enthusiasms, which looks far better now, in retrospect, than it did in the German poems of the past: it is a city
"on whose battlements my youth's glow lies / like a rosy drapery,
like a light overture, / like the veil of dreams upon the titan's
sleep." The "titan's sleep" foreshadows the change which has taken
place, a change described in terms which are ambiguous, as is customary in her statements about the Revolution: "It was the time before
the deep wounds, before the mighty scars, / before rejuvenation's
bath of oblivion."

    The poem's second section is built upon questions, the first
taking a prophetic stance ("What befalls me as I speak?"), and the
subsequent ones predicting the isolation of revolutionary Russia--
without attempting to say whose fault the isolation was: "Do I have
presentiments of immeasurable tragedies? / Do my fairytale viaducts
never climb over your roofs, / do trains not flash by with ecstatic

flags / to Berlin-Paris-London? / Does all that I see become an immeasurable pile of ashes?" No expresses with signal flags "ecstatic" in the wind of speed (that favorite thought of rapture again) roared through the Raivola station; the border had been closed. Thus the prophetess now looks westward, toward another "new" state--toward a replacement vision, as it were. The lines are inspired by the effective newspaper photographs of the raising of the flag of Mannerheim's Finland over the bastions of Sveaborg: "Does not our wonderful fortress emerge from the sea in Helsingfors? / Do sentries not stand there with blue and red banners the world has never seen! / Do they not stand leaning on their spears, gazing out over the sea / with fate's granite in their features of stone?" It is hardly a real Sveaborg she beholds: the soldiers in the photographs did not lean on mythic spears, nor could the flag have been "blue and red" (her own colors of the dream and of eroticism and vitalism). The flag first raised on Sveaborg after the Civil War was the red-and-yellow Lion-Banner of the Grand Duchy of Finland, the new Finnish national flag was a blue cross on a white field. The dream persists here, as in the views of St. Petersburg: "Or is everything merely a reflection in the sleepwalker's eyes, / do I dwell in dreams on another planet?"

The third section of the poem discloses, at last, its intent; in her open letter to Dagens Press, Edith Södergran said that the "fragment" must clearly reveal "the new...I cannot help the person who fails to feel that the wild blood of the future courses through these poems." The future for Edith Södergran lies not in political constructions, but in Zarathustra's higher world, which will now descend to the earth. Mankind is told to "love nothing smaller than infinity," to "dream nothing smaller than to kiss God's little finger," but to remember, at the same time, that it is not yet ready for the task. The "children below" are told to "do penance"; "Zarathustra awaits within for chosen guests." The admonition which follows is directed, like that of Nietzsche's Zarathustra, to his "strange guests" at the banquet, to a set of "friends" not as base as the "children below," but unworthy, all the same. (Zarathustra's guests, it will be remembered, are not the "loftier men" he expects.) "Friends, we are as low as the worms in the dust. / Not a line by us will survive before the glance of the future. / With all that is past we shall plunge into Lethe." The prophetic speaker is quite willing to include her own work ("not a line by us") in the destruction of the present world: "our cheap beggar's wares" and "we are not worthy that the crosses remain upon our graves" continue this current of self-rejecting thought. It must be noted that the pronouns "we" and "our" are used throughout the section--in other words, the address is made as though before the time of the great change, subsequently announced with a return to the singular pronoun. As a mere poet she is willing to be thrown into oblivion; as a prophetess, her words must be heard: "Friends, I predict a festival in the sign of beauty.../ Where can it take place if not in the Engadin?" The scene of the dream is changed to the Alps where "old peasant houses" are destroyed by "beauty's restless, greedy, demanding spirit...," by Zarathustra's thaw-wind ("Föhn"): "Tearing down our many-colored flowers. Crushing the pane where geraniums stand. / No idyllic paths

lead any longer to homes hundreds of years old.../Eternal Föhn leaves
no stones upon our roofs, / the storm will not cease on earth..."
Again, as in the case of the locomotive's signal flags, Edith Södergran employs "real" details to great effect: the tidy Swiss geraniums and the stones, placed on the roofs of houses in the high Alps
in order to keep shingles in place in high winds, will be blown away;
at the same time, there may be a suggestion of Christ's "There shall
not be left here one stone upon another." These will be "days of
creation"; in order to illustrate what the "beauty" of the festival
will be, the houses, personified (the prophetess quotes their
speech), turn from a Nietzschean and biblical tempest to another
realm of Edith Södergran's imagination, the fairytale: "Has not
this beauty lain dead among us for a thousand years? / Like the
maiden Snow White sleeping in her case of glass." The owners of the
neat houses (and the whole race of men) have been a Lilliput folk,
desecrating her slumbering form: "We have trodden upon the bridge
of her nose, we have trudged upon her eyelids." At last, they are
ready to accept their well-deserved destruction: they offer a salute
(with gladiatorial echoes as surprising as those of the fairytale
have been) to the new world aborning: "Perishing, we salute you,
incomprehensible starry night, / which will give birth, of course,
to a new man: / The human being will emerge from the mountains, like
unto them, / with the eternal shimmer of greatness upon his forehead.
/ Then the Cosmos will open. The riddles fall ringing / into
Minerva's immeasurable bowl of sacrifice." At this climax, the figure of the wise virgin goddess is introduced, a tutelary deity (and,
simultaneously a high priestess) for the whole and puzzling course
of events. (In her vision, Edith Södergran has not neglected any
of the aspects of her personal mythology.) The poem's coda, an
address to mankind, proposes that, in accordance with the dictum of
Die Geburt der Tragödie, the 'principium individuationis' will be
abandoned: "we shall forget ourselves and be united with the Cosmos
again." The winds return: "Go streaming through us, eternal winds.
/ Honey of heaven, blessing of the all!" The poem ends with an
injunction for the reporter-prophetess who has beheld the long
vision: "He who has heard this and he who has seen this, / shall
ascend to sacrifice on holy mountains," an injunction that would be
followed in the next collections. (Once more, the "modernist" Edith
Södergran shores up the sublimity of her vision with oldfashioned
rhythmic devices: clearly discernible dactyls[42] begin ten lines from
the poem's end. Rilke would employ the same device in the Duino
Elegies four years later on.)

   The "Fragment" is one of the great visionary poems in a Northern
literature. It is odd that her contemporary critics noted neither
the poem's extravagances nor its grandeur in their reviews; perhaps
they were put off by the poem's very length, and the difficulty of
its allusions. Yet it may have been to Edith Södergran's advantage,
in post-Civil War Finland, that the poem went unnoticed; for, of all
her works, it could most convincingly--if quite incorrectly--be
interpreted as a call for political revolution from the left. Perhaps Jumbo was thinking of it as he wrote about "literary Bolshevism." Evidently, she was quite oblivious to this danger; as
Nietzsche said, Dionysian emotions encroach upon the political

instincts.[43] Dionysian emotions, as we have seen, play a large role in the fragment, her proclamation, she liked to think, to the world, and, at the same time, a chronicle of the stages on her own life's way.

5.

The Aesthetic Nietzschean:
Rosenaltaret

The completion of Rosenaltaret only four months after the publication of Septemberlyran may be attributed in part to Edith Södergran's sense that she was still possessed by her 'September-rapture';
her message had to be brought to the world a second time and, perhaps, clarified. It is doubtful, though, that she would have had
the courage to finish Rosenaltaret so quickly if Hagar Olsson's
sudden intervention in her fortunes had not inspired her. Later on,
Hagar Olsson expressed a rather tepid liking for the new book,
excepting the section dedicated to her: "Save for the beautifully
lyrical Fantastique, (it) did not bring much that was new."[1] Edith
Södergran herself was more enthusiastic as she described it to Hagar:
"My collection opens and closes gracefully, and 'Fantastique' in the
middle is a gracefully woven wreath, it came upon me like a sweet-
smelling white veil, there is something painful and burning about it.
The book's first part is even and strong, save for 'Conjuration' (a
reference to the poem 'Besvärjelsen'), which is characteristic, however, for one side of my nature" (EB, p. 74).

The dating of the poems in the collection is easy enough. Four
are from the marvelous September, but were not included in September-
lyran at the publisher's decision ("Rosenaltaret," "Botgörarne" ("The
Atoners"), "Gudarna komma" ("The Gods Are Coming"), and "Förvandling"
("Transformation")). Three more ("Lidandets kalk" ("The Cup of
Suffering"), "Jorden blev förvandlad till en askhög" ("The Earth Was
Transformed to an Ash-Heap"), "Mina sagoslott" ("My Fairytale Castles")), and a portion of a fourth, "Var bo gudarna?" ("Where Do the
Gods Dwell?"), were entered in a letter to Hagar Olsson of January
1919, together with a version of "Rosenaltaret."[2] The "Fantastique"
poems were written between January and March 30, 1919, when the whole
manuscript was given to Hagar Olsson for examination; one of these,
"Syster min syster" ("Sister My Sister"), was then omitted from the

final version at the suggestion of Edith Södergran: "it is not strong and can weaken the cycle." In the same letter, she says: "the sequence of the poems in the volume is of no importance" (EB, p. 70).

The choice of "Rosenaltaret" as the title poem of the new volume is a challenge thrown in the face of the critics; it states once again the tenets of the September poetry and, rather pathetically, tries to recruit followers for the new faith, of which the poem's speaker will be the priestess (SD, p. 223): "In the twilight I am / (a) temple priestess, / initiate, guarding / the future's fire." There are sideswipes at Christianity: "I step forth to you / with a glad message" (the tidings of great joy in Luke 2:10)--"God's kingdom begins, / Not Christ's dwindling empire, / No, higher, brighter human forms / step forward to the altar," which is crowned with roses, "a mountain of beauty." Here, discounting the past, "Lightly / the spirit of the moment will sit / drinking / a toast to the moment / from a fragile golden glass." The "higher beings," the worship of beauty, the denial of the past, and the implied fragility of the beautiful dream, are all elements quite familiar from what has gone before; Hagar Olsson was correct in her opinion about the lack of novelty.

The recruitment, and the exhortations, continue in poem after poem. "The strong" are told that they should flee into isolation ("Be men! / Do not remain dwarfs with shrunken limbs") and follow "the stars' unwritten laws."[3] Or "human beings" are instructed to bow before those powers, "the gods," so that they may be lifted up ("The Gods Are Coming"); that the gods are products of the human spirit, however, is clear enough from the second line (SD, p. 243): "Kneel, oh humans. The gods are coming. / The gods arise from dust-weighted brows," and the old-fashioned sublimity of this poetry is signalled not only by the "biblical imperative" in -en (knäböjen) but by Edith Södergran's use of the poetic word "änne" ("brow"). She admonishes mankind (or the candidates for "God's realm," at any rate) again and again; in "Conjuration" she tries to bend her audience to her will, in order that they may receive a higher and wilder strength (SD, pp. 245-246): "I would wish that you grow weak from my will, / I would wish that you tear apart your hearts, / and that the demons would find a place in your limbs, / wild, inhuman, bursting all life asunder." The "demons" are the relatives, in Edith Södergran's world, of the "light devils" whose typographical fate caused her such embarrassment in Septemberlyran; they have also been companions of the giants and monsters in "Framtidens tåg" ("The Procession of the Future" (SD, p. 197) in Septemberlyran), who put oil beneath the "kettles of the future," and, in the St. Petersburg "Fragment," they descended upon the Alps ("the demons' way is the suns' heartless flight through space"), as spirits which bring about the destruction of the old. In the second part of the present poem they are summoned again: "demons, yearned-for: do I conjure you forth with my strength?" Elsewhere, in "Facklorna" ("The Torches"), the message of revolution seems quite close to that of the "Internationale": "Oh my torch, shine in the face of the terrified, / the person racked with tears, darkened, defiled"; the torch will burn in every "nocturnal farm / in the Alps, where the air is blessing, / in the tundras, where the sky is melancholy"--St. Petersburg, the sleeping titan, was inhabited by people from the gray steppes. However, the revolution here, as in "Fragment," is not political but spiritual. "A gentle god stretches out his hand to you. / Mankind cannot live for a second without beauty" (SD, p. 251).

Membership in the new army is not a guarantee of ease, however. The demands for purification and atonement, made in "Fragment," compose the whole of another of the poems intended for Septemberlyran, "The Atoners"; "We shall do atonement in the lonely forests"--it is a kind of course for missionaries, in which the candidates learn a Nietzschean "strength" and "superiority" (SD, p. 233): "When some day we resemble one another as siblings / in strength and superiority, / then we shall go to the people." The troop is given, in fact, a marching song, "Det fasansfulla tåget" ("The Terrible Procession" (SD, p. 231)), which Schildt made a point of excluding from the collection. The first part is inspiratory enough, and no harder to grasp than Henry Cutler's martial hymn about the "blood-red banner" of the Son of God ("Bravery is the highest thing... / God's realm stands on our strong side, / Unfurl the redness of your heart...The angels seize our banners"); but the second, where the terrors of the march are described, has bizarre qualities: that the parade is "like one's own funeral procession" means, to be sure, that the old self should die willingly and gladly, as in "Fragment," but now the very dead seize their own wreaths. (Edith Södergran had already thought better of a particularly gruesome description, "poor emaciated bones lumber along," and left it out of the fair copy[4].) Schildt's rejection of the poem is regrettable, though, for the sake of its fine conclusion: a reminder that the struggle for the future has been waged, thus far, only within the prophetess herself ("All the terror, the future's highest fear, / (are) pressed together in a single breast"): her reactions have been both those of the "normal" being and the visionary, a mixture which emerges as paradox ("one can only mourn in this procession / one's joy is all too great").

A similar double perspective pertains in "The Storm." Edith Södergran was afraid that she and her mother would be swept away in a sudden Bolshevik invasion of the Isthmus; on March 26, she wrote to Hagar Olsson that "perhaps the wave of the Bolsheviks will come, and we shall never see one another again" (EB, p. 65) and, on May 11, "perhaps everything that is old will suddenly collapse now..." (EB, p. 75), a statement which seems to refer to her own poetry and program, although the letter begins with the sentence "World events give one strange thoughts..." Again, there is the patent fear of the actual, or "political" future, and the desire to welcome the coming of the "new," a realm never clearly conceived, but described in lines of a peculiar grandeur (SD, pp. 229-230): "Now the earth wraps itself again in black. It is the storm / which arises from nocturnal cliffs, and dances / its ghostly dance alone across the earth." The Nietzschean burden is readily detectable; Enckell points to the passage in Ecce Homo where "a war of spirits" is predicted: "there will be wars such as the world has never seen."[5] As an adolescent versifier, Edith Södergran had uttered the same message: "The autumn storms will come / and then the iron of castle and keep / will rust and be undone" (ESD, p. 27). The poem's emphasis is different from that of the first "Storm" (SD, p. 181), written during Finland's Civil War a year before: there the main figure was the hero descended suddenly from the heights; here, attention rests with the storm's victims, although the poet does not sympathize with them. Instead, she simply describes what becomes of them in their blindness and confusion (SD, pp. 229-230): "Now men are fighting again-- phantom against phantom. / What do they want, what do they know? They are driven / like cattle from dark corners, / they cannot pull free from the tether-chain of events... / the great ideas drive their prey before them." Even these ideas (which may be an allusion to the events beyond the Finnish-Russian border) are powerless, subject to the highest life force of all, the Dionysian urge to action--the great tempest of which Zarathustra speaks, the wind of Nietzsche's poem "Mistral,"[6] the "eternal thaw-wind" of Södergran: "The ideas stretch out their arms in the storm, imploring in vain, / he, the dancing one, knows that he alone is master on earth." The result of the Dionysian storm is apparent chaos: "The world no longer controls itself. The one shall / fall like a burning house, like a rotten tree, / the other will remain, spared by unknown hands." Yet there is a consolation for humanity, to be found, we assume, when the purifying tempest is over: "And the sun looks at all this, and the stars shine in icecold nights, / And mankind creeps along his lonely way toward boundless happiness." If Edith Södergran's readers found this distant goal to be cold comfort, however magnificent the verse in which the message was couched, they had to remember that the priestess of the collection's first poem had announced that she knew and saw more than they: "I separate myself from you, for I am more than you." In his memorial written after Edith Södergran's death, Jarl Hemmer reminded his public that the Swedish tradition[7] had included a Saint Birgitta and a Swedenborg.

In fact, in the closing poem of the collection's first part, "Martyren" ("The Martyr" (SD, pp. 254-255)), the poet sees herself as a proud victim. The martyr speaks, looking pityingly and not a little scornfully at the crowd which watches his death: "What do you / who swarm back and forth / with ugly movements, / know of your well-being or woe, (or) how it feels to lift one's head freely." With a play on words (from "fritt" to "frikänd"), the martyr welcomes the hemlock (SD, p. 254): "He whom the whole world condemned / is spoken free. / The black beaker / is purest sun." If the mode of the martyr's death suggests Socrates, his dress suggests the sanbenito in which the victim of the auto-da-fé was traditionally clad or, simultaneously, a jester's hood; Tideström has proposed that the poem was written at the time when the furor concerning Septemberlyran was at its cruellest.[8] The martyr falls silent while he is described: "Lightly he takes upon his shoulders / the victim's many-colored cloak," and then he speaks again, gladly accepting his fate, in which he is sustained by his will: "you caress like velvet, like softest velvet-- / my will's raiment." The purple cloak of the "artiste," the velvet dress of the "triumfator," has undergone another transformation: it has become the Nietzschean garment par excellence.

The claims of the priestess-poetess are made again and again.
In one of the most often quoted poems in the book, called after its
first line: "First I shall ascend Chimborazzo in my own land" (SD,
p. 226), she is not content with national triumph; she will climb
"the mountain of fame" and "the mountain of power." In "Vägen till
Elysium och Hades" ("The Road to Elysium and Hades" (SD, p. 225)),
she will ascend "a mountain of fate," while men "wander below, in
the midst of clouds"; somewhat more modestly, the speaker of "På
Himalayas trappor" ("On the Himalayas' Staircase" (SD, p. 247)) makes
another mountain ascent in order to address the solar deity Vishnu,
offering "to sacrifice my life for a single moment of your dreams."
Conversely, in "The Earth Was Transformed to an Ash-Heap" (SD,
p. 236), the speaker has faced down death. (Edith Södergran attached
great importance to the poem, insisting that it be retained when
Schildt wished to drop it.) "I am strong, / for I have risen from
death's marble bed. / Death--I gazed into your countenance, I held
the balance against you. / Death--your embrace is not cold, I myself
am the flame." She will share her triumph with mankind, a generous
priestess now: "From silver goblets I shall pour out pleasure over
the earth, / compared to which Aphrodite's dreams grow pale." What
the priestess has to offer is greater than the joy of physical love,
a claim which fits, as well, with Edith Södergran's anchoritic concept of herself: "I live the life of a saint...I avoid all influences of a baser kind."

Nonetheless, the priestess is beset by an enormous longing;
seven poems in the first part of Rosenaltaret have "my heart" as
their central image, a replacement of the lyre of Septemberlyran.[9]
But "heart" is a more emotionally charged word than "lyre"; implications of poetic inspiration (and poetic technique) give way to implications of sheer affective power: in "Förvandling" ("Transformation"), she addresses herself, "Fortunate fairytale princess, / your
heart storms harder than the oceans" (SD, p. 244), and in "Conjuration" she asks: "How shall I speak to you from my deepest heart?"
The heart is an instrument of communication, seeking contact with
others like itself, and the journey to find this mighty heart has
been an overwhelmingly long one. In an untitled spiritual autobio-
graphy, the mission has not yet been completed (SB, p. 232):

> On foot
> I had to walk through the solar systems
> before I found the first thread of my red attire.
> I already have a sense of myself.
> Somewhere in space my heart hangs,
> sparks fly from it, shaking the air,
> to other boundless hearts.

The remarkable little poem not only uses the boundlessness of space
(traversed on foot!) to suggest the immense difficulty of the poet's
search for her identity, at once creative and emotional;[10] it also
says that the goal has not yet been reached--only a thread of the
red garment of true existence. The inconclusive "I already have a
sense of myself,"[11] followed by "somewhere in space," can only indicate a still more taxing pilgrimage to come. It is an unforgettable

expression of the artist's and the human being's smallness confronted
by the task of finding "my heart."

The dimensions of "I feernas hängmatta" ("In the Fairies' Hammock," another of Södergran's almost painfully childish titles) are
cozier, surely, than limitless space. The speaker of the poem is
lying down, as so often before ("Days and nights I lie / thinking..."[12]
and "I lie the whole day, awaiting the night"). It was a simple
fact of the tubercular's existence--she had to spend much of her
time at rest: "Nights and days / I lie in the fairies' hammock /
and dream strange things." Of all the poems in Rosenaltaret, this
is the one most closely associated with the erotic wound of Dikter,
and the turn toward the "choruses of Diana" (SD, pp. 410-411) which
followed upon that experience (SD, p. 227): "The heart is not born
which loves me: / he will never climb over reality's threshold. /
Diana's lamp shines through my nights / from thin fairytale gauze. /
I cannot love, I cannot sacrifice my great heart," lines which can
be taken as one more echo of the old, unhappy affair. But the poem
is not limited to physical longing and regret; the heart, as the
place of poetic creation, is the element in the speaker's existence
which cannot be abandoned. The quasi-erotic revery is continued:
"But one day I shall lie down beside the earth's most splended
son... / A little child / shall drink from my breast of stone /
earth's strangest milk. / I shall call him--Diana's gift." As in
the cosmic search for the heart, the poem looks into the future:
the speaker will find the love that matches hers; it would not be
unreasonable to think that "the earth's most splendid son" is
Nietzsche (or Zarathustra) as inspiratory force, the Nietzsche-
Zarathustra who says "'I never yet found the woman from whom I should
want children.'"[13] The product of the union will be her coming
verse, fed at the breast that has had to be as hard as stone in its
resolve.

The question of the poem, "Where Do the Gods Dwell?" (SD,
pp. 239-240) is answered directly in its second line: "In my heart
/ in my tattered, strangely blessed heart / when the song rises."
The center of the poem is simply a description of the circumstances
of inspiration (or, thinking of the hammock poem, of conception),
given in a kind of disorder, corresponding to the very rapture of
the event: after "the gods" have come to her, she lies "tired,
dreaming of them" (once more the use of the erotic to describe
poetic creation); when they visit her every day, "she is full of
power," when her blood "has gathered itself to hear their voice,"
they whisper "immortal words" to her: "Oh gods, gods! / In all my
weakness I find mighty words-- / words for you." (There is a resemblance between her phrase about the gathering of the blood and a
line from the uncollected "Blekhjärtade natt" ("Pale-hearted night,"
SD, p. 284) from the same time: "Pale-hearted night, / when your
blood is up, and forward, and ready to go to attack / then your
veins are an empty fortress, hideously abandoned." Poetic creation
was exhausting; it literally made the heart grow pale and empty.)
"Where Do the Gods Dwell?" seems to contradict previous claims of
her revolutionary power: "Is not the world unsayable (outsäglig) /
since you (the gods) touched things with your enchanted hands?" and

"No one has seen the world as yet. You concealed it behind curtains." But the poet understands the very inexpressibility of the world, thanks to the perception she has been given; seeing and saying more than others, she realizes how little she can see and say. Then, after the line of dashes (the inspiration has ended), there is a famous statement of thanks for what she has been vouchsafed: "A beam of light fell on my poor way."

Edith Södergran told Hagar Olsson on March 26, 1919, that "I wish I were quite healthy and had twice as much genius and that suffering were accessible..." Earlier in the same letter, she said: "It is as though flames burst out of me, I long for storm, suffering, and pregnancy" (EB, p. 64). In the light of the poems just discussed, the confession is clear enough; and the search for "suffering" reminds us of the praise accorded "pain" in Dikter. Her meaning is that she fears she has been unable to accept Zarathustra's dictum about suffering as "a primal source of being"; Zarathustra had called himself the "advocate of life, the advocate of suffering."[14] "Lidandets kalk" ("The Chalice of Suffering") is a palinode, a poem retracting or correcting a position once held. In it, Edith Södergran states what she has believed in the past (SD, p. 235): "Weaker hands may seize the cup of suffering / setting it to paler lips, / my victor's lips still do without it." The next line abruptly makes the correction: "But--no"--another example of the dialectical or self-argumentative process at work in many of these poems. In "my heart" there are "giants with dark countenances, / with tightly clasped hands of stone." Someday they will step forth from their twilight and summon pain. The end of the poem is an extended imperative: "(Bring) hither the spark-striking hammer against the stone image. / Hew out my soul / that she may speak words which have never sat on the tongue of man." She has said that her breast is of stone ("In the Fairies' Hammock") and yet it will give milk; now the stone giants of her heart will move and summon pain, and her soul, liberated, will say unheard-of things.

It is a paradox of artistic creation, as Edith Södergran sees it: the breast, the heart, must be of stone in order to endure the rigors of the sublime calling ("This hardness is necessary for every mountainclimber," Zarathustra says[15]), yet the required hardness must be overcome. "Verktygets klagan" ("The Tool's Lament") ponders the enigma at some length. Once again, the poet is elevated (SB, p. 241): "For me, the earth sank back into blue smoke. / I stand raised above all, / with nothing above me but the threatening copper sky, / which I rule," but the sense of power, in the midst of danger, is directly followed by a lament at the inevitable hardening of the heart of the chosen one: "Why was this burden placed on human shoulders? / Why was my heart encased in iron armor? / I wander amidst rosy clouds, a homeless god." The image of the hammer returns, but altogether transformed; an "overmighty god" (not to be confused with the "homeless god," the speaker of the lament) has shaped her into his tool: "Piece by piece you broke from my heart, oh overmighty god, / And made me into your instrument." Although the speaker weeps ("tears of the stone-hard one"), she realizes that she belongs utterly to her calling: "Where does my mouth still find words for lament / in inexorable overabundance. / My days and my nights / are written in your book, oh god..." The key words of the poem ("övermäktig," "överflod") carry us back to the punning on Nietzsche's Übermensch of "The Whirlpool of Madness" (see p. 73); there the perils had been described which the gift, the super-abundance of perception, entailed for the poet. The end of the poem turns to another paradox of the creator's lot; having all, she has nothing: "Naught belongs to me on earth, / not as much as a flower." Chosen to sing, she is deprived of a part in life. In "The Special Mark" (see p. 77) she had had a black-red mark on her dress; now it is on her forehead, a poet's mark of Cain: "Oh, being the richest one of all! / Having it written on one's forehead (,) / playing fate's strange game / at necessity's behest."

But the chosen one also bears a happier mark. The rose-altar of the book's title poem is so named because it is to be crowned with roses, and rose-words appear passim in the collection. The realm of the triumphant mountain-climber (in "First I shall ascend Chimborazzo") is one of "rosy visions," the homeless god of "The Tool's Lament" wanders amidst "rosy shadows," the frozen waves of [16] "The Song of the Ocean" reflect the rosy light, in the small poem "Fråga" ("Question"), the poet ("who (goes) through life in intoxication") wonders if there is some vessel to receive her "few drops of oil of roses" which she will distill from her fleeting existence, "Oh strangely flashing reality" (SD, p. 250). The rose-symbolism of Rosenaltaret is quickly deciphered; if the heart is the birthplace of poetry, the rose is beauty itself. The matter is stated at some length in the programmatic "Skönhetens stod" ("Beauty's Statue"): "I beheld beauty. / It was my fate! All lies within it. / How can I offer thanks for it? / I strew fresh roses every day / plucked with hot hands / before your statue..." The poem goes on to say that the poet seeks roses "which do not defile my dreams," another of the many indications of Edith Södergran's concern that her poems were inadequate expressions of her poetic vision; beauty is her queen, before which she lies "sobbing"--questioning the validity of her work, Edith Södergran falls into an almost risible sentimentalism (as in the "No, a thousand times no," of a poem in "Fantastique"). At the finale of "Beauty's Statue," she abandons herself altogether to the conventional phrase: "When shall I arise, light as a feather, / to fetch the rose, the one which never dies?" The rose which never dies is the perfect expression, the poem sought for so often, the work of the future, "words which have never sat on the tongues of men." All hesitations and doubts are overcome, though, in the jubilant outburst of the book's last poem, "Rosor" ("Roses" (SD, p. 279)): "The world is mine, / Wherever I go, / I cast roses to all." Edith Södergran's remark concerning the unimportance of the order of the poems in the book is disingenuous; "Roses" is intended to close off the book as "The Rose-Altar" had opened it: serving beauty, the poet will serve the whole of mankind. "Without beauty, man does not live a second."

If she dreamed of the supreme expression, the rose that would not die, she was painfully aware, all the same, of the transitoriness of the rose's beauty, the fragility of the poems she created. In

"Outsägligt är på väg till oss" ("Something Unutterable Is on the Way to Us"), a part of "Fantastique," she asks her "sister" (Hagar Olsson) if they are not mocked by "beauty's statue, around which the roses crumble" (the phrase, "skönhetens stod," is the same as in the poem of that name): beauty will persist, man's tributes to it will die (SD, p. 265). The subject had been brought up early in the friendship, in the revealing poem "Mina sagoslott" ("My Fairytale Castles"), which she sent with her first letter; the allusion at the poem's outset, as Edith Södergran explained in a note, was to the German aphorist, G. Chr. Lichtenberg, who compared the intellectual dwellings men build for themselves to "das Wohnhaus der Schnecke," "the dwelling of the snail": "I looked into the philosopher's house / and realized that he was happy... / But my fairytale castles / stand on fragile pillars indescribable" (SD, p. 237). The final word ("obeskrivliga") can belong, grammatically, either to the castles or the pillars, an amphiboly which serves to fasten the reader's attention upon the image of the structures poised in air, ready to collapse, as they are then told to do: "Plunge, plunge / in golden ruins. / I love you too well--die." At this point, a strophic break is indicated in the later editions, but not in the manuscript sent to Hagar Olsson or in the first printing[17]--the direct continuation of the poem is, in fact, more effective, since the process of rebuilding is immediately begun again: "I build you up again / trembling / in order to slay you--all too beautiful." There is a link between this poem and the title poem, "The Rose-Altar"; there, the "spirit of the hour" sat drinking the "toast of the hour" from a "fragile golden glass," here the castles fall into golden ruins: the beauty, the "goldness," of the moment or the vision is enhanced by the perception of its fragility. The creator of beauty--even though he searches for "the rose that does not die" and laments the fact that his roses, or poems, will crumble--knows very well how to rejoice in (and draw artistic profit from) the thought that the "deathless" verses cannot be attained. Indeed, creativity itself is spurred by the sense that the search must be continued, that the dreams are constructed, only to collapse. The poem has, literally, a dark ending: "My dream castles / You will stand upon the earth one day... / Then, dark, I shall put away hammer and chisel... / The world will end for me." The realization of the dream would mean the end of longing, and, for Edith Södergran, the cessation of the force that kept her alive--another reason, then, for her hesitation to think of her poems as immortal. The psychological insight of the poem is one worthy of a Lichtenberg, and of a sort rather rare in Södergran, who, however, had read something quite similar in Die Geburt der Tragödie: "In order to live, the Greeks had to create the gods, out of the deepest urgency...as roses burst forth from the thorny bush," and "The dream must have validity for us as a still higher satisfaction than life itself of the primal desire for illusion."[18]

"Fantastique" was called the "sister-cycle" by Edith Södergran in an accompanying letter to Hagar Olsson: "Are you satisfied with it?" (EB, p. 68). It begins with "Vårmysterium" ("Spring Mystery"), which Edith Södergran said was not "a strong poem, but it belongs to the whole, it has the aroma of violets and gracefulness and the same delicious, burning atmosphere" (EB, p. 75). The poem is reminiscent, not surprisingly, of the schoolgirl verse to Paula and Claudia; the very presence of the beloved makes the world enchanted ("the violets in the shadow smell of delicious fulfillment"), and secret conversations will take place, now not "in the broad warm bed" or "on the wild, free sea," as in the German verses, but in the woods (SD, p. 257): "I shall lead you to the forest's most delicious corner, / there we shall speak to one another about secrets..." (SD, pp. 99-100). In "Fantastique," the next poem, "Brev från min syster" ("Letters from My Sister"), is in the same vein, but less sentimental (the favorite word of the first poem, "ljuv" ("delicious"), disappears) and more empassioned. "What can letters say, / when I see you? / Does not your hair fall lightly around you in golden waves / when you enter / in order to tell me of your life? / Do not your hems freeze with rapture when you walk?" (SD, p. 258). Why do others not have "the eyes to see" this beauty (again, there is an association with the language of the New Testament: 'seeing they see not'); "why does a single hand draw from the well of the gods?" (The Song of Solomon, 4:12-15 says that "my sister, my bride" is "a spring shut up, a fountain sealed...a well of living waters.") The poem ends with a pointe, a trick smacking of anacreontic verse: the poet has not seen the sister, but has only received her picture, enclosed in a letter.

"Letters from My Sister" was not submitted to Schildt for publication, and it survived only in a pencil copy, belonging to Hagar Olsson; Tideström gave it the second place in his edition because of its allusion to an early stage of the friendship. "I mörkret" ("In the Dark"), the next poem, continues the narration (SD, p. 259): "I did not find love. I met no one. / I went trembling past Zarathustra's grave on autumnal nights: / who hears me any longer on earth? / Then an arm was gently put around my waist-- / I found a sister." (In the penultimate line, Edith Södergran is punning again: "liv" can mean either "waist" or "life." An American translator has rendered it as "Then an arm was laid lightly on my life,"[19] which blurs the physicality and the naturalness of the expression.") After tugging at the golden curls of the sister, to make sure that the "impossible being" is real (those "golden locks" are mentioned thrice in the cycle, twice as belonging to the sister, and once as the property of young birches, reminiscent of her), the speaker still cannot convince herself of her good fortune: "Doubting I look into her face... / Do the gods play thus with us?"

"Jag tror på min syster" ("I Believe in My Sister"), the longest of the poems in the cycle, is misleadingly titled; or, rather, the title makes an assertion which the body of the poem disputes. This time, the sister is described by means of Edith Södergran's fairytale apparatus: "The elves wove her silken dress / The moon-maid sprinkled dew upon her breast" (SD, p. 260). These allusions are apt enough here, for it is the intention of the two to tell "fairytales to one another, / unending fairytales for a thousand years" until one day "the dawn will come, our new dawn." The prediction is not fulfilled, however; the very outset of the poem has shown that all is not well: "I walk in the wilderness and seat myself alone in the mountain, / on the devil's stone, / where cares have waited / a thousand years," a period corresponding exactly to that allotted to the happy telling of fairytales. No doubt unintentionally, Edith Södergran uses time-honored material from European love poetry--the Petrarchan topos of the lover alone and wretched, in a desert place-- which she combines with a vague Scriptural memory, the temptation of the hungering Christ in the wilderness, where the devil challenges Him to change stones into bread (Matthew 4:3). In her emotional starvation, the poet succumbs to the temptation to doubt her beloved, and so sets free the army of cares that wait in the stone; the poem's third section (after the predictions of happiness) is one of the most painfully melodramatic outbursts in her poetry: "My sister... / Has she betrayed me? / Does she bear the dagger in her bosom--the lightfooted one? / Answer me--laughing eye," and the answer is the "No, a thousand times no" mentioned above.[20] "I do not believe it, / though angels wrote it with unerring styluses / on the sheets of time."

"Alla ekon i skogen" ("All Echoes in the Forest" (SD, p. 262)) continues the theme of despair, and engages again in negative excesses: "No, no, no, all echoes in the forest cry: / I have no sister." It continues, as it were, the story of "The Maiden's Death": the poem's speaker finds a "white silken dress" and embraces it, asking the "thoughtless fabric" if it remembers "her rosy limbs"; "her shoes" have been left in the sunlight, and "the gods warm their hands at them." The climax is an appeal to nature to join in the lament, like Shakespeare's "Blow, blow, thou winter wind" and Fröding's "Säv, säv, susa" ("Reed, reed, sough"): "Fall snow upon my sister's remains. / Blow over them snowstorm your bitter-heavy heart." The omission of punctuation makes these lines, the best in the poem, all the more immediate; it then descends into melodrama once more, with "shudders" at "the hideous place where beauty is buried."

In her letters to Hagar Olsson, Edith Södergran is circumspect about her fear of losing her "sister": she praises the work of Hagar Olsson's fiancé, Eklund, and never asks her about the details of her life in Helsingfors. The poems, however, are much more outspoken; the lonely imagination has the upper hand. In "Systern" ("The Sister" (SD, p. 263)), the girl with the golden hair vanishes once again: "I once had a sister, a golden child, / in the city she disappeared from me in the crowd." The poet is reminded of her when she sees the young birch shaking its golden locks among the black firs; she wonders if the birch--or the sister--stretches out her hands toward her in wistful appeal. There are broad hints that innocence has been defiled: "Sister, my sister, whither did they lead you?" and "What dreams of lust can you dream upon tired beds?"--and an attempt is made to restore that innocence with fairytale allusions: "Heroic child, good fortune's child! / We wait together / for the fairytales' day." The situations of the adolescent lyrics are repeated: there, in "Autumn," a friend (evidently Claudia) was seen in the Raivola woods (where the wind "played with (her) rich and golden locks, / which streamed across (her) ivory neck") before she departed for the city (ESD, pp. 43-44).

"Outsägligt är på väg till oss" ("Something Unutterable Is on the Way to Us") mingles themes and mixes tenses, however, in a fashion quite beyond the reach of the St. Petersburg schoolgirl (SD, p. 265):

> Who can love you, sister?
> Will not a god with a dark countenance enclose you in
>   his arm?
> Does the same one not stand at the foot of your bed
>   when you fall asleep?
> Shall our eyes behold him, sister?
> Did we not live in the fairytale, where everything
>   impossible is possible, did I say so, sister?
> Does not beauty's statue mock us, around which the roses
>   crumble?
> Do not these lips promise everything on earth?
> Does not this forehead know that something unutterable
>   is on the way to us?

The final words, which provide the title, are of some importance; the whole poem is an attempt to say the unsayable, to describe the promised realm of happiness for the sister. Using present and future tenses, the poet summons an image of the dark god of the dream (and an erotic god); using the past, she speaks of the fairytale world into which she has already led her sister; using the present again, she implies that, because of her failure to persuade her sister, and of the sister's failure to listen, the goddess of beauty, life's only permanent and precious force, mocks them, and the roses, offerings to the goddess, crumble. The referent of "these lips" and "this forehead" at the conclusion is purposefully ambiguous; they belong to the "statue," but they belong equally well to the speaker herself: after all, she has made the promises, and conceived the vision of the future, and has tried to put it into the terms at her disposal—of the erotic phantasy, of the fairytale, of the cult of beauty.

In contrast to the effervescent tone of the letters from the spring of 1919, the cycle's last poems—"Gudabarnet" ("The Divine Child") and "Syster, min syster" ("Sister, My Sister") betray a growing resignation or hopelessness. In "The Divine Child," the disposition of tenses is once again noteworthy; the first two lines have the past (SD, p. 266): "The divine child sat with me. / The golden lyre sang from my hands," but the two middle lines are in the present: "the divine child stares out into endless twilights. / The song circles over her head with broad wings," in what may well be valedictory benediction. Then (another of the many queries put to the "sister" in the cycle), the question is asked: "What do you see in the song?," and the reply, moving into the future, is frightening: "It is your own future which rises (there) / from the icy twilights, / your own future, admonishing, calling, waiting." In his biography of Edith Södergran, Loup de Fages comments that the "sweet meeting" had to come to an end; Hagar Olsson had to return to her work, her friends, her fiancé.[21] It appears that the "empire of my dreams" of the adolescent poetry, where the friends sat beside a "free wild sea" (cf. ESD, p. 73), has collapsed: the twilights are "icy," the

repetition of "your own future" places a dividing wall between them,
and the inspiratory companionship, as the tense of the opening shows,
lies in the past.

Like "Letters from My Sister," "Sister, My Sister" (SD, p. 267)
survived only in the pencil copy in Hagar Olsson's drawer, and was
inserted by Tideström at the end of the cycle. Edith Södergran
thrice stated her own hesitation: "(it) seems quite tired to me, I
am not enthusiastic about having it included" and, "Follow your conscience: if (it) is tired, don't include it," and "perhaps it can
be included in the cycle, but it can't hurt to let it wait, it is
not strong and can weaken the cycle" (EB, pp. 68-70). These fears
(which also served to make Hagar Olsson concentrate her attention on
the poem) may have arisen not only from worries about artistic value,
but from the poem's criticism of Hagar Olsson's spiritual standpoint.
It is concerned with that "sick" interest in the transcendental which
Edith Södergran found so upsetting. "If it lies within my power, I
shall save your art from the transcendental," she wrote in February,
and enclosed some fragmentary verse in her letter: "The strange pro-
claimer--was she my sister?/Do transcendentalists and gypsy women now
become my sisters?" (EB, p. 52). The verse was meant "to annoy
Hagar," as Edith Södergran said; "Sister, My Sister" goes farther
still, no longer hinting but lecturing. There are, as usual, vaguely
biblical tones, which could seem almost ironic: "Sister, my sister,
you are still small / but you have already seen God. Blessed is
your brow, it beams so"; now, she informs her sister that this very
gift has estranged her from man and nature: "Since you saw God, you
fell away from men. / You sat lonely among the trees, / but the brook
was silent to you, the birds sang no more." The lesson is spelled
out: "He who has seen God sees nothing more on earth, / he is at
home in heaven." It was a message which Edith Södergran very badly
wanted her friend to understand; when she first brought up the poem
in the correspondence, she made a proposal about it by means of which
she hoped to underscore its importance: "It can have a stronger
effect if one reads it the way Sonja reads the Gospel to Raskolnikoff" (EB, p. 68). With some perversity, Edith Södergran chooses
a major "Christian" passage in Crime and Punishment (Part IV, Chapter 4) in order to make her anti-Christian point. What she means
is that she wants Hagar to listen to the poem with the same intensity as Raskolnikoff listened to Sonja's reading of John 11: "he
knew...that she herself was most anxious to read to him, and to him
alone, and to make sure that he heard, heard it now."²² Shortly, of
course, Edith Södergran would read the Gospels with a devotion equal-
ling Sonja's own.

As Hagar Olsson was about to hand the collection to the publisher, her friend told her: "I do not wish anyone to know who the
sister is. Be crafty, act in such a way that the Schildts can guess
nothing." Her injunction was well-reasoned; these intimate documents
could have been embarrassing to both the friends, and could have
compromised Hagar Olsson as the public champion of Edith Södergran's
works. But the poet did not attempt in any way to deceive herself
about the personal nature of the poems, and, indeed, about their
element of physical passion; she laughed at Karl Bruhn when he wrote

about "ethereal sister poems": "He talks the way Lenore does with the Princess in Tasso. He does not know the least thing about the laws of poetry. Nothing comes from nothing, but in order to write poetry about you I need only a lock of your hair" (EB, p. 92).

The third section of Rosenaltaret is given over to several fig-ures from Edith Södergran's actual life or from her mythology. The elegy on the death of Ludwig von Muralt, "Fragment av en stämning," (Fragment of a Mood" (SD, pp. 271-274)), repairs what Edith Södergran seems to have regarded as her failure to estimate the physician pro-perly when he was alive; "It happens at times that one neglects to express one's entrancement (hänryckning) in relation to someone. That is what happened to me, for example, with Muralt" (EB, p. 95). In Septemberlyran she had included a brief poem on Muralt's passing, "Trädet i skogen," ("The Tree in the Forest"), which builds upon the topos of the mighty tree struck down by the tempest, or, in this case, by lightning--a tree ascending, of course, toward the Söder-granian heights: "It rose above the mists of the depths to the peaks of the earth in lonely splendor" (SD, p. 173). In the elegy, the Alpine background is given in more detail, and the subject of the poem is the "son of the high land" ("höglandets son") whose memory is illuminated by the "high land's sun" ("höglandssolen"), while the "summer of the high land" ("höglandets sommar") looks forth from the forest, and the "gods of the high land" ("höglandets gudar") play their melancholy pipes. The poem is unabashedly confessional about Edith Södergran's experiences at Davos, and equally unabashed in its dramatization of the events: "If I love mountains, the love of my youth lies in them. / Over tender, green crocus, over my first bud-ding love / memory walks with triumphant feet. / Thus one pulls along, reluctantly, a young / barbarian prisoner,²³ with flashing yellow locks." The prisoner is the Alpine spring, come violently and against his will; at the same time the prisoner is the speaker herself, the unwilling captive from the North in the sanatorium. It is impossible to miss this self-identification: early in the poem, she has referred to the "high land's sun shining wildly in my locks" and, then, to "my wild longing," and says finally (after the descrip-tion of the springtime's coming) that: "Was I not young in those days with flashing yellow locks." The idea is broken off, and four lines of dashes ensue; then a statement is made about the happy result of the captivity: "It happens at times that the briar-rose blooms / that the briar's dry tangle is covered with rosy wonders. / That is what befell me, too---." More dashes follow.

The poem has begun with traditional elegiac tones ("Wind, wind, wind! / strew roses and narcissi from my memory's garden... / The taste of the bitter narcissi on my tongue repeats: parting, parting, parting, parting..."), and the second part enters the realm of detailed recollection (the story of her love), where not loss but gain is emphasized. Belying its fragmentary appearances (the pleni-tude of dashes), the poem closes with a mingling of the two streams, regret and emotional profit. The loss has been bitter, the memories of the brief and happy episode are themselves insubstantial, in their coming and going: "My memories flame up even as the pyre / of those in retreat over stretches of land laid waste, / even as bogs in the

North are covered with white bloom in springtime / even as the fata
morgana lifts its mute marching flag / for the converted, believing,
giddy wanderer," but the memories' intensity is what counts.

The physician to whom the elegy is directed has not been named;
he has merged with another Alpine hero, Nietzsche, whose teaching of
a Dionysian affirmation of life in its short moments of ecstasy
stands behind the ending: the retreating army lights a pyre in the
wasteland, the morass swiftly blooms, the wanderer pursues a vision,
and (SD, p. 274): "When does one see such things? When life will
show its power. / When it shall ascend its boldest mountain top / in
giddy adoration." Tideström thought that the elegy was reminiscent
of Nietzsche's Dionysian dithyrambs;[24] the young barbarian captive
can also recall Nietzsche's admiration for "another sort of barbar-
ians, who come from the heights,"[25] and his observation that, to the
Apollonian Greeks, the Dionysian element itself was "titanic" and
"barbaric." (Also, Enckell's suggestion that the foundation of
Södergran's passion for Nietzsche was laid in the Davos library
should be borne in mind.[26]) Is it possible that the "elegy"--which
deserves that designation less and less as it goes along--was completed not in 1917, upon Muralt's death, but two years later, when
Edith Södergran clearly recognized her need for "Dionysian rapture,"
and sought it?

The "Dionysian" statements by Edith Södergran in the letters of
early 1919 are shot through with distress at her inability to give
voice to what she feels. "The Dionysian (element) lays claim to my
whole soul, but I cannot sing of it...I am unhappy about the Dionysian" (EB, pp. 61-62). The poem called "Dionysus" is an attempt to
describe the experience; it is written from the standpoint of the
worshiper who waits to be taken up into the chariot of the god--in
short, the poem completes the hidden Ariadne-myth of Dikter (SD,
pp. 269-270): "Dionysus, you come with the sun's team from distant
space. / The earth, tired with weeping, waits, a praying woman. /
O Dionysus, Dionysus! / over our heads we hear the thunder of your
team. / Liberation, liberation / the quick reins sing." The speaker,
"with insane hands," seizes the chariot's wheels, and, "a beam of
spring sun," climbs into the chariot. (It is one of the many athletic feats the invalid describes.) The god and the speaker go off
through space together, and the team that pulls them is like the
storm: "All realms of space sing of resurrection (uppståndelsen),"
a surprising word in the present, Dionysian context: we think of
"I am the resurrection and the life," the climactic sentence in the
passage from John which Sonja read to Raskolnikoff. Ecce Homo (the
work of Nietzsche which Olof Enckell believed to have fired Edith
Södergran's first enthusiasm) ends with the line: "Did you understand me?--Dionysus against the Crucified One..."[27] She uses the
Christian term, or reference, in service of her present, hostile
belief.

In October 1921, well on her way from Nietzscheanism to Steiner-
ism, and Christianity, Edith Södergran wrote to Hagar Olsson about
seizures she had had: "...violent Dionysian attacks, with a need of
physically casting myself in the air and dancing, dancing. If I were

healthy, I should run in the forest and dance tens of kilometers, and the superman is a thousand times stronger than man, and I am a wreck" (EB, p. 172). In the poem "Scherzo," her athletic dreams take a special form, that of dancing on a tightrope of stars stretched in space itself, a stellar cord bearing a special affinity to her creative heart: "Stars above unambiguously clear, my heart on earth unambiguously clear" (SD, pp. 277-278). Indeed, the dance has already taken place, and she is tired, like Esaias Tegnér of "Mjältsjukan" ("Spleen"), tired of the poetic art itself: "I have grown weary of beholding its tightrope walker's toils / its leaps into the air."[28] She sits on the rope, looking down into the "sleeping abyss of time," which will someday claim her; this moment of exhaustion (after the creative act) represents the danger of destruction: "Danger for tiring dancer's feet, / danger for slackening dancer's arms, / danger for recklessly stretched band of pearls." But time itself is told to pass away: "Time--perish," an imperative which has much in common with the "Time--get you hence" of "Triumph of Existing." Time is held at bay by desperate commands. The acrobat, her femininity clearly indicated by the Swedish noun-forms ("danserskefötter" and "klättrerskearmar"), is surrounded by the stars, which tell her "'I am you'" and "'Stay with me'," forming a ring around her in this scherzo or jest of a vision, so that "all the upper part of my body is in star vapor." With the poem's last section, a new figure enters the starry world: "The sea-king drinks a toast from a conch (mussla)." Space has become a great sea, whose ruler (in astrology, Neptune is the ruler of the "boundless sea of space") drinks the dancer's health, encouraging her. (The erotic import of the shell should be recalled here, as in "The Maiden's Death.") In this perilous situation, the dancer still sits, exhausted, on her rope: "No one shall stir. But let the dancer go forth on midnight toes / and fall on her knees and stretch out her arms / and kiss the fair one"--who is, grammatically, masculine, "den sköne," the handsome king. The god combines the several elements of the speaker's longing--for perfect love, for perfect art, for the infinite. The dancer will continue her acrobatic deeds, the perilous task of the creation-of-art will be resumed.[29] We should be thankful that Edith Södergran decided to omit a proposed final line from this fine poem, which combines so many of the elements of her work: her Nietzscheanism (in the figure of the artist-acrobat), her love of the fairytale (the mortal who falls in love with the magic being), her overriding concern with the difficulties of creation, and her ability to fill the aerialist scene with elements of the cosmic and the deeply personal. She instructed Hagar Olsson to delete the following prosaic description of the dancer's descent: "awake: Consciousness. Sister Fantasia descend to earth" (EB, p. 70).

"Offrets timme" ("The Hour of Sacrifice" (SD, pp. 275-276)) can be dated by the fact that a phrase, "Our bell rings," resembling the poem's first line, "Hear the clock strike,"[30] is part of a pencil sketch, called "Hagar," from February 1919. Thus, it is from the time when Edith meant to cure her friend of her mysticism, and when she burned up "The Star Child": "One does not come to the rose altar (italics added) with such gifts, you know that well," and "The dread-

ful path you walk is not the path of human beings" (EB, p. 51,
p. 55). Like "Sister, My Sister," the present poem criticizes the
recipient. The sacrifice of oneself is "no torment"; the addressee
is asked "what else" or "whom else" she will sacrifice. Unquestion-
ably, the poem is directed to Hagar Olsson; the opening of the second
strophe closely resembles the description of the mute nature surrounding "my sister" who beheld God and became estranged from mankind: "After all, you gave the whole of earth away / you learned to
walk on the ways of heaven. / In your hand the rose is dead, / the
wind does not touch your cheek." The identity of the other victim
to be placed on the sacrificial table is kept silent (the question
of the first strophe returns in the second, "Whom will you still
sacrifice?"); but the end of the first strophe implies that the
speaker thinks of herself: "you love still, you love still, / do
not say more." The poem, then, is one more of the exhortations to
Hagar Olsson: Edith Södergran did not intend to be sacrificed by
her on the "transcendental altar." "Do not hinder my creating,"
she told Hagar Olsson in the letter of February 20 (EB, p. 51). That
Edith Södergran so persistently engaged in this personal campaign,
in Rosenaltaret as in the letters, is not a sign of the tug-of-war
of wills alone; the fear that she would lose the ability to create
poetry, her life-support system, was overwhelming, and made her
assaults on Hagar Olsson's "transcendentalism" all the more stubborn,
or desperate.

The last poem in Rosenaltaret is "Roses," the statement of the
artist who "loves each marble ear which perceives his words." In
"The Martyr," the crowd, with its ugly movements, had not compre-
hended the martyr's calling; the "marble ear" is, we assume, a
beautiful one, that can hear beauty. That poem, put at the end of
the collection's first section, was a jab at uncomprehending critics,
and a praise of the poet's difficult task; this one is the envoy for
those who have ears to hear--or who are worthy of worshipping at the
rose-altar. As for the poet, or the priestess at the altar, she
survives--or, indeed, overcomes (SD, p. 279): "What are pain and
misery to me? / Everything collapsed with a crash: / I sing. / Thus
pain's great hymn ascends from a happy breast." Haranguing Hagar
Olsson, Edith Södergran said that she herself had been "un-liberated"
("oförlöst") until she was "able to begin to create from my fullest
heart...I am become bliss and the light itself" (EB, p. 55).

6.

Cosmic Visions and Crisis:
Framtidens skugga

Framtidens skugga reached the publisher in two parts. In November, 1919, Edith Södergran mailed a notebook to Schildt's, containing the collection as it was subsequently printed, save for the last eight poems. (The notebook ended with "Materialism"; a loose sheet contained two more poems, "Extas" ("Ecstasy") and "Hamlet.") After the crisis described above (see pp. 19-20), an annex of nine poems was sent off, with the title "Sol" ("Sun"). Perhaps because of misgivings about a political mininterpretation, Schildt's omitted one of these from the printing, "Ögonblicksbild" ("Snapshot"): "There are people of various kinds in Europe / but let those be saluted who are of our kind. / Bolshevism's victory is very swift, but ours will arrive before them (sic), for it is the last one..." (SD, p. 414).

An aggressive tone prevails in the collection's first part, "Planeterna stiga" ("The Planets Ascend"). The speaker of the opening poem, "Mysteriet" ("The Mystery"), announces that she will "convert everyone to a more holy god, / sweeping away all superstition with a soundless broom; / slaying all pettiness with mockery." The Nietzschean tone is unmistakable, but the culmination, from medieval legend, is what made Hagar Olsson call the time of Framtidens skugga the "Saint George period"[1] in Edith Södergran's life (SD, p. 310): "I will climb up onto your mighty serpent. I will pierce his head with my sword. / Oh my good sword which I have got from heaven, I kiss you." The poem is not a rose, as before, but a weapon.

Nietzsche becomes the title-figure of "En gammal härskare" ("An Old Ruler" (SD, pp. 313-314)), who, addressing his youthful warriors, passes the task of conquest along to them. Even though it has been built "for conquerors," his castle seems not yet to have dispatched the army on its campaign: "These melancholy windows stand / and speak of fallen fates." His young followers, "...untrembling, people

of bronze like me," wait impatiently inside its walls; Edith Södergran makes a surprising reversal of her window-image in the second
strophe, where youth's impatience is said to beat on a window pane
from without: "And your breast will sing like a spring storm, which
whips the glass with wet wings." Next, the old ruler predicts the
behavior of his warriors, once they have left his castle: "Blessed,
laughing, you seize a new star with your hands, / then your features
darken, your glance falls upon the earth, an earth that must be pun-
ished: / What power this arm puts into the sword, / which will
pierce...," a verb which is left dangling, without an object; two-
and-a-half lines of dashes ensue, as though silently indicating the
evils that must be destroyed. The poem's last line stands alone:
"Young breast...why is it so bright within you?" Is the "young
breast" filled with light at the prospect of the punitive expedition
against the earth? Or has the work of the sword been accomplished
during the grand pause (the dashes), and so it is pleased at what
it has wrought? "Skaparegestalter" ("Creator Figures" (SD, p. 316)[2])
is more specific about the campaign's objectives ("Force, force /
the seas of mankind / form, form / mankind's huge mass into a joy
for the gods"), and about the participants, who approach like
Nietzsche's riders:[3] "We come rocking in loose saddles, / the
unknown, the frivolous, the strong," and utter Zarathustran sounds:
"Like mocking laughter our voices ring from afar, afar." And the
Nietzschean weapon's material is again present, if not the weapon
itself; "Creator Figures" is the song sung by "my heart of iron."

These poems are often minatory, for example, "Tolerans" ("Tolerance" (SD, p. 311)), whose title is utterly misleading; it demands
tolerance for its own supreme intolerance, the intolerance of the
chosen one, "the star which climbs toward the heights / can you measure its flight? / Do not stop it from climbing." The star has a
color which could have made the anxious Finland-Swedish reader of
the early 1920's (with Bolshevism just next door) wonder about Edith
Södergran's political views; its "redder shine," however, only sig-
nifies preternatural vitality: it tells others, literally, to get
out of the way ("ur vägen"), it is "a hand which follows its own
law, / (and) will topple what others preserve. / A victor comes,
inaudible lips speak the forcer's name." The victor (and "forcer")[4]
is then defined more closely in the aptly named "Makt" ("power"):
"I am commanding strength...I follow no law. I am law in myself. /
I am the human being who takes" (SD, p. 312).

All these unvarnished praises of arrogant strength and power--
recalling Edith Södergran's several aphorisms on Napoleon from the
same time--are interwoven, nonetheless, with worry: how can a star
be sure that it has pre-eminence? This is the problem of "Fientliga
stjärnor" ("Hostile Stars" (SD, p. 315)), where no solution is found;
a long anaphora tells us that: "Every star has an icy glance. /
Every star is proud and lonely in its strength... / Every star comes
marching like a red shine from afar / in order to destroy, devour,
consume, exercise its power." But, in their rivalry, they bring--
as "Stjärnorna vimla" ("The Stars Abound" (SD, pp. 318-319)) says--
a "golden madness" to man who, hearkening to a voice that sings on
high, forgets all else: "With a bold hand, every star casts its

mite onto the earth: ringing coin. / From every star infection comes
over creation: the new sickness, the great happiness." (It is
characteristic that Edith Södergran describes even the spread of her
teachings in pathological terms.) These stars, teeming as a
bedazzled mankind stares at them, are creative intellects, each making exclusive claims ("Every star wishes to seduce one into believing
that she (sic) is all"), each wishing to set the world afire, each
preparing the future: "The stars ascend. The stars abound. Strange
evening. / A thousand hands lift the veil from the countenance of
the new age." In reading this pair of star poems, we must remember
not only the doubts which beset Edith Södergran about her own calling, but her transference of allegiance from one star, one teacher,
to another. Nonetheless, her hesitations are put aside in the finale
of the book's opening suite, the grandiose "Planeterna" ("The Planets"). In its feat of the imagination, it is comparable to the ode
of Klopstock, "An die nachkommenden Freunde" ("To the Friends Coming
After"),[5] which tries to capture the sensations of a planet as it
hurtles through the cosmos; "The Planets," in fact, represent the
apotheosis of Edith Södergran's poetic athleticism: "Wild earth
that rolls forward in burning, smarting space, / blissful[6] that the
air strikes against your cheek, / blissful that the speed makes you
turn. / The planets wish naught else but swiftness in their course."
Beauty has been forgotten, as have the lyre and the heart; instead,
as poetry's symbol, the pitiless sword has been joined by the equally
pitiless planet, "swifter, quicker, more merciless."

The euphoria of imaginary action ends quickly. The book's next
section, which gave the collection its title, "The Shadow of the
Future," suggests that the shadow is a first sign of the happiness
which Edith Södergran insists will fall to mankind's lot, if it will
listen to her; but the title also has an ominous personal note. In
a letter of July 22, 1919, Edith Södergran complains to Hagar Olsson
that she has lost her poetic gift: "I have no inspiration. I hear
wonderful tones within me, but have nothing which lifts them forth,"
a writer's block for which she seems to blame her friend: "You put
a mute (en sordin) on me." After another appeal for friendship, she
alludes to the title of her new book: "They say that coming things
cast their shadow, is it true?--you are familiar with the dark," and
she finishes with a renewed complaint that no letter has come: "I
suffer quietly cruelly intensely" (EB, p. 86). (The line contains
no commas.)

An untitled poem in the second section has been quoted[7] as an
indication of Edith Södergran's sense of isolation from her Finnish
milieu (SD, p. 324):

> What is my homeland? Is it distant Finland, star-strewn?
> No matter what. Low stones, sprawl on flat beaches.
> I stand on your gray granite as on a certainty.
> You certainty, you will always cast laurel and roses in my
>   path.
> I am the divinity that comes with victorious brow,
> I am the blessed conqueror of the past.

As usual, the seminal Nietzsche-text can be identified: Zarathustra predicts his "great, distant kingdom of man, the Zarathustra-kingdom of a thousand years," saying that it does not matter how far away it is: "What do I care! After all, it stands no less firm for me on that account-- I stand sure on this ground, on an eternal ground, on hard primeval stone, on this highest, hardest primal mountain-range..."[8] Yet, as usual, the source has undergone Södergranian transformations: both prophets are sure of their calling now, but the one, Zarathustra, implies that his age is not ready for him, the other, Södergran, that her own land is not. (With the adjective, "distant," she alludes to her own distance, physical and intellectual, from the country's heart, and to what she, and the other modernists, perceived as Finland's distance from the continent's intellectual currents; that Finland is "star-strewn" suggests, to be sure, the promise that Finland still may hold--after all, it was the land of her "companion stars," Hagar Olsson and R. R. Eklund.) Another change is that the mountain-range of Zarathustra has turned into low boulders on flat beaches, a landscape which formerly (in Dikter) had been that of stultification, of inability to do poetic work--see "Two Beach Poems" ("a place of silence without echo") and "The Low Beach" ("my thoughts were not born in this place" (SD, pp. 68-69; 87)). Now, though, slowly moving toward independence from Nietzsche, Edith Södergran no longer needs the imaginary Alpine --or even Himalayan--scenery; her confidence is so great that the "low" world becomes a place of triumph.

A free employment of a Nietzsche text can also be found in "Nätet" ("The Net" (SD, p. 330)), the source of which is Zarathustra's reflection, in "The Honey-Sacrifice," on his being a fisher of men. (In Also sprach Zarathustra, the passage immediately follows the one, just quoted, on Zarathustra's "great, distant empire"; both passages borrow their images from the Gospels--i.e., the rock on which the church is to be built, and the Kingdom of Heaven that is "like unto a net cast into the sea." Was the attention of Edith Södergran--already become a reader of Scripture, though still an unwilling one--drawn to the lines in Nietzsche precisely on account of this similarity?) "I have the net into which all fishes go. / Blessedly the fisherwoman's calm breast rises / as she pulls the silver burden unto her. / I lift the riches of the earth up onto my shoulders. / I bear you, I bear you to a fairytale pond." Yet the fisherwoman is not the only figure in the poem; "up on the beach a fisherman stands with a golden fishing rod." Again, Södergran makes significant changes. In the German text, Zarathustra himself, with his "golden fishing rod,"[9] makes his "catch on this high mountain," in the Swedish poem, it is a fisherwoman who collects the fish at seaside or riverside, to deposit them, evidently, in a pond for the delectation of the fisherman--he, like the old ruler in the castle, allows someone else to do his work, or to carry his mission into the future. Abruptly, then, the poem turns to suggestions of what the purpose of this work of collection--of recruitment for an expedition--may be: "Gods exist somewhere behind the thickest forests, / we straying children of men want to go nowhere but there. / Up to look for the future's flaming sun beyond the forest." The goal is as alluring, and as difficult to define, as that of the wandering boys in H. C. Andersen's tale, The Bell, whose quest (in pursuit of the bell's sounds) leads them beyond the forest, to a place where the sun sets "like a shining red altar."[10]

Memorable as their central images are, both "What Is My Home-land?" and "The Net" fall back onto the (by now) all too familiar rhetoric about "certainty" and about "the future"; similarly, two other poems from "The Shadow of the Future" express familiar doubts about the validity of the calling. The one, "Tantalus, fyll din bägare" ("Tantalus, Fill Your Cup" (SD, p. 326)) denigrates the poet's work itself ("Are these poems? No, they are rags, scraps, / Paper-slips of the everyday"), the other "Den förlorade kronan" ("The Lost Crown" (SD, p. 327)), talks about the "fairytale crown," which the poet fears she must renounce. The last two lines of the latter poem ("I have found everything. / Deny the victor, teach him humility") are particularly obscure because of their laconicism; to Enckell, they mean that "the disciple of Nietzsche had learned to see through everything, even her own production."[11] It was a dan-gerous perception; the poet was on the way to the long silence of her last years. But, in both poems, there are also signs that another and still deeper fear lies behind the intimations of unworth-iness--the fear that death will come. "The Lost Crown" puts the question: "shall this pale forehead bow?", and "Tantalus" ends: "dying, I shall cast the wreath from my locks into your eternal emp-tiness." Having failed as poet and prophet, Edith Södergran will fall into oblivion; she will not have existed at all.

The initial poem of the series, "The Shadow of the Future" (SD, p. 321), tries bravely to confront the inevitability of death, stated in its first line: "I sense the shadow of death." Some ameliora-tion, or consolation, is sought in the customary anaphoric catalogue, with a reference to the Nordic fates (an isolated example in Edith Södergran's work) and then the fatedness, and so the importance, of all deaths; "I know that our fates lie piled upon the table of the Norns, / I know that not a drop of water is sucked into the earth / which is not written into the book of eternal times." However, the last item in the catalogue is, in fact, a cry of anguish: "I know as certainly as the sun rises / that I shall never behold the endless moment when it is at the zenith." The adduction of the sun, though, affords the chance to make death's prospect bearable, at least for the Dionysian: it will be a death in exaltation. (The source is again from the vadecum, Also sprach Zarathustra--Zarathustra's vision of his own end, "a star, ready and mature in its zenith, glowing, pierced, blessed by destructive arrows of the sun."[12]) "The future casts its blessed shadow upon me; / it is nothing other than the streaming sun: / pierced through by light I shall die, / when I have trampled all chance with my foot, I shall turn away smiling from life." The thought that mankind is at the mercy of forces quite beyond its control had been brought up by Edith Södergran in "The Storm" in Rosenaltaret, where it "is driven like cattle from dark corners"; now, she convinces herself that she can rise above life's accident and death's necessity by the very act of willing an accep-tance of death--actively, in exaltation, not in resignation or despair.[13] "Oh you, my will! You turning of all necessity, you my

necessity!", Nietzsche says in an untranslatable pun ("Du Wende aller
Not, du meine Notwendigkeit!") at the opening of the pertinent passage in Also sprach Zarathustra.[14]

The sun-theme will return with a vengeance in the annex to the
collection; presently, in the book's second section, it is represented by a poem "Solen" ("The Sun," (SD, p. 329)), which, in its
scenery, seems almost to copy "The Song from the Cloud" (see p. 71);
but instead of directing a quasi-playful attack against the earth,
the woman on the clouds now wants to float upward, toward what will
become her immolation: "I stand as on clouds in a bliss without
compare. / The clouds' edges burn red. It is the sun. / The sun has
kissed me. Nothing on earth kisses so." The gently erotic foreplay
with the sun does not satisfy; being a witness to the sun's power is
not enough, and she is not meant "...to live eternally as a witness
of this moment, / oh no, to ascend the vertical beam / nearer to her"
(i.e., the sun).[15] The being on the cloud must employ its will to
climb even higher, to its death: "One day, I shall spin myself into
the sun like a fly in amber." The image of the dead insect has been
employed by Edith Södergran before, in "A Life" (see p. 61). The
remains, although captured in amber, will not be the whimsical poet's
equivalent of a Horatian monument outlasting bronze; poetic immortality means little or nothing, a life's concluding ecstasy means much,
or all: "it will be no jewel for posterity, / but I have been in
the glowing furnace of bliss." Those who see her crown will fail to
understand that it is her ability to achieve a splendid annihilation,
and not her poetic work, that counts: "Oh woe, you crown that shines
around my forehead, / what shall they know when they behold you?"

In "The Sun," the word "bliss" appears twice; it is also the
central word and the title ("Sällhet") of still another poem that
deals with death and utter happiness. There is no sun-imagery; the
poem is reduced to a set of euphoric funerary visions. A decade
before, the teenager's "Frau Petrow" had been beautiful in death,
but unmoving (see p. 29); the deceased speaker of "Bliss" is hyper-
active, dying (the laws of reason are suspended for the oxymoron's
sake) for very joy in the midst of her own funeral (SD, p. 325):
"I die--for I am all too happy. / From very bliss I shall bite into
my shroud. / My foot will curl with bliss in my white shoes / and
when my heart stops--it will be rocked by pleasure." She will become
an example for all the world to see: "Let me be carried to the market place-- / here lies the bliss of earth." The last line has the
force of an epitaph; her corpse will show that she incorporated joy,
and died in it. Still, the poet does not mock the paraphernalia of
death, as Edith Södergran's Swedish contemporary, Birger Sjöberg[16]
(1885-1929), did in "Bleka dödens minut" ("Pale Death's Minute");
living with death so close at hand, Edith Södergran never tries to
disarm it by making fun of it. Her tack is to make it altogether
splendid, or playfully graceful, as here: "Small genii will cover
me with white veils / and they will strew red roses on my bier."

Blissful death has a related theme in the cycle, "The Shadow of
the Future," that of Eros--not the degrading lust of "To Eros" (see
p. 40), but a sustaining or even an ennobling factor in life. Olof

Enckell points out that Rolf Lagerborg's Den platoniska kärleken
(Platonic Love) had created a sensation when it appeared in 1915,
and suggests that Hagar Olsson may have called the book, and its
longwinded analysis of the penetration of the erotic into every facet
of life, to her friend's attention.[17]   Edith Södergran then changed
Lagerborg's concept of Eros as an omnipresent and vital force into
Nietzschean terms: "It is Eros which holds a divine service in his
temple--it is Eros which is The Will to Power," a statement which
Edith Södergran makes to Hagar Olsson in connection with the new
book planned for Christmas publication: "Its name will be Köttets
mysterier (Mysteries of the Flesh)." After a summer when she had
been able to write but little (and when she was excited by the prospect of your coming"), she had begun to compose again: "I've felt
such an electricity within me the whole time that it was almost
difficult to endure it. As if I lay in very Eros' arms the whole
time. I feel myself as the most blessed of everything (sic) which
has arisen from the depths of existence" (EB, p. 92).

The first of the two erotic hymns in "The Shadow of the Future,"
called "Du store Eros" ("Thou mighty Eros" (SD, p. 323)), is a proclamation; mankind has known this force, that "breathes of marriage,"
since time's beginning; but, thus far, lust has merely joined two
bodies together. The erotic drive has not yet reached the mind of
mankind: "the lightning has not yet attained man's forehead." "Eros
tempel" ("The Temple of Eros") continues the complaint--Eros' power
has not yet been understood (SD, p. 328): "No one knows what his
lips offer, / No one knows what his innermost thoughts are; / His
glance merely whips those carelessly youthful bodies / which play
with one another. / We do not know his pleasure--------------------"
(Edith Södergran uses her interruptive device: a second full line
of dashes ensues.) Those who are "Eros' comrades in play" (to be
contrasted to the bodies which "play with one another") have but a
single wish, readily connected with the wish for death "pierced by
the sun": "we wish but one thing: / to become flame of your flame,
and to be consumed." The Finnish poet Aale Tynni says that "Edith
Södergran's Eros arises from the bosom of her Dionysus";[18] both
divinities require a dissolution of the individual, but a dissolution in what is a highly individualistic way, even a theatrical one.
Edith Södergran may hint, or assert, that her concept of eroticism
is novel, something not yet understood; however, it can be easily
connected with her favorite myth from antiquity, that of Ariadne,
and with a favorite myth of the nineteenth century, the Wagnerian
love-death--save that in Edith Södergran's case, the love-partner
is imaginary.

The cycle, "The Shadow of the Future," ends with a melodramatic
"occasional poem" (in Edith Södergran's subtitle), "Uppståndelse-
mysterium" ("Resurrection Mystery" (SD, pp. 331-332)), about a dead
woman, around whose bier great candles burn, and "on whose face there
is a lust for Life." Heavenly choruses summon her, and she replies:
"Yes, Lord, I come." The imagery and language seem patently Christian, but we must wonder if the poem perhaps makes a blasphemous
point not unlike that of D. H. Lawrence's "The Man Who Died": there,
Christ, taken from the cross, is aroused by the Priestess of Isis,

here, the summoning lord is the male lover. This bizarre work
("Suddenly, a fire flames over the dead woman") is directly followed
by the most bizarre of Edith Södergran's necrophiliac visions, "Älvdrottningens spira" ("The Elf-Queen's Wand" (SD, pp. 333-339)). (It
is inspired by the memory of Muralt; the first of the Muralt poems
(see p. 52) speaks of the great tree struck by lightning; the present
fragment has the following closure: "One cannot believe that lightning can fell a thick tree / with titanic noise.") The fragment
opens with a series of questions, a search for the lover: "Where is
he, whom I have beheld in an ecstatic dream... / Where is he / who
lifts up a tired flower from the road / and shrouds her in transparent silk / and wraps veils around her feet / and watches her for a
long time, wondering: how did you die, child?" Then the speaker of
the poem (on whose forehead it is written: "She is sleeping") begins
the poem's second section, a series of admonitions to the man who
found her in the dream, and who has vanished: "Your tears will fall
upon my feet / they will trickle between my knees / as though they
would cause an awakening unto life." The phantasy substitutes tears
for semen; instructions are supplied, one after another, by the girl
(dreaming a continuation of the "ecstatic dream") to the imaginary
savior: "You will arrange the golden locks on my forehead, you will
smooth the silk on my belly." The mourner will pluck the pinkest
roses, and place one of them in the girl's hand; "And a fine green
leaf you will place on my bare breast / that I may prop my chin on
it as on a psalmbook"--the mourner is told how to prepare the corpse
for burial, even as he tries to awaken it to life. The erotic imaginings grow still more detailed: the mourner will play with the
girl's hair and brush her lips with a duster of silver-down, place
her in the grass, and, taking a diamond ring from her finger, press
it into the flesh of her upper arm. She bleeds: "Through red veils
you see that I still live." The instructions given to the mourner
now are unambiguous: "And you unlace my dress / and you put your
hand on my heart to listen. / You disrobe me, / the silk falls from
my shoulders." But all the mourner's efforts are in vain; the
dreamer, albeit alive, sleeps on, and her "marvelous head" falls back
"lifelessly." Still, the lover will not give up: "Yet, you have
more courage," and he plays with her fingers "as with a child's."

The poem has been, of course, a sultry recasting of the story of
the prince's efforts to revive Snow White; now it grows almost por-
nographic, yet, simultaneously, the fairytale elements are also more
pronounced. A "blue tower"--a structure with obvious physiological
implications: think of Rilke's "column" and "tower"[19] in his so-
called "Phallic Hymns"--rises in the mourner's garden: "the elves
dance around it. / The elf-queen walks back and forth on its battlements." These miniature beings ascend both "bridegroom" and
"bride", clambering onto his "brown foot" and into his hair, climbing
over her body as though she were a mountain (a similar vision of the
giant girl appears in the St. Petersburg fragment). Yet the elves
(who have the stimulating and ornamentative function of the amoretti
or cupids in the classical epithalamium) also fail to arouse her,
even as the mourner has; and "he turns away, (saying): what does it
avail me, / that the elves comb her golden hair, / that they place
silver poppies upon her breast./ I let the ring fall back into the

casket, resounding." His abandonment of the task, however, makes the elves turn on him, crying: "There you have the faithfulness of men," one more allusion to Edith Södergran's belief that men are scarcely dependable lovers. Finally, the "cat Elektrus" is summoned by the elf-queen to purr the "dead girl" back to life. After a grand pause, in the course of which the cat apparently succeeds in its task, the lovers are united in a duet which talks of pleasures to come (he calls her "a wonderful toy," she calls him "a large-eyed savior"), and the question is asked: "Can we still die?" The fragment ends with the question about the mighty tree, mentioned above, which led Tideström to conclude that the dream-lover was the late Muralt. In a way, it does not matter whose features the dream-lover bears; the poem is a remarkable autoerotic display, and it is particularly worth noting that the cat succeeds in rousing the girl where the man has failed. The cat's name is not taken out of a hat; he is Elektrus, "electrical," the term which the letters used, in the summer months of 1919, to describe that intense and self-engendered eroticism in whose grasp Edith Södergran found herself.

The fragment is an intimate and intentionally playful document, an arabesque which such an erotic visionary as the Dane, Jens Peter Jacobsen, would have appreciated--Jacobsen, who created the figure of the tubercular Edele Lyhne (in the novel Niels Lyhne) with her carefully arranged setting for her own phantasies.[26] The distribution of the roles in the phantasy is revelatory. While the girl is ostensibly lifeless almost until the poem's end, she is the director (and the poet) of the whole play, and, albeit a semi-corpse, is strikingly beautiful (even her teeth "stand white" before her "shining lips"). In a manner grotesque but fascinating, Edith Södergran has put on stage some chief figures of her real and her imaginary life: the desirable but moribund girl (who makes her lover obey her will), the marvelous lover (who fails), the more efficacious beings of the childhood world (the elves, the magical cat), and finally the dream of a transfiguration in love--Bacchus carries Ariadne aloft, in flames, the lovers sing of "life with violet-colored waves."

There is a sharp break in tone between "The Elf-Queen's Wand" and the poems about Eros which follow it. The language is often more brutal, sometimes more elevated and more proclamatory; Eros appears as a simple force: this is, in fact, "Eros hemlighet" ("Eros' Secret" (SD, p. 342)): "You are not man and not woman. / You are the force / which sits squatted in the temple, in order then, rising up, wilder than a moan, / more violent than a cast stone / to cast out the striking words of the message across the world..." The linguistic devices are of an elementary nature; the single semi-rhyme ("skrän / sten," "moan / stone") calls attention to the violence of the act, as do the repetition of the verb, "slunga," "to cast" ("slungad sten / slunga ut," "cast stone / cast out") and the implication that "striking" modifies "stone" as well as "words." Just so, the poem's first lines have blared out the poem's message: "I live red. I live my blood. / I have not denied Eros." It is not a long way from the overwhelming and humiliating Eros of 1916 (see p. 40) to the new standpoint--save that now the force has been accepted without reserve, just as a death in ecstasy has been. Variation after variation is made on the theme. "Eros skapar världen ny" ("Eros Makes the World Anew" (SD, p. 343)) emphasizes the potentiality of the force, as yet unrealized: "in his hand the earth is filled with miracles" and "on (his) forehead great wonders are already dawning"--a play on the Swedish "under" and "underverk." "Vattenfallet" ("The Waterfall" (SD, pp. 340-341)) opens with a description of the "creative anguish" around the speaker's heart, and after a middle section of doubt ("I will go to a fortune teller"), comes to a joyous acceptance: "Oh you thundering waterfall of pleasure." In "its thundering, plunging rush," the cascade is filled with surety; like Eros, like poetic inspiration (which are equated here), it cannot be resisted, nor can the lightning (in the poem of that name, "Blixten" (SD, p. 344)) be turned aside. "My body lies like a rag / in order one day, seized by electric hands, / more firmly than all the ore of earth / to send the lightning." The speaker's very person will become a transmitting agent, more dependable than metal, to convey to lightning's force onward--the poem does not say toward what goal. "Lightning" shows the speaker in the familiar creative position, prone, limp, a position which returns in "Instinkt" ("Instinct" (SD, p. 345))--intended, it may be assumed, to be the epigraph, or the programmatic poem, of The Mysteries of The Flesh: "My body is a mystery. / As long as this fragile thing lives, / you (plural) will know its might. / I shall save the world." That is why "Eros' blood hastens in my lips / and Eros' gold in my tired locks." The word "trött" ("tired") appears three more times in this poem about the poet's power: "tired or downhearted: the world is mine" and "When tired I lie upon my couch, / I know: in this tired hand (a past participle now: 'tröttnade') the world's fate lies." The four appearances of "tired" are balanced, however, by four appearances of "might" ("makt") in the poem: one in the third line, already quoted, and the other three clustered triumphantly at the end: "It is might that trembles in my shoe, / it is might that moves in the pleat of my garment, / it is might, for which no abyss exists, that emerges before you." The paradox of the situation cannot be ignored: the mortally ill woman who imagines that the message of erotic power--a message nourished by her own phantasies, and expressed in the minority language of an obscure land in the marches of the West--will seize and save the world.

"Aning" ("Presentiment" (SD, p. 349)) speaks of the fragile body in which so much power rests, or through which power passes: "Oh you most splendid of all splendors, my body, / why do you know that you have might?" The speaker on the bed concedes that, as in the case of the rival stars, "I am but one among others, and others are stronger than I"; but "I am the shield on which one will look, / I am the nucleus and the link that combines." "Shield," "nucleus," "link"--these semi-technical words are used to demonstrate, as though in an elementary physics class, that the poet is the gathering point of power, its concentrator, its transmitter--for those who are to see the "blue shine" of the lightning and "to understand." (The line, "Man skall se (blixtens) bleka sken och fatta" contains another of Södergran's earnest and untranslatable puns: "fatta" may be parsed here as an intransitive verb, "to understand"; but it may also be taken as "to grasp," i.e. to seize the lightning itself.) In "Vid soluppgång" ("At Sunrise" (SD, p. 350)), the speaker herself has seized the lightning: "I caught the lightning in my right hand, / might, might flows over my lips," a line whose verb ("flödar över") emphasizes the abundance and the ineluctability of the gift bestowed on her. She has been given a vital task: "Fate stationed me to guard the rising sun. / May the expanses around us be greeted-- / a new day enters."

The plural "expanses" ("vidder") of "At Sunrise" are turned into the singular and become the central word of the companion poem, "O du mitt hjärtas vidd..." ("Oh, You, My Heart's Expanse..." (SD, p. 351)), a title praising the poet's enormous heart, the seat of her visions, which will be transmitted to the waiting world: "I will speak, my words shall fall like glowing brands in the mob." The mighty heart exists in fearful isolation, of course ("There is no hand that touches its surface so that it trembles"); but it is sure of its calling--or so the poem repeatedly asserts, in language echoing the Biblical description of the seven angels of the apocalypse (Revelations 15:6), "girt about their breasts with golden girdles": "I believe I collect the belt of thunderbolts around my breast." For the Biblical girdles, it substitutes the thunderbolt which is the sign and instrument of Zeus, in his role as Dionysus' father, and of Dionysus himself. Finally, the poet calls herself the god, no longer merely his instrument: "I am a god in whom the tempests rage, / with sucking eyes I draw all (people) into my soul."

Nevertheless, more hints of doubt appear in the midst of these assertions of power--most plainly in the ambiguous close of "The Waterfall": "Melancholy surety: that you are irresistible and superfluous (överflödig)." "The Tool's Lament" in Rosenaltaret (see p. 90) has already brought up the "inevitable superfluity" ("obevekligt överflod") of poetry, coming in its rich over-abundance, and "At Sunrise" speaks of the might that "flows over" the poet's lips; now, in the adjectival form, the double meaning of superfluity (in Swedish as in English) is made all the clearer. Not only does the rush of inspiration come over the falls unceasingly, like Eros, but it is also irrelevant--in the world's eyes. (The last word in the line gives a wry double-meaning to the preceding adjective, "irresistable"; the poet cannot resist inspiration's force, but the world can.) "The Waterfall," in fact, is a good deal less confident in its attitude than its forerunner in Septemberlyran, "The Whirlpool of Madness" (see p. 73), which ends with the speaker's complete surrender to the Dionysian force; in the later poem the speaker, although still aware of the divine madness of exaltation ("The foam which bubbles on (the waterfall's) edge makes a mind mad"), is afraid that the surrender has been to no purpose. The question is put to nature, and to the audience: "Clouds, do you know what will become of me?"

At the same time, Edith Södergran continued to watch a seductive foe, more dangerous than the world's indifference. "Den starkes kropp" ("The Strong Man's Body" (SD, p. 348)) opens with the usual message of coming victory: "I know, I know that I shall conquer."

The speaker identifies herself as "the star of the future," who has "awakened on an ancient throne." The second half of the eight-line poem is composed, then, of a four-fold anaphora on the word "mystery": "The mystery moves in my veins. / Mystery, I recognize you, I, the anti-mystic, the foe of ghosts. / Mysteries have no clear boundaries, mysteries have no stated names, / the mystery rises in the strong man's body when he, blind with intoxication, strides to action." The "mystery," we may assume, is once again "the mystery of the flesh," the erotic power to which the book was to be dedicated; and, once again, the kernel of the poem lies in a pun, on "mystery" and "anti-mystic." A bearer of mysteries, Edith Södergran detests mysticism--in short, she returns to the battle against Hagar Olsson's "mysticism," which she identifies with Christianity. "Ensamhet" ("Loneliness" (SD, p. 347)), placed just before "The Strong Man's Body" in the collection, is a reproach, in fact, sent to her transcendental friend in Helsingfors: "Alone I have come, alone I shall go. / My free heart has no brother. / Christian ghosts sit in all hearts and stretch out poverty's hands. / The sweetness which flows to me from all sides is inaccessible to you." The second-person pronoun is in the plural; Edith Södergran aims her poem not just at Hagar Olsson but at the myriads like her who follow "Christian ghosts." On the other hand, those who understand Edith Södergran's message are "few among the sand in the sea."

There was a patent lure in what Edith Södergran thought Hagar Olsson stood for; Edith Södergran polemicizes all too violently against "mysticism," and in favor of what was presently her own faith. On August 30, announcing the genesis of The Mysteries of the Flesh, she told her friend (and opponent) that it is "Eros who holds divine service in his temple. It is Eros who is the 'Wille zur Macht'" (EB, p. 92). The full confession of the Nietzschean-erotic faith came, at last, in "Ecstasy" (SD, pp. 353-354), the middle poem of the triptych which closed the original version of her book. The poem is laid out with great neatness, as though the poet wishes to make sure its message will not be missed. First, there is a jeremiad against a world that will not listen (in a five-fold anaphora on "woe," beginning: "Woe, the past is dreaming, / woe, we hold the unopened bowl of the future in our hand"), then a minatory section, a threat that the world will be destroyed for its inattention ("With tears in my eyes, I pronounce the words of bliss over the condemned world"), and finally, the description of the priestess: "Bliss touched this forehead which calls itself mortal, / through my lips there streams the heat of a god, / all my atoms are open and are afire..." (The poem's concluding aposiopesis indicates still greater transports of bliss, beyond the power of words to describe.) The priestess, or poet, is ready once more to receive the lightning; the language has an incontrovertible sexual import: "åtskild" means both 'open' and, more literally, 'parted.' Looking back, Hagar Olsson said that the ecstasy was rapidly becoming more than Edith's strength could bear.

On either side of "Ecstasy," there are poems of paralyzing self-insight and terrible despair, "Materialism" and "Hamlet." "Materialism" (SD, p. 352) makes the case with frightening clarity; it is only

the exercise of her will, culminating in these erotic visions, that
keeps her alive, and takes her mind away from her death: "In order
not to die I must be the will to power. / In order to avoid the
atoms' battle during dissolution." The "most splendid of splendors,"
her body, was failing her; she put this realization--as well as her
conviction that her body was all she owned--into a couplet with
strangely clumsy language and an almost childish rhyme: "I am a
chemical mass. I know so well (Jag vet så väl), / I do not believe
in illusion and soul (sken och själ)." The remainder of the poem
has, justly, been the object of considerable critical attention:
"...the game of games is so strange to me. / Game of games, I play
you and do not believe for a moment... / Game of games, you taste
good, you have a wonderful odor, / yet there is no soul, and there
never has been a soul. / It is illusion, illusion, illusion and mere
game." Edith Södergran chose the poem's last four words, "sken och
idel lek," as its title, meaning to drive her point home; in the
manuscript, a strange hand crossed this title out, replacing it with
"Materialism," an outsider's--and a moralizer's--judgment on the conclusion to which the poet had come.[21] According to Enckell, the same
materialistic, or nihilistic, conclusion had been reached before, in
"Nothing" (see p. 59); noting the resemblance between the "game of
games" and the "plaything of playthings" ("lekarnas lek" / "leksaker-
nas leksak"), a phrase in "The Elf-Queen's Wand," Olof Lagercrantz
proposed that, in "Materialism," Edith Södergran saw through and condemned the erotic fantasy of the long poem.[22] Edith Södergran admits
that she will continue, now and then, to play the resurrection game,
but she does not believe in it (as she says) "a single moment."
Hagar Olsson, replying to Lagercrantz, took him to task for implying
that "Materialism" represented a firm intellectual stand when, in
fact, it expressed only "the mood of the moment."[23] However, on
another occasion, she herself said that "Materialism," together with
"Hamlet," reflected the "feeling of nothing with terrifying clarity."[24] There is no ignoring the awful plainness of its language,
and the repetition, at once contemptuous and desperate, in the last
line ("sken, sken, sken").

The immediate source of "Hamlet" (SD, pp. 355-356) is a passage
in Die Geburt der Tragödie where Nietzsche expands upon a theme
introduced early in his tract--that of the "terrible wisdom" of the
wood-god Silenus, who has seen through the "illusion" of life and
realized that it would have been better not to have been born. "The
Dionysian man resembles Hamlet in this sense: once upon a time, both
have had a clear glance into the essence of things, they have understood, and they are sickened by action. Now, no consolation helps
any longer, their yearning goes beyond a world after death, beyond
the gods themselves, and existence, together with its deceptive
reflection in the gods or in an immortal world to come, is denied...
now the human being perceives everywhere only the horror or the
absurdity of existence, now he understands the symbolism in Ophelia's
death, now he understands the wisdom of the wood-god Silenus: (existence) sickens him."[25] The opening of Edith Södergran's poem is a
reduction of the passage; the poet addresses herself: "What does my
mortal heart wish? My mortal heart is silent. My mortal heart
wishes nothing. / Here lies the whole earth. You turn away con-

vulsed. / A magic wand has touched the earth and it became dust."
The earth had been reduced to dust once before, in Rosenaltaret (see
p. 88), where, however, a kind of resurrection followed: "I am
strong, for I am arisen from the bed of death." In "Hamlet," the
meeting with death will not end in triumph: "And where I sit on the
ruins, / I know that you are coming, unforeseen hours," unforeseen
not only because its time is uncertain(Matthew 24:36:"of that day and
hour knoweth no man"), but because the speaker of the poem had not
wished to foresee it. The reader of the correspondence with Hagar
Olsson will remember Edith Södergran's horrified greeting of the
story of the white door behind which death lurked in Själarnas
ansikten.[26] Now, the door is named again: "I know that you are
waiting behind a bolted door, / that I am near to you and you can
reach me your hand," words which sound like a terrifying reversal
of the consolation of the 23rd Psalm: "Thou art near me, thy rod
and thy staff will comfort me." It is likely that the episode in
Hagar Olsson's prose poem coincided with an old fantasy about the
"room of death" entertained by the adolescent Edith, a fantasy
expressed in the final poem to Cottier (see p. 34); the figure of
speech has a Biblical source in Ecclesiastes 3:20: "All goes unto
one room, all is of the dust, and turns to dust again." Another
allusion, or set of allusions, follows; Edith Södergran makes her
commentary on the to-be-or-not-to-be of Hamlet's soliloquy, and his
musings about the "undiscover'd country": "There is no choice for
me, / truth, I follow you if you walk in the land of mists. / Truth,
truth, do you dwell in a corpse-room amid worms and dust? / Truth,
do you dwell where there is everything I hate? / Truth, do deplorable
lanterns light your way?" To Tideström, the poem's climactic anaphora is both "an expression of revulsion at death" and of "anguish
at the religious submission from which (she) had begun to see that
she could not escape"; Enckell detects more clear-cut pairs, the
first two lines describing the gruesome end of the "chemical mass,"
the second pair accepting, however reluctantly, the "metaphysical
and transcendental alternative" which Hagar Olsson's vague Christianity represented.[27] Yet, examining the poem, we should not forget
its Shakespearian origin; Hamlet has a choice, of being or not-being,
but Edith Södergran does not--she is confronted by imminent death,
a "truth" (repeated five times) which will befall her whether she
thinks of it as physical dissolution, or, unwillingly still, as a
way--illuminated by "deplorable lanterns"--into another world. (With
her adjective "bedrövlig," Edith Södergran again makes a wry play-
on-words: the lanterns may be deplorable or, quite simply, sad, as
befits the path of the dead.)

After "Hamlet"'s composition, Edith Södergran read Hagar
Olsson's Kvinnan och nåden. It would be too much to say, however,
that Edith Södergran accepted Hagar Olsson's "mysticism" without
demur; instead, she made a compromise between it and a newly won
concept of her own, to which, she hints, she will win Hagar: that
death is a part of a natural process, a Goethean "Stirb-und-werde":
"There is no one, no one in the world whom I admire the way I do my
little Hagar. And if you are not already on the way to complete
liberation, I shall not let go of you before you are. Nature has
answered me: one does not ask if God exists or does not exist, one

quite simply puts his little power of reason aside. To know and to
believe are not words suited to God's conditions. God's law is simpler than everything. One can breathe only in absolutely pure air,
physically as well as morally. The knowledge of God has a very
strong effect on heart and lungs. One breathes as if it (sic) wished
to go straight through one's body. Vis-à-vis God I feel myself,
above all, a being of nature." She continues: "I have had to fight
against my aversion to mysticism, religion, and Christianity," and
"I have gone my way soberly, and my healthy, intimate feeling for
nature has led me to mysticism" (EB, pp. 95-96). But, by mysticism,
she means, of course, her "natural" version: "Goethe as a mystic
entrances me now. He is healthy..." (EB, p. 101). (As in other of
her programs, Edith Södergran emphasizes both the health of her
teacher and her expectation of getting healthy heart and lungs herself; we are tempted to say that what Enckell calls the great "lyric
of ideas" is, rather, a pathetic poetic diary of the search for a
miracle.) The poem "Hyacinten" ("The Hyacinth") formulates the
latest consoling program, after the despair of "Materialism" and
"Hamlet"; in the midst of the withered brown blossoms of the past,
still covered with snow, the new blooms appear (SB, pp. 357-358):
"I stand so valiant, so full of expectation, and blissful. / Shall
fate throw snowballs at me? / Let snow run in my brown hair, / let
snow cool my blessed neck. / I lift my head. I have my secret. What
can prevail over me? / I am unbroken, a hyacinth which cannot die."
The background of the poem remains obscure; Edith Södergran's prose-
poem on Princess Hyacintha has been lost, but her description of her
sensations upon reading Kvinnan och nåden is extant: "there is such
an aroma within me of hyacinths, lilies of the valley, and young
birch leaves" (EB, p. 95). Quite possibly, Edith Södergran had also
read Strindberg's Ghost Sonata, with its homage to the hyacinth's
"virginal form" and its "aroma, strong and pure from the springtime's
first winds, which have passed over melting snow."[28] The symbolism
of Edith Södergran's hyacinth is not as complex as Strindberg's; her
flower is the spring perennial which emerges "from ironhard ground,"
as the second part of the poem says—an expression of a brave confidence in life ("I am unbroken") which at the same time accepts life's
end: "Break me with your mighty, sap-filled hands—Life... / Break
me as an adornment for a queen." Hagar Olsson called the poem "one
of the most gripping celebrations of life";[29] still, there is the
conditional sentence that concludes the poem, and which might betray
(as so often with Edith Södergran's announcements) a lack of complete
confidence in what has just been said: "If there is a queen without
worries and cares, she may hold the hyacinth in her hand, / the
spring's frail symbol, related to the sun." The fragile plant, dying
only to be reborn each year, the sun's coursing—these are nature's
signs that life continues. The letter of November 25 contains another chiding of Hagar Olsson for her unwillingness or inability to
read the signs: "I do not want that which is not but that which is.
Your mysticism has the fault that it is sick, you draw upon nature's
fresh spring and believe that you drink mist..." (EB, p. 101).
Thereupon, she makes her recommendation of the "healthy" Goethe to
Hagar Olsson, and in her next letter (December 28, 1919), after mentioning Steiner and "his master" (Goethe), whom, she says, Steiner
"met in living life when he was twenty," she subjoins a fragmentary

poem (EB, p. 103), not included in any of her works, which is a hymn
to nature, but whose adjectives have the masculine vocative ending--
does she think of Goethe here, too? "O you mighty one, you are in
everything. In the tree and in me. / My dust wishes to fall into
nothingness, when I sense you behind these shadows / O you mighty
one, clear mirror of all things..." The thought that the individual
is a part of the great cycle of nature (compare Goethe's Wanderer,
and his apostrophe to nature, "Nature, / Eternally budding one"[30])
held up more or less well during these months, when Edith Södergran
worked on her book's supplement. The "Fyra små dikter" ("Four Small
Poems" (SD, pp. 359-361)) employ the thought variously. The speaker
of the first of them is "blessed" ("säll", the word also used in the
first line of "The Hyacinth"): "How can it be so blessed within one
breast? / That's the only question in my philosophy," a noun allud-
ing, perhaps, to Hamlet's remark to Horatio about the thinness of
the latter's "philosophy": Edith Södergran has found a simple answer
to Hamlet's queries about existence: "And my only answer is:
therefore, therefore that I know. / What do I know? / That I shall
be swooned (avsvimmad) in the sun / and not be dead and not be
victor-- / a sun which does not endure its own rising." Zarathustra's sun-pierced apotheosis is transformed into a trance-like (or
vegetative) state, where the individual, gone back into the whole
of nature, is neither death's victim nor its conqueror. Wishfulness
and wistfulness are combined in the paradox: returned to nature,
the individual--its individuality gone--will not know of its next
appearance in life. It is a hard-won sort of serenity, permeated in
the second poem by a sense of loss at what had existed before, the
cult of the body and its sustaining erotic electricity; the word
"body" is replaced here by the grimmer term of the burial service,
"dust." Snared again in the self-contradictions which must arise in
a creative intellect seeking to accept the inevitable, Edith Södergran says that "My crown is too heavy for my strength," then, in the
next line, that she "can lift it easily," and then, "but my dust will
fall asunder."[31] Her poetic gift, her "crown," is at once readily
lifted by inspiration and yet too much for her physical strength to
bear; her body fails her, and she addressed it with some irony: "My
dust, my dust, you are splendidly bound together. / My dust, I think
you begin to long for a coffin. / Now it is not the electric hour, /
my dust, you do not hear me." The "electric hour" of inspiration no
longer comes to so frail a vessel. (The search for electricity was
not readily abandoned; in a letter of the next autumn, she wrote that
she "had surrendered herself to (her) all-powerful flesh...I bathe
in blue electricity" (EB, pp. 146-147).) The habit of the victorious
proclamation was likewise not easily shaken; in the third poem of
the little cycle, the speaker says: "I am triumphant as life itself
/ ...and once again my heart stands above abysses and knows triumph";
and in the fourth: "I am success (medgången) itself. On my forehead
it stands written: / The sun cannot weep for an instant. He who will
slay the sun must surrender." The success she claims, however, is
that of her victory over herself, and her surrender to the sun, her
recognition, as she says, of "that which is stronger." The sun, in
its turn, does not weep at the natural course of life-and-death, or
at a simple human fate.

Slowly but surely, self-assertion, or Nietzsche's 'principium individuationis,' is weakened. In "Animalisk hymn" ("Animalian Hymn" (SD, p. 352)), the word "jag" (I) does not appear, and the speaker has become one of the human animals to whom the sun gives equal treatment: "The red sun rises / without thoughts / and is the same to all. / We rejoice in the sun like children. / A day will come when our dust will crumble, / it does not matter when. / Now the sun shines into the innermost corners of our hearts / filling everything with thoughtlessness / strong as the forest, the winter and the sea." Years before, the adolescent poet, writing in German, had made a similar statement about the sun's importance as compared to man's: "We have been given the sun and the sky and the earth and the sea, / Yet we in our tormented longing wander eternally" (ESD, p. 132).

The second sun-poem of the appendix, called simply "Sol" ("Sun" (SD, p. 363), also the original title of the whole new section of the final volume), repeats the lesson of humble acceptance. The poem begins with a grammatical progression from "my prideful heart" to "my heart becomes more prideful with every passage of the sun" to "the most prideful of hearts." The old arrogance seems to reappear, in a reminiscence, intentional or not, of the threats hurled at the earth in "The Song from the Cloud" (see p. 71): "It is as though I held the sun's disk in my hands / merely to crush it. / It is as though I visited the earth accidentally, lightly, fleetingly, / in order to awaken it with a hail of mocking words." But the echoes from the past are only preparations for the poem's volta, its dramatic turn: the most prideful of hearts is told to stretch out its arms toward the sun: "fall on your knees and let your breast be penetrated by the sun, the sun." The poem, "The Shadow of the Future," has had almost the same formulation--"Pierced by the sun I shall die"--but there it was a description of the supreme ecstasy in which the speaker meant, "someday," to leave life; now, the emphasis lies rather on a reverent acceptance of the sun's warmth--"shine in my face, touch my forehead."

On March 9, 1920, about two months before the dispatch of the appendix to Schildt's, Edith Södergran wrote: "A limitless devotion has broken out within me. I shall abandon everything, art too, for it is unholy" (EB, p. 114). And, a month later: "No one really owes anything to my poems, it (sic) is the purest trash, and my almost ancient book (she means that her book has not kept pace with her spiritual development) will turn out to be the same trash. Now I know how a mature person looks" (EB, p. 118). The poem "Beslut" ("Decision" (SD, p. 364)) uses the same phrase: "I am a very mature person, / but no one knows me, / my friends make a false picture of me." Both Tideström and Enckell have caught the allusions to Zarathustra's "Song of Melancholy" in "Decision";[32] Zarathustra, despising the mere poet's calling ("Only a fool! Only a poet!"), prefers to think of himself as a wild animal or an eagle, plunging downward hungrily onto lambs. Edith Södergran likewise puts herself into the eagle's role: "I am not tame. / I have weighed the tameness in my eagle's claws..." Addressing herself, she gives a directive: "Do you wish, perhaps, to write poetry (dikta)? You shall never write poetry again. / Every poem shall be the tearing-apart of a poem, /

not poem but claw-marks." The next poem, "Blixtens trängtan" ("The Lightning's Pining"), repeats the image (SD, p. 365): "I am an eagle. / That is my confession / not a poet / never anything else / I despise everything else." It is noteworthy that, with "confession" ("bekännelse"), Edith Södergran uses the term for a religious faith. Young Elmer Diktonius, the voice of the political left, would shortly take the panther-imagery of Nietzsche's "Song of Melancholy" for his poem of revolt, "The Jaguar."[33]   But here Edith Södergran means that the creative spirit enters a higher and uncommunicative realm: "What happens in the eagle's flight? Always the same, the eternal. / A lightning-bolt shoots down the sky in endless desiring, / secretly loving as when a new world is created." The lightning-bolt shoots down the sky but does not aim at earth, the love is secret and without object, these things happen not in order to create a new world, but, rather sadly, "as when a new world is created." The creative urge has become intransitive.

Yet the project of making the world anew died hard; the penultimate poem in the collection, "Den stora trädgården" ("The Great Garden" (SD, pp. 366-367)), talks of drawing together the "homeless wanderers," the poet's "siblings," in a special place: "Since we have no homeland we could become a people. / We shall build a latticed fence around our garden / so that no sound from the world reaches us." The dream is compounded out of two parts Nietzsche ("among the Europeans of today, there is no lack of those who, in a distinguished and honorable sense, have the right to call themselves homeless" (Die fröhliche Wissenschaft), and "You lonely folk of today, you seceders, some day you shall be a people" (Zarathustra)),[34] and one part Raivola, with its tumbledown villa and its fairytale garden. But like the lightning and the eagle, the dwellers in the garden are glad to be cut off from the world: "We have nothing else to do with the rest of creation / save to give it our soul." The little band's purpose is not intervention but example. Like a child planning a secret club, Edith Södergran tells Hagar Olsson of possible candidates for her "fate-group"--Rudolf Steiner, R. R. Eklund, and T. K. Sallinen, the Finnish artist (whose face, like that of the German general Ludendorff, had impressed her). This catalogue was given in the letter of April 16, 1920, in which she included the poem (and where she characterized herself as "a mature person"); on July 29 she came up with other names and ideas: "We shall have a home somewhere in Europe, a big hotel, for example, and to this home we should attract sympathetic people, Steiner, Barbusse, Branting,[35] and so forth" (EB, p. 141). Realizing that "we need a very large capital," she proposes the Bolsheviks and the Ruhr industrialist Hugo Stinnes as possible sources--only to withdraw the idea of such an odd couple directly.

In the letter of April 16, she also called the poem about the garden sanctuary "antiquated," adding that "I believe my career as a poet is over"; she casts about almost desperately for some new mission, telling Hagar that "I am nothing but a sword" and "I will not commit actions with motives other than religious ones" and "I do not wish to die until I have done something which is not a drop in the sea" (EB, p. 121). There is a kaleidoscopic shifting of idols:

Steiner's dreams are praised to the skies, and "Nietzsche's value
has risen for me, although he is so poverty-stricken in comparison
with (Steiner)...Sallinen, of course, is much greater than Nietzsche"
(EB, p. 129). The Goethean 'anthroposophist,' the poet-philosopher,
the contemporary Finnish artist (with his brutal paintings of religious hysterics and peasant dancers) have all become "message-
bearers with the word of power on their lips." (The term "message-
bearers" ('budbärare') had been taken from Kvinnan och nåden, where
it is employed passim.) Suddenly, a central figure emerges from the
letter's verbal swirl: "...the Message-Bearer who said: 'Where two
or three are gathered together in my name, there I am among you.'
And you, (Hagar), are the one with whom I shall see the eternal
Message-Bearer...We shall sacrifice our genius on the altar of the
other world" (EB, p. 130). Edith Södergran has embraced Christianity, which recently she had so much despised, and has now decided
to abandon poetry for its sake.

A sense that her poetic powers were dwindling must have played
some role in this decision. "Stjärnan" ("The Star" (SD, pp. 168-
169)), the final poem in Framtidens skugga, may first seem to be as
bold as "The Planets Ascend" at the book's opening: "I belong to
those who believe in their star: / that is to seize the secret powers
of fate. / What can the secret powers of fate do if one seizes them
with hands made strong by truth?" Yet these brave words immediately
have doubt cast on them: "Pernicious words, pernicious." The
speaker does not deny that she has been chosen, but she has been
unworthy of the call: "But my star does not deny itself. / In the
presence of my star, which stands threatening / I feel my insufficiency." In "An Old Ruler" (see p. 101), the spokesman of the young
generation praised the easy strength which "this arm puts into the
sword"; in "The Star," strength is sought for again: "Where shall
I get the heavy hand that seizes the sword?" The poem's concluding
line gives a reassuring answer: "your own, your own (det egna, det
egna) shall give you power"--it must be assumed that the abstract
formulation refers to Edith Södergran's poetic gift. Nevertheless,
the poem itself offers a demonstration of how the gift has failed;
it is built upon repetitions, as if trying to overcome doubt by
means of the elementary rhetorical device of reduplication: "What
do you know? What do you know?" // "I feel fortune in my hand, fortune itself" // "I have luck, great luck, in my fingers" //
"...fate's secret powers...fate's secret powers" // "but my star does
not deny itself...my star", and, at the end, "your own, your own."
Words, indeed, are not only "pernicious...pernicious" (the seventh
of the poem's anadiploses); they have lost their power. The old
magic of the Södergranian repetitive devices--the anaphoras intro-
ducing varieties of definitions, the effective parallelisms, the
puns--has vanished; now words are simply set up twice, close to one
another. The spiritual insufficiency which is conceded by the poet--
who no longer knows ("What do you know?") what message it is she has
to proclaim, nor what instrument she will use--is matched by an
insufficiency of language.

Olof Enckell has wondered why "Zigenerskan" ("The Gypsy Woman"
(SD, p. 377-378)) was not included in the annex to Framtidens
skugga;[36] the manuscript is dated February, 1920, which would place
its completion immediately before the announcement of the decision
to abandon "art, too, for it is unholy" (March 9). It is a last
demonstration, before the hiatus, of Edith Södergran's old poetic
strength, and has rightly attracted much critical attention.[37] Tideström advanced the idea that the poem was Edith's attempt to make
ammends to Hagar Olsson for having so long refused to accept the
latter's Christian transcendentalism; he cites the earlier piece of
verse written to "torment" Hagar, the "little gypsy": "Do transcendentalists and gypsy women now become my sisters?" (EB, p. 52). More
convincingly, Enckell sees the gypsy woman as a relative of Edith
Södergran's Hamlet, who has perceived the hideous truth about life,
but who, unlike Hamlet, is able to bear it. Gunnar Ekelöf thinks
that the gypsy woman's cards are Edith Södergran's own poems, and
that the poem, thus, is a kind of self-portrait--or wish-dream,
infused with health and strength, with maturity, and with the exoti-
cism which Edith Södergran liked to display on those rare occasions
when she had an audience: "I am a gypsy from foreign lands, / in
brown, secret-filled hands I hold the cards. / Days pass after days,
monotonous and varied. / I look defiantly into the faces of men: /
What do they know of how the cards burn? / What do they know of how
the cards live? / What do they know of every card's being a fate? /
What do they know about every card which falls from my hand, / having
a thousandfold meaning?" An answer to Enckell's reasonable query
about the poem's exclusion from the annex to Framtidens skugga can
very well lie in the atmosphere of defiant individualism surrounding
the gypsy woman: Edith Södergran had decided to renounce her calling, a decision taken with the utmost seriousness, and the gypsy
woman (with whom Edith Södergran nonetheless identifies herself) has
not decided to do so--the poem was an all too vivid contradiction of
the program of silence. The gypsy woman is an individual beyond
compare, not a part of a mass, nor even one star among rivals:
"there is only one such pair of hands in the whole world." The
poem's ending (which may well contain an allusion to the cry of literary defiance from two years earlier, "The Bull" (see p. 66)), is
a summary of the qualities that once characterized Edith Södergran's
oeuvre--boldness,melancholy, endless longing, even the "carelessness"
which she had cultivated with such care: "These wonderful hands of
prey (rovhänder) / I conceal beneath the red cloth / in defiance and
melancholy, adorned with rings and strong. / These brown eyes look
out in endless longing. / These red lips burn in a fire that does
not go out, / these careless hands will do their task in the gloomily
fire-flame-colored night." The unique hands are hidden beneath the
gypsy's apron; the card game, or the telling of fortunes, is ended
for the present. Had Edith Södergran not been so much at the mercy
of her newly found quasi-religious convictions, "The Gypsy Woman"
might have been chosen as the envoy of Framtidens skugga--a departure
from poetry made with poetic strength, a departure promising new
treasures to come. Erik Kihlman was not off the mark when he said

that "The Gypsy Woman" is reminiscent of the poems of <u>Dikter</u>[38]--it has a humanity, and a color, which is sometimes missing from the pages of <u>Septemberlyran</u> and, more often, from <u>Rosenaltaret</u> and <u>Framtidens skugga</u>. A fortune teller is more accessible than a priestess or a prophetess.

7.

The Return to Poetry

The poems from 1922 and 1923 are nine in number. "Min barndoms träd" ("My Childhood's Trees") is from June, 1922, "Kyrkogårdsfantasi" ("Churchyard Fantasy"), "O himmelska klarhet" ("Oh Heavenly Clarity") and "Månen" ("The Moon") are from September, "Hemkomst" ("Homecoming") and "Novembermorgon" ("November Morning") from October --for the latter, Edith Södergran also proposed "'Late Autumn Promenade' or whatever." The nameless poem about "the old woman and the cat" cannot be dated; "Landet som icke är" ("The Land Which Is Not") and "Ankomst till Hades" ("Arrival in Hades") are perhaps from the spring of Edith Södergran's death. The theme of "My Childhood's Trees"--as of "Oh Heavenly Clarity," "Homecoming," and "November Morning"--is a return to a relationship with nature as simple as a child's. In one of the early Swedish verses from her adolescence (ESD, pp. 146-147), she had written: "I believe that I have gone astray / from my childhood's path / for all the pines and firs / have lost their fresh aroma"; now the prodigal returns. The trees of Raivola are inclined to scold, as they shake their heads in fairytale-like anthropomorphism: "What has become of you? / Rows of pillars stand like reproaches: unworthy you walk beneath us, / You are a child who ought to be able to do everything. / Why are you fettered in the bonds of illness? / You are become a human being, strange (,) detestable. / When you were a child you carried on long conversations with us, / your glance was wise" (SD, p. 379). In the trees' straightforward argument (which indicates penalties like those befalling the sister in "Fantastique" (see p. 96) for her transcendentalism: "the brook was silent for you, / the birds sang no more"), the only ambiguity lies in "the bonds of illness": does the poet think primarily of her physical ailment (which kept her fettered to her bed) or of the spiritual weakness which had led her to follow what she now deemed to be strange masters? The trees mean to heal her by telling her "your life's secret: the key to all secrets lies

in the grass on the raspberry hill"--in other words, they suggest
that she should embrace the truth perceived in "The Hyacinth,"
acceptance of life and death as a part of nature. (Tideström
observed that Raivola's "raspberry hill" lay "close beside the fence
of the churchyard."[1] Edith Södergran attached a simple symbolism to
her little world, and the changes which took place in it; on October
7, 1921, she wrote: "Now we are united with the churchyard, the
fence fell down in the storm" (EB, p. 173).) The trees' last words
describe what they, having scolded her, would like to do with her:
"We would strike you on the forehead, you sleeping one, / we would
awaken you, dead one, from your sleep." In effect, the story of
Snow White's awakening has been told once more; however, the overtones are not a mixture of the erotic and the resurrectional (the
poem is not a playing of the "game of games"). Rather, Edith Södergran tells how her existence has been passed, and, in part, sadly
wasted: the clear-eyed child has fallen into a spiritual sleep,
from which the trees awaken her. A passage from Paul's epistle to
the Ephesians comes to mind: she was once in darkness and now "walks
as a child of light."

The reproaches of "My Childhood's Trees" are put aside in "Home-
coming" (SD, p. 385); the trees welcome the prodigal: "My childhood's trees stand around me, exulting: Oh human being! / and the
grass bids me welcome from foreign lands." Johanne Birch-Jensen
notes that the trees of Dikter (which urged the poet to assail
heights she could not reach, "with inaccessible cones," and caused
the question, "how shall I ascend the slippery trunks?") have now
become her protectors.[2] The position of the speaker has become
different, too, neither stretching upward nor lying tense, "in
ambush,"[3] but at rest: "I lean my head in the grass: now at home
at last / Now I turn my back on everything that lies behind me: /
my only companions become the woods and the beach and the lake."
The poem is quite clear in its message and language, natural in its
return to nature; yet it has its small touches of artistry: the word
"now" appears five times in the poem, so that the reader will be
aware of the immediacy of the poet's happiness, and the contrast to
a past on which she, quite literally, has turned her back. The poem
is written, furthermore, in (to be sure, not very strict) dactylic
and anapestic hexameters and pentameters. This use of classical
prosody is not inadvertent: Edith Södergran visibly transgresses
against normal word order to obtain the meter: "och gräset mig häl-
sar välkommen ur främmande land. / Mitt huvud jag lutar i gräset."
Can it be that Edith Södergran wishes to give the poem an air of the
idyll, by means of its strong present tense (the idyllic tense par
excellence, as Tore Wretö shows[4]) and its suggestion of the distich?
The poet's parched past is reflected in the key words of the lines
describing what she does now: "Now I drink wisdom from the sapfilled
crown of the firs, / now I drink truth from the dried-up trunk of
the birch, / now I drink might from the least and the frailest of
the grass-blades." The "wisdom," the "truth," and particularly the
climactic "might" of these lines were once sought for in a different
context; now--to the extent they are needed, or wanted--they come
from nature, or from nature's creator: "A powerful protector gra-
ciously gives me his hand." To Birch-Jensen, the protector in this

world of childlike piety is the Creator who has made both the human
being and nature; in two of her aphoristic "Thoughts about Nature"
not included in Ultra, Edith Södergran says that "Nature is under
God's protection" and "Nature is God's darling" (SD, p. 372).

Edith Södergran had become a close student--and imaginative
interpreter--of the New Testament. On May 24, 1921, she wrote:
"Just read Paul, Second Corinthians, on God's surpassing clarity.
The truth exists only in the New Testament and nowhere else in the
world" (EB, p. 164). Quite apart from what the sentence tells about
the convictions at which Edith Södergran had arrived, it provides
evidence to show how, once more, a passage of a beloved document
could be put to poetic use at some remove from the document's
original intent. Corinthians 2, 3:10, has to do with the superiority
of the New Law over the Old: "For though the former ministration
was glorified, yet in this regard it is without glory, because of
the surpassing glory of the latter," a passage which, in the Swedish,
has "klarhet" ("clarity") for the English "glory" and the Greek dōxa.
Ignoring Paul's proselytizing argument against the Jewish faith,
Edith Södergran takes his remark about the New Law's "surpassing
glory"--"surpassing clarity"--absolutely, without comparison, placing
it in conjunction with Christ's instruction (Matthew 18:3, Luke
18:17) that man must become as a little child: "Except ye turn and
become as little children, ye shall in no wise enter into the kingdom
of heaven." (In "Thoughts on Nature," she says: "If we do not
become children of nature, we shall not enter into the kingdom of
heaven, for the religious secrets are nature's secrets" (SD,
p. 372).) The poem with the key word from Paul's epistle, "Oh heavenly clarity," begins: "Oh heavenly clarity on the child's fore-
head--/its angel beholds the father in heaven" (SD, pp. 383-384).
The angel is not mentioned again in the poem; presumably, Edith
Södergran recalls childhood's (and the Eastern Church's) belief in
a guardian angel, who serves as intermediary between the child and
the Almighty. Also, in this return to the simplicity of childhood,
Edith Södergran returns to rhyme ("invid" / "frid"; "stor" / "år")
and, as in "Homecoming," to a dactylic-anapestic pattern: "And the
light which streams from the eyes of the saint is darkness beside /
the peace, that heavenly peace, which on a child's forehead resides.
/ And the glory which shines round the brow of the saint is neither
so plain nor so great / as the crown which crowns a child of man in
its tender state . . . ." Then, in the two four-line stanzas which
close the poem, she changes to a hymnal form; the first stanza, about
a community of language between nature and the child, has identical
rhyme (språk / språk)--nature and the child speak, literally, the
same language: "And the earth and the flowers and the stones to the
child / do speak their tongue, / and the child--it answers and bab-
bles back / in creation's tongue," while the second is rhymeless,
but has a perceptible iambic pattern: "And God is hid in the smallest flower / and the things proclaim his name. / But the heart of
man, expelled by the Father, / knows not how near he dwells." In
its innocence, the child is holier even than the saint; and the exile
from God's realm can be reunited with that realm, if he will but
learn to speak, and to understand, as a child once more.

"Homecoming" receives the prodigal, "Oh Heavenly Clarity"
describes the method to follow, if one is to return from the outer
darkness of 'adult' life. "November Morning" (SD, pp. 388-389),
from the same autumn of 1922, offers remonstrances once again, as in
"My Childhood's Trees." This time, instead of the trees, the
"water's edge" ("stranden") speaks, as "the first snowflakes fall."
The poem's opening is in a narrative past tense ("we walked rever-
ently"); then the water's edge begins its homily: "See, here you
have walked as a child and I am always the same. / And the alder
which stands by the water is always the same. / Say, where have you
walked in foreign lands and learned your bungler's habits? / And
what have you won? Nothing at all." The avuncular strand then tells
the listener how to behave: "Your feet shall walk upon this earth, /
here is your magic circle, from the alders' catkins / surety will
come to you and the answers to riddles." The apparently naive poem
betrays a certain plan; key words of Edith Södergran's poetic and
philosophical past, "the magic circle," "surety," and "the riddles"
(which fell resoundingly, it will be remembered, into Minerva's bowl
in the infinitely grander, Nietzschean world of the St. Petersburg
fragment) are recalled, but now incorporated into the world of childhood rewon, where the poet's task is a praising of the Creator who
lets him, or her, enjoy nature's riches. The echoes of the typical
church-song of thanksgiving for nature's gifts (for example, Israel
Kolmodin's "Den blomstertid nu kommer" ("The Flowering Time Now
Cometh") or Gabriel Lagus' "Se, över allt den räcker / Din allmakt,[5]
Herre Gud!" ("See, Everywhere It Reaches / Lord, Your Omnipotence!")
are palpable enough: "And you shall praise God who lets you stand
in his temple / amidst the trees and the stones," as are the echoes
of the church-song which thanks God for release from spiritual blindness: "And you shall praise God who has let the scales fall / from
your eyes," an allusion to Acts 9:18, and the miracle that befell
Saul on the way to Damascus. The poem's conclusion is the directive
(from the strand's mouth) which may--no doubt correctly--be regarded
as a final turning-away from the old teachers, Steiner, and before
him, Nietzsche; the disciple is told: "All vain wisdom you scorn, /
for now the fir and the heather are your teachers. / Bring the false
prophets here, the books that lie, / in the dale by the water / we
shall light a merrily flickering pyre." It is a drastic ending,
like that of "My Childhood's Trees," with its blow to the sleeping
girl's forehead; but violence--ameliorated in both cases by the dis-
ingenuousness of the poem's tone--is a part of the fairytale. Further, "November Morning" is built out of the four elements, air
(through which the snowflakes fall), earth (the beach), water (the
stream), and the bonfire. What Edith Södergran treats in these late
palinodes is a primary theme of major western literature--for example, of Hölderlin's Hyperion, with its command: "Go again to that
place from whence you came, into the arms of nature, unchanging,
still, and fair"[6]--but her treatment of it is unmistakably her own,
willfully naive and earnestly playful, not sentimental.

One more celebration of simplicity appears among the late poems,
the titleless verses which begin: "There is no one who has time here
in the world / save God alone" (SD, pp. 390-391). Since He does have
time, the forget-me-not asks Him "for a brighter shine in its blue

eyes," the ant "for greater strength to seize the straw," the bee
for a "stronger song of victory over the crimson flowers." The catalogue of requests, the imputation of boundless generosity to an all-
caring Divinity, the implied eulogy of a simple God attentive to
simple things, belong to the tradition of the pious children's story
(as practiced by H. C. Andersen and, in Finland, by Topelius), and
have their scriptural origin in the Sermon on the Mount, with its
account of God's attention to the birds of the heaven and the lilies
of the field. Yet, the hymn to simplicity has called forth some
complex comment, especially the strophe which concluded the poem in
the first printed version: "And God is present in all connections. /
When the old woman met her cat at the well, / and the cat its mistress. / It was a great pleasure for them both, / but greatest was
the pleasure that God had brought them together / and vouchsafed
them this wonderful friendship / for fourteen years." The Swedish
philosopher Hans Larsson saw "an unconscious Spinozism" in these
lines; Olof Enckell perceived resemblances to William Blake and to
Whitman; his brother Rabbe Enckell called attention to the likeness
between the poem and the situation depicted in "Gallen's painting,"
in other words, Akseli Gallen-Kallela's Akka ja kissa (The Old Woman
and the Cat). To these observations, it may be added that, as in
"November Morning," fun is implicitly made of the earlier Edith
Södergran, and her overriding urge for beauty, power, and victory:
the wishes of the flower and the insects are infinitely more legiti-
mate than hers had been. And it goes almost without saying that the
poem's climactic strophe reflects the large--the equal--role which
household pets had got in the Södergrans' little world.

    In the pencil manuscript which Edith Södergran sent to Diktonius
in 1922, and which survived only in Diktonius' typed copy, the poem
has still another strophe, printed for the first time in Tideström's
edition (SD, p. 391); it continues the tale of the benevolent God
Who, as in the spiritual, has His eye on the sparrow. The cat of
strophe three has been a good friend to the old woman; yet it is
also, qua cat, a beast of prey: "And meanwhile a redstart flew out
of the ash tree by the well, / happy that God had not let it fall
into the hunter's claws." Although these two lines have a connection
with what has gone before, the remainder seems joined to the poem's
main body only by the theme of death--which the redstart has escaped:
"But in a dark dream a little worm saw / that the moon-sickle cut
his being in two parts: / the one was nothing, / the other was everything and God Himself." (The moonsickle can be understood by reference to another poem of the last days, "Månen" ("The Moon") (SD,
p. 387), where "the sickle of the moon mows flowers down / in late
autumn nights.") The worm (or man himself, Job's "son of man, that
is a worm") has a dim awareness that death will come, as a part of
God's order, and that he then will be divided into two parts, the
one the chemical mass of "Materialism," the other the soul. That
this "other part" is "everything and God Himself" may be an indication, albeit laconic to the uttermost, that Edith Södergran--forced
to reckon with her own imminent death--has stated a concept of Christian mysticism: man is composed of worthless flesh and precious
soul, and the soul, as God within man, God's emanation, is God Himself and immortal. Yet the worm beholds this vision only darkly;

and it would be risky indeed to argue that the poem represents a "final" and affirmative thought of Edith Södergran about an after-life. (Why did Diktonius omit the strophe from his printing of the poem? Did he, an atheist, think it was indeed a statement on the immortality of the soul, and so to be deleted as an aberration of the mortally ill poet? Or did he drop it for artistic reasons, con-sidering its last four lines to be obscure, verily a dark dream?)

Two of the last poems deal more transparently with death. The one is "Kyrkogårdsfantasi" ("Churchyard Fantasy" (SD, pp. 380-382)), written, it may be surmised, with a thought to publication in Ultra: Edith Södergran gave Hagar Olsson extensive instructions about its text. The source of the poem was an experience Edith Södergran had had in the Raivola cemetery; she wrote to Hagar that: "A woman's voice which I heard here in the moon's twilight caused my fantasy to make a combination between her and a dead woman buried with her child" (EB, p. 195). The poem's central fiction is that the dead woman, her child in her arms, hurries to join her dead husband; it opens and closes with the following lines: "What is it that echoes in the churchyard: / My own! My beloved! / Who is it that cries out in the mist? / It is the warrior's wife, hastening to join her hus-band." An odd detail in the original version is the term which Edith Södergran used to describe the soldier, "jägare"--(literally "hunts-man"). To a Finnish reader of the early 1920's, the noun "jägare" would have meant a "light infantryman," a member of the battalion of volunteers from Finland, trained in Germany, which then formed the cadre of the White Army; we know from the letter to Hagar Olsson that a veteran of the force resided in Raivola, with his wife; a (no doubt unfounded) fear that the wife would see the poem caused Edith Södergran to propose the emendation to "warrior." Whether the poet had had some thought of winning sympathetic "White" readers with her original noun, we shall never know; the poem's body, wholly apoliti-cal, is a long description of the dead woman, in the form of an address to her. Her forehead is "colorless and pale," her hand "careless and light," she is beautiful, of course, but no one will caress her black locks again, and her feet, in "thin velvet shoes," feel nothing--the lovely corpse yearns for a lover (as in "The Elf Queen's Wand") to try to awaken her. The remainder of the address has to do with an existence after death, a flight into some distant region, "farther away" than where (in a fairytale formula) "the moon stands in the crown of the birch" or where "the sun itself, the sun shines"; carrying the child, "you ran as fast as you could, leaving the stars beneath you." All this is put into a past tense; pres-ently, the woman has reached a goal that smacks of holy legend: "Where the Infant Jesus sits in the lap of the Virgin, / you have come / and everything that a human heart can win / you have won." In this poetry of would-be Christian belief, Edith Södergran has used--once again--a regular metrical pattern, and, in the climax, a rhyme: "dit har du hunnit...det har du vunnit." Form is meant to strengthen faith--there is something consolatory about rhythm and rhyme. The churchyard poem was sent to Hagar Olsson on September 27, 1922; on October 20, Edith wrote that: "I shall certainly write for Ultra, if Ultra will take what I do. But I'm turning away from materialism now in all earnest....I must go to God. Otherwise, I

shall die of grief. Now I'll really leave what's old behind me"
(EB, p. 205).

"The Moon," Edith Södergran said in her letter of September 16,
was written "with blood--all the way to 'endless longing,' and then
by hand" (EB, p. 194). What she meant was that she thought the first
sixteen lines of the poem were inspired;[8] the rest of the poem, another sixteen lines, was omitted by Hagar Olsson with her friend's
permission. What was omitted (and subsequently printed by Tideström
(SD, pp. 415-416)) deals, again in the manner of a church-song, with
nature's praise of God, its creator ("and all flowers rest in the
creator's bosom / and praise his will"). That the poem's first half
was written with blood has a kind of gruesome factuality; on October
4, Helena Södergran told Hagar that "Edith is bedridden at present--
she has been coughing up blood" (EB, p. 201). Hagar Olsson held the
poem in high esteem: "She wrote one song concerning death--'The
Moon'--which perhaps was the most beautiful of all her poems, and
surely the one most filled with secrets. It was no longer a poem,
it was the shadow of her own death, drawn in the uncertain light of
dawn. Other poems (from the last months) were merely a child's conversation with God, a hymn-of-praise of the flowers of the Creator."[9]
Did Hagar Olsson suspect that the poems of simple nature-faith were,
in their way, avoidances of what pressed in more and more closely
upon Edith Södergran these last months--circumlocutions about death,
further playings of the "game of games"? But "The Moon" is an
attempt to beautify, and to affirm, death, too, while trying to look
it in the face. The moon, according to the simple division which
Edith Södergran made in "Thoughts about Nature," means death: "We
behold life and death with our eyes, they are sun and moon," and
"Thus the suns course through the cosmos bringing life, the moons
slaying it, the earths submitting themselves to life and death" (SD,
p. 271). At first, the poem sounds a little like "The Moon's
Secret," where the moon illuminates, and beautifies, violent death;
the moon and its victims are made to appear marvelous, if not beautiful: "How wonderful is everything that is dead, / and inexpressible:
/ a dead leaf and a dead human / and the moon's disk" (SD, p. 387).
Another of those "secrets" of Edith Södergran is mentioned, not the
secret of the happiness to be found in a sense of unity with nature
(the secret of the raspberry patch) but: "All flowers know a secret
/ and the forest preserves it, / it is that the moon's circling
around our earth / is the path of death." Death will come as surely
as the moon; the nocturnal world waits for death, knowing it will be
caught: "And the moon spins its wondrous web, / which flowers love,
/ and the moon spins its fairytale net / around all that lives."
Nets had long fascinated her--the "net" with which she caught fish
for the fisherman Zarathustra, the "nets, in which Steiner wants the
whole world to wriggle with him" (in a letter of August 29, 1921
(EB, p. 170)); in "The Moon" the net becomes a cobweb which will
catch everything that lives. She repeats the idea of nocturnal,
death-bringing cobwebs in "Thoughts about Nature": "The moon spins
its net, around everything which is sick, until the full moon comes
and fetches it some fair night." In another of the "Thoughts," she
is franker still about her own condition, combining it expressis
verbis with one of her major theses--that she is a child of nature,

and so must share gladly in nature's great process: "Dying children of nature love death, they long for the moment when death takes them." In the poem, it is said less flatly; the sick being, or the dying child of nature, is turned into the flower--the game of beautification is played again, after all: "And the moon's sickle mows flowers down / in late autumn nights, / and all the flowers wait for the moon's kiss / in endless longing." The parallel prose texts, continuing, talk about the corruption of death, the thought of the chemical mass, something which the poem only touches between the lines: "Death is a sweet poison--corruption, but there is nothing unhealthy in death. Nature is health itself and perceives death as healthily as it does life... The quick work of destruction in the autumn is admirable." A decade-and-a-half earlier, Edith Södergran had written a German poem about a hateful, death-bringing moon, "Since, when someday I have perished / Your cruel light will flit from above / Onto my death-touched features, / I shall deny you my love" (ESD, p. 115). Enckell says that "the whole battle of her life can be measured in the distance between this poem and 'The Moon'."[10] It is true; she has learned how to love death. Nonetheless, even now, death has to be beautified, romanticized--with fairy-tale cobwebs, in a Midsummer Night's Dream atmosphere--in order for it to be accepted.

In her Clarté essay, where "The Moon" is praised, Hagar Olsson does not mention "Landet som icke är," by name, appearing to regard "The Moon" as the major accomplishment of the last phase. In the Ny Generation version of the essay, however, she lists "The Moon," "The Land Which Is Not," and "Arrival in Hades" as the poems over which "the shadow of her death lies." In Ny Generation she then goes on to say that "the words are wrapped in a trembling light, portending the new morning's commencement," turns of phrase which Hagar Olsson perhaps felt were inappropriate for Clarté--among its editorial policies was "the removal of the old religious superstition." The relationship of "The Land Which Is Not" to "The Moon"-- the moon of death--is readily discernible; the speaker yearns for a "land which is not," about which the moon tells (SD, pp. 292-293):

> I long for the land which is not,
> for I am tired of desiring all that is.
> The moon tells me in silver runes
> about the land which is not.
> The land where all our wishing is marvelously fulfilled,
> the land where all our chains fall,
> the land where we cool our lacerated forehead
> in the moon's dew.
> My life was a hot illusion.
> But I have found one thing, and I have truly won one thing,
> the way to the land which is not.

(The penultimate line of this first strophe echoes the rhyme-words of "Churchyard Fantasy" (hunnit / vunnit), in the description of what the dead woman has found: "Men ett har jag funnit, och ett har jag verkligen vunnit.")

The poem's first half may be taken as a statement, building on "The Moon," of longing for death; at last, the speaker has learned not only to accept the thought but to yearn for the end. It is the poem's second part that has aroused extensive debate, especially concerning the identity of the "beloved":

> In the land which is not,
> there my beloved walks with a glittering crown.
> Who is my beloved? The night is dark
> and the stars quiver in reply.
> Who is my beloved? What is his name?

In 1953, Hagar Olsson wrote that: "It was Christ. Not the churches', not faith's and not reason's Christ. But love's Christ, the Christ of the cosmic mystery, the prince of the land which is not."[11] What she said was in reply to Olof Lagercrantz, who in fact had made two proposals about the identity of the beloved--first, that he was the chief player in the "game of games" (in other words, the Christ who said: "I am the resurrection and the life"). "Or was it death that bears the glittering crown?"--Lagercrantz's second possibility meant that the speaker of the poem had accepted death as release, the strong implication of the poem's opening.[12] The problem has fascinated other commentators as well, Erik Kihlman saying that the beloved might well be "love itself, forever sought, leading man onward and outward";[13] certainly, the sublime conclusion of the poem could support this idea:

> The skies arch higher and higher,
> and a child of man drowns in endless mists
> and knows no answer.
> But a child of man is nothing other than certainty.
> And it stretches out its arms higher than all heavens,
> And an answer comes: I am the one you love and forever
>   will love.

Olof Enckell thought that Edith Södergran may, among other things, have been thinking of Hagar Olsson as she wrote these lines, "the beloved 'sister' whom she missed, and whom she almost never got to see";[14] the repetition of the phrase, "the land which is not," calls to mind her chiding of Hagar Olsson's mysticism: "But I do not want that which is not, but that which is," during the Hamlet-crisis; thus, according to Enckell, Edith Södergran makes amends to Hagar, the princess of the land which is not. (Obstacles to this theory lie in the masculine pronouns.) Finn Stein Larsen suggests that the beloved is the "power of poetic creation" or a "belief in poetry," which lures the speaker ever outward;[15] and in a poem which Edith Södergran may well have known, Severjanin--the object of Edith Södergran's little tribute from the fall of 1922--speaks of himself, the poet, as "the emperor in the land which is not."[16] Without attempting to make an identification of the "beloved," Gunnar Ekelöf senses a resemblance to the Swedish pietists' song, "Till Österland vill jag fara / Där bor allra käresten min" ("To the East I will travel / There my most beloved dwells"), a song in which the "most beloved" is Jesus, albeit described in amatory terms;[17] and, as long ago as 1920, Edith Södergran herself had sent Hagar Olsson a pair of verse-lines which sound very much like an extract from a church song: "Oh, how I long for the eternal homeland of men. / Oh, how I long for the eternal homeland of men" (EB, p. 129).

None of these proposals or suggestions lacks validity; the fact that all of them can be supported, in one way or another, may lead to the suspicion that Edith Södergran did not want the beloved identified, any more than Walt Whitman, in the climax of Song of Myself, wished to be precise about "the great Camerado, the lover true for whom I pine"; Gunnar Ekelöf, by refusing to make an identification, showed his instinctive poet's respect for the ambiguity. The only information given the reader about the beloved concerns his sex and his "glittering crown"; in addition, there is the reply which, it has been assumed, comes from his lips: "I am the one you love and forever will love." These details led Tideström, proceeding less apodictically than Hagar Olsson, to join her in identifying the beloved as Christ the victor.[18] Yet the "glittering crown" may as well be the stars which give their mysterious signal two lines farther on in the poem. After all, the refrain of the second strophe is interrogative: "Who is he?" (twice) and "What is his name?"

The quest, the "endless longing," pervades all Edith Södergran's verse, and creates much of its imagery: the speaker is led out into a space that grows larger and larger, into endless mists, drawn on by the certainty of the uncertain quest, stretching out her arms, "higher than all heavens"; and "there comes an answer" (the poem, in reality, does not reveal who or what speaks it): "I am the one you love and forever will love," an answer which leads farther still. The situation is closely related to that of "Scherzo" (see p. 99), where the dancer kneels--on her precarious tightrope in space--before the "king of the sea," "the fair one," lures the tiring "acrobat" onward. The acrobat descends (in Edith Södergran's planned conclusion of the poem); the "child of man"[19] will go on--into a land which is not. We must be fair to Tideström; having made his identification of "Christ the victor," he adds that the beloved is clad in a form not remarkably different from the prince in the fairytale, the saviour of whom the young woman had dreamed.

What is assumed to be the last poem by Edith Södergran, "Ankomst till Hades" ("Arrival in Hades" (SD, pp. 394-395)), continues the outward trip--not into space now, but into the land of the dead. The poem resembles some of the other pieces of late and intentionally simple verse in its conservative prosody (trimeters, tetrameters) and its occasional rhymes; it may betray--if we think of illustrations from journals as a source of Edith Södergran's poems--some promptings from the enormously popular art of Arnold Böcklin: Self-Portrait with Death as a Fiddler and The Isle of the Dead:

> See, here is the shore of eternity,
> and here the stream rushes along,
> and death plays in the bushes
> his same and monotonous song.

Death, why did you fall silent?
We are come from far away
and are grown hungry to listen,
we have never had a nursemaid
who could sing like you.

The wreath which never adorned my forehead
I silently put at your foot.
You shall show me a wondrous land
where high the palmtrees grow,
and where among rows of columns
the waves of longing go.

In what seems to be the almost apathetic artlessness of the deathbed
poem, there are still small subtleties of structure. Like death's
song, the meter is monotonous; as the view from the shore of eternity broadens out,[20] so does the poem, the stanzas increase from
four lines to five lines to six. The fiction is based upon the
Charon-tale; a band of the dead (the "we" of the second stanza),
reaching the Styx, wishes to keep on hearing the song of death--a
song which has been heard, it is implied, since childhood, underlying
every thought. The poem's events take place in the breaks between
stanzas; in the first pause, death's music stops, in the second the
speaker prompts him to play (or sing) again--in this final stillness,
even death's song is consolation. The poem's dependence upon its
own stillnesses is in keeping with its scene, and its words--the verb
"tystnade" ("fall silent")--of the central question, the adverb,
"tyst," ("silently"), modifying the deposit of the wreath at death's
foot. That the wreath has "never adorned my forehead" is another
sign of the end: the poetic gift, the maintaining force of the
poet's existence, is surrendered--a gift never really owned by the
speaker, who has doubted its value again and again, while speaking
of it in exalted terms. Nonetheless, it is her only bribe. Finally,
she gives a set of instructions to death--instructions resembling,
in their imperative tone, those much more detailed ones given the
lover of the sleeping (or dead) girl in "The Elf Queen's Wand": "you
will show me a wondrous land" where longing's waves will "go," forever unceasing. But her voice must stop (she has put down her
wreath), and the poem does not provide death's answer, only her own
last words about the Italianate deathland, with palms and pillars,
a "wondrous land" that does not exist. The vision, a last beautify-
ing of death, is brief; the poet cannot imagine death's world any
longer, and the reader is left to wonder if death obeys her command.

8.

Conjectures in Conclusion

Long ago, the critic Bengt Holmqvist expressed a not unreasonable fear--that Edith Södergran would fall into the hands of cultists
or, at any rate, uncritical enthusiasts.[1] The pathetic and yet
exotic circumstances of her life, the efforts of some of her contemporaries to surround her earthly existence, and her production, with
sanctity's odor, the strong emotional appeal some of her poetry makes
(to such disparate groups as unhappy adolescents, radical feminists,
and fundamentalist Christians), the visionary quality of many poems
in the middle collections--it is readily understandable how, and why,
a canonization may occur. But we have seen what damage the cultic
approach did to the study of Rainer Maria Rilke, obscuring his place
in literary history, diverting his audience's attention from his
remarkable poetic means to his several 'philosophies,' and, what was
worst, driving away potential readers who were unprepared for full
enlistment among his worshippers. It is to be hoped that, in the
future, scholarship will grapple with Edith Södergran's language, in
all of its aspects, with an expansion of our knowledge about the circumstances of her life (Tideström has had no successor thus far),
and with the complex story of her reception in the North and abroad.

Certainly, she has been a major liberating force on Scandina-
via's poetry, even as Rimbaud was on that of France. Holmqvist--who,
by the way, does not hesitate to mention Edith Södergran in a single
breath with Rimbaud and Rilke--speaks of "the great revolution" which
her work caused;[2] and poet after poet has willingly confessed an
indebtedness to her. In Sweden, Gunnar Ekelöf's (1907-1968) works,
from Dedikation (1934) to his great En Mölna-elegi (1960) are never,
as it were, out of contact with her; the first section of the Elegy
closes with a line quoted from Edith Södergran's "My future" ("A
capricious moment / robbed me of my future"), phrases which Ekelöf
then combines with others from Rimbaud's Une Saison en enfer, and

later on, near the Elegy's close, Ekelöf quotes the six opening lines
of "Nothing" (see p. 59).[3] Nor is Ekelöf the only major Swedish poet
to have learned from Södergran, or to have been inspired by her; Finn
Stein Larsen says that Karl Vennberg's (1910-   ) belief in poetry
as an instigation to "fitting action" can be directly traced from
the example of Edith Södergran's lyric self-analysis[4], while Werner
Aspenström's (1918-   ) gift for remarkable yet unstrained imagery
must have been encouraged by a reading of such Södergran masterpieces
as "Love" or "Hope."[5] In Finland, several stages in the story of
her impact may be discerned: on the other Finland-Swedish modernists
(Diktonius, Björling, and Rabbe Enckell, to be followed by Solveig
von Schoultz (1907-   )), and then on her Finnish semi-contempo-
raries, who followed her lead in the tongue of the nation's majority
(her translator, Uuno Kailas (1901-1933), and Katri Vala (1901-
1944)). Subsequently, Finnish lyricists of both language groups
became more interested in her spirit than in her form: Marja-Liisa
Vartio (1924-1966), whose "Södergran-like intensity" has been
remarked by Kai Laitinen[6], or Bo Carpelan (1926-   ), whose programmatic poem, "Det stumma gräset" ("The mute grass," 1966) alludes
to Södergran's "My Childhood's Trees," and carries its thought farther, or Lars Huldén (1925-   ), whose "Gräsets grammatik" ("The
grass's grammar," 1962), utters the same belief--in the human being's
precious bond with nature--as a graceful and convincing jest, thus
emulating that playful side of Södergran which all too many of her
imitators have ignored.[7] In Norway, to which an abandonment of fixed
metrical and rhyme patterns came tardily, Paal Brekke used her (in
an article of 1947) as a guidepost to a new style of verse;[8] however,
she had long been known to Tarjei Vesaas (1897-1970), who had been
given a volume of Edith Södergran's verse in 1931[9] by his wife-to-be,
the lyricist Halldis Moren Vesaas (1907-   )[10], and so, by his own
admission, had had his concept of poetry radically changed; Edith
Södergran transformed, or transfigured, other poets as well, from
Aslaug Vaa (1889-1965), another late-come disciple, to Astrid
Hjertenaes Andersen (1915-   ). Less inclined to aesthetic con-
servatism than their Norwegian counterparts, Danish poets, and Danish
critics, took to Edith Södergran's work fairly early, with an enthusiasm that has never abated: we may think of Tom Kristensen (1893-
1974), and his poem "Optimism," full of Södergranian immediacy and
built with Södergranian anaphoras,[11] or Paul la Cour (1902-1956)[11], or
Gustaf Munch-Petersen (1912-1938)[12], or Thorkild Bjørnvig (1918-   ),
who called her a "shaman, gypsy woman, prophetic child."[13]

    The extent of Edith Södergran's influence in Scandinavia, then,
can be measured, however roughly. But what of that final and probably unanswerable question: how does Edith Södergran rank in the
outside world, in the 'museum of modern poetry' (to use the title of
the Enzensberger anthology[14] where the German poet helped bring her
to the attention of an international audience)? For example, had
she written in her "best language," German, would she have been
accorded a rank as high as the one she holds in the North? Or had
she been born in the English-speaking world, would her poems have a
place, say, in every anthology of imagist poetry? (The Danish critic
Poul Borum has observed a tone which is "astonishingly reminiscent"
of Edith Södergran's in the verse of D. H. Lawrence; in the same

volume, Borum has given Edith Södergran a chapter, called "Three
Priestesses," in which she is coupled with two stars of German
poetry, Elsa Lasker-Schüler (1976-1945), and Nelly Sachs (1891-1970)
in a trio of "the century's great women lyricists."[15]) The making
of such comparisons, the uttering of such praise is as exciting, of
course, as it may be misleading; Edith Södergran does possess a
Lawrence-like sense of the magical moment (for example, Lawrence's
"The Gods! The Gods!" could well be from her hand), she has the tormented erotic perceptivity of Lasker-Schüler, and, sometimes, Sachs'
air of the tragic prophetess—but she is not just a Nordic version
of any of these poets, rather the owner of a special genius. Still,
how can that genius be defined to someone who does not know her work?
Telling W. H. Auden about Edith Södergran, even Gunnar Ekelöf had to
take recourse to comparisons:[16] "she is a very great poet, as far
as I can judge of Achmatova's[17] class, or even beyond, a young Swedish woman in the diaspora, one of our Byzantines, brave and loving
as your Emily Brontë. It is a pity that such a rare bird should be
buried for the world in a grave over which the war has passed several
times. She belongs to the world though her language might seem an
Old Aeolian dialect."

Notes and References

Preface

1. Bo Carpelan, "Edith Södergran," in Matti Kuusi et al., eds., Suomen kirjallisuus (Helsinki, 1967), VI, 225.

2. Kai Laitinen, Finlands moderna litteratur (Helsingfors, 1968), p. 59.

3. Mirjam Tuominen, Besk brygd (Helsingfors, 1947), p. 125.

4. Lars von Haartman, in Merete Mazzarella et al., eds., Författare om författare (Helsingfors, 1980), p. 195.

5. Rabbe Enckell, in the introduction to Modärn finlandssvensk lyrik (Tammerfors, 1934), p. 20, p. 27.

6. P. O. Barck, "Kommentar till Södergran," in Ansikten och möten (Helsingfors, 1972), p. 94.

7. Among others, by the Swedish poet Anders Österling, Dagens gärning (Stockholm, 1931), p. 248.

8. See bibliography, p. 156.

Chapter One

1. On the family background, see Gunnar Tideström, Edith Södergran (Stockholm, 1949), pp. 11-31. (Hereafter ES.)

2. ES, pp. 31-57, and Olof Enckell, Edith Södergrans dikter 1907-
1909, I: Inledning och kommentar (Helsingfors, 1961), pp. 83-117.

3. Jarl Hemmer, introduction to Edith Södergran, Min lyra: Dikter
i urval (Stockholm, 1929), p. 10, and Hemmer, "Edith Södergran," in
his Brev till vänner (Helsingfors, 1936), p. 215.

4. Hagar Olsson, ed., Ediths brev: Brev från Edith Södergran till
Hagar Olsson (Stockholm, 1955), p. 123. (Hereafter EB.)

5. Bertel Jung, ed., Gustaf Mattsson berättar om sig själv: Brev-
växling (Helsingfors, 1942), p. 372.

6. On February 7, 1928, Helena Södergran gave Hagar Olsson an
account of what she remembered of her daughter's literary enthusi-
asms: apart from "the classics" (unnamed), their library contained
the contemporary Russian poets Konstantin Balmont and Igor Severjanin
(see note 18). Also, Edith Södergran "admired Swinburne, Musset,
Rilke, Max Dauthendey, Daudet, Vilhelm Ekelund, and others, Tegnér,
Strindberg, Fröding, Almqvist, and others...among the Finland-Swedes
Gripenberg, Mörne, Hemmer, and others...Yes, she read much: J.
Ruskin, Schopenhauer, Maeterlinck" (quoted in ES, p. 131 and p. 304).
This account cannot be taken at face value; for example, the state-
ment about Fröding is contradicted by Hemmer (see p. 9). Among Swed-
ish poets, the case of Vilhelm Ekelund (1880-1949) is especially
vexing; resemblances do exist, and Tideström (ES, p. 62) assumed that
Ekelund played a particular role in her poetic development; yet Algot
Werin, in "'Mitt liv var en het villa': Ett brev från Edith Södergran till Vilhelm Ekelund," in his Vandring kring en sjö (Lund,
1967), pp. 169-177, and in "Vilhelm Ekelund och Finland," in P. O.
Barck et al., eds., Festskrift till Olof Enckell (Helsingfors, 1970),
pp. 57-59, has shown that, as late as 1921, she knew only two of his
works, both in prose.

7. "Almqvist och Södergran," Bonniers Litterära Magasin 8 (1933),
48-50.

8. Brev till vänner, p. 215.

9. ES, p. 76.

10. Thomas Tottie, "Edith Södergran och förlaget," Bonniers Litterära Magasin 29 (1957), 241-251.

11. The Norwegian impressionist (1866-1901), whose work was often
used as an illustrative comparison by early critics and reviewers of
Edith Södergran's work.

12. Tideström (ES, pp. 139-145) gives a resumé of the reviews of
Dikter.

13. Quoted by Matts Rying, "Optimism trots allt," in his Galleri:
Möten och porträtt (Stockholm, 1972), pp. 52-58; a somewhat different
account is in Ruin's diary, quoted in ES, p. 156.

14. In the introduction to Min lyra, pp. 9-11, and Brev till vänner, pp. 215-216; Tideström (ES, pp. 153-154) shows that Hemmer erred in placing the visit in the late winter of 1917.

15. For Södergran and Mombert (1872-1942), see Chapter 4, Note 24. For Russian literature, particularly Severjanin (pseudonym of Igor Lotaryov (1887-1941)), see Göran Lundström, "Edith Södergrans för- hållande till rysk lyrik," Poesi 3 (1950), 43-53, and Martin Nag, "Russiske impulser hos Södergran," Ordet: Tidskrift for fri sprogut- vikling 22 (1971), 196-212.

16. EB, p. 206 and pp. 222-223. Hans Ruin defended his late friend Hemmer (who died by his own hand in 1944) in "Sliten mellan ljus och mörker," Världen i min fickspegel (Stockholm, 1969), p. 44.

17. Samlade dikter, ed. Gunnar Tideström (Stockholm 1950), p. 174 ("Grimace d'artiste"). (Hereafter SD.) Ture Janson, who met Edith Södergran in 1917, recalled that she urged her new friends to walk around in "purple mantles" as a sign of "intellectual superiority" (Janson, "Modernismens genius," in his Den litterära hjulångaren (Stockholm, 1950), p. 164). Olof Enckell, Esteticism och nietzsche- anism hos Edith Södergran (Helsingfors, 1949), p. 68, notes that the "red raiment", the poet's special garb, "was a part of Oscar Wilde's and Stefan George's European eighteen-nineties." (Hereafter Esteti- cism.)

18. For instance, Tideström, ES, p. 165, Enckell, Esteticism, p. 81, and Hagar Olsson, EB, pp. 36-37. Recently Tua Forsström has made a witty refutation of Hagar Olsson's attempts to show that Edith Söder- gran sympathized with the Bolshevik regime; cf. "Den heta villan" in Merete Mazzarella et al., eds., Författare om författare (Helsing- fors, 1980), pp. 120-126.

19. Reprinted in ES, pp. 206-207, and EB, pp. 15-17.

20. See the resumé of reviews in ES, pp. 208-211.

21. Grotenfelt was a poet of some stature; Edith Södergran included his poem, "Det röda och det vita vinet" ("The Red and the White Wine"), in her planned anthology of Finland-Swedish verse (EB, p. 175).

22. Partly reprinted in ES, p. 211.

23. The open letter is reprinted in ES, p. 214; Hagar Olsson's pub- lic reply ("Fåvitska betraktelser") is reprinted in her Tidiga fan- farer och annan dagskritik (Helsingfors, 1953), pp. 19-23.

24. "Våra litterära hemmaexpressionister," Nya Argus 12 (No. 13/14, 1919).

25. Translated with an introduction by G. C. Schoolfield, The Wood- carver and Death (Madison, 1965).

26. The aphorisms are included in SD, pp. 288-305.

27. Esteticism, pp. 166-167.

28. Kvinnan och nåden, reprinted in Hagar Olsson, Tidig prosa (Stockholm, 1963), p. 176.

29. Tidig prosa, p. 184.

30. Tideström, ES, p. 253. The opinion of Jens Bjørneboe, "Edith Södergran," Horisont (Oslo), 9 (1963), 24-27, that "Steiner's anthroposophy surely forms the fertile soil for the basic mood in her poetry" seems ill-taken: most of Edith Södergran's poetic work lay behind her when she began to study Steiner.

31. Unpublished letter to Diktonius (September 4 (incorrectly dated August), 1923, Swedish Literary Society in Finland).

32. Hagar Olsson, "Modernistisk morgon," Hufvudstadsbladet (December 8, 1957).

33. "Radikal dikt," reprinted in Tidiga fanfarer, pp. 31-38.

34. "Edith Södergran: Kritisk hyllning," Ultra (No. 4, October, 1922), 52-53. This "critical salute," together with Elmer Diktonius' other writings on Edith Södergran, has been collected in Elmer Diktonius, Meningar, ed. Olof Enckell (Stockholm, 1957), pp. 206-223. On the relationship between Södergran and Diktonius, see Hans Ruin, "Diktonius och Edith Södergran" in his Den mångtydiga människan (Stockholm, 1966), pp. 93-108.

35. Cf. Johan Wrede, "Tidskriften Ultra," in P. O. Barck et al., eds., Festskrift till Olof Enckell, pp. 145-165, and Johan Wrede, "Illusion-utopi-realism: Edith Södergran, Hagar Olsson, och Finland omkring 1920," Finsk Tidskrift 195-196 (1974), 273-282.

36. "Igor Severjanin," Ultra (No. 5, October, 1922), 72-73.

37. The story of the ceremony of 1933 is told by Diktonius in unpublished letters to Emil Zilliacus of July 2 and July 22, 1933 (Swedish Literary Society in Finland), and in Diktonius' article for Göteborgs-posten, reprinted in Meningar, pp. 220-223.

38. Gunnar Ekelöf, "En vallfart--1938," in his Blandade kort (Stockholm, 1957), pp. 92-99, and "Landskapet bakom Södergrans dikt," in Hård höst: Debatt och värdering (Helsingfors, 1943), pp. 71-79, both reprinted in his "Edith Södergran studier," Svenska Akademiens Handlingar 75 (1967), 3-26, esp. 19-26. (Hereafter SAH.) See also Johannes Edfelt, "Karelsk sommar," Hård höst, pp. 80-93.

39. Ragna Ljungdell, "Diktarmodern i Raivola," Det oförstörbara (Stockholm, 1940), pp. 229-238, and Inez Frank, "Om böckernas magi," Bokvännen 24 (1969), p. 133-134, an account of a visit to Helena Södergran in the same summer.

40. Unpublished letter to Elmer Diktonius of June 23, 1943.

41. Tito Colliander, "Avtäckning av en gravvård," Horisont (Vasa) 7 (1960), 4: 8-9; Lars Hamberg, "Rodzino tur och retur," Nya Argus 53 (1960), 286-287; Lars Hamberg, "Resa till Edith Södergrans minne," Studiekamraten 55 (1974), 65-66.

42. P. O. Barck, "Minneshögtid i Raivola," Hufvudstadsbladet (June 27, 1973).

Chapter Two

1. Olof Enckell, Edith Södergrans dikter 1907-1909, II: Texten (Helsingfors, 1961). (Hereafter ESD.) There had been discussions of the adolescent poetry before Enckell's edition: Paavo Talasmaa, "Edith Södergranin lapsuudenrunous," Nuori Suomi 48 (1938), 42-47 (an article which contains a poem not included in the oilcloth note-book, but quoted from memory by Helena Södergran for Talasmaa), Gunnar Tideström, "Edith Södergrans skolflickspoesi," Poesi 1 (1948), 3-17, and Tideström in ES, pp. 31-57.

2. ES, p. 57.

3. The notebook has several entries with the castle motif: "Mär-chenschloss" ("Fairytale Castle," pp. 24-25), "Im Schloss" ("In the Castle," p. 76), and the suite, "Im Schloss" ("In the Castle," pp. 121-122), among others.

4. The cycle consists of eleven poems: VIII salutes a lofty figure ("to whom I look up"), IX is transitional (describing a "copper moon"), X addresses a being with a "charming glove," a "tender hand," and "the blackest eye," XI says: "I have borne you through autumn storms."

5. Cf. Hellmuth Petriconi, "La Mort de Venise" and "Der Tod in Venedig" in his Das Reich des Untergangs: Bemerkungung über ein mythologisches Thema (Hamburg, 1958), pp. 67-95, and Hans Hinter-häuser, "Tote Städte," in his Fin de siècle: Gestalten und Mythen (München, 1977), pp. 45-76.

6. In his anthology, Lyrik des Jugendstils (Stuttgart, 1964), Jost Hermand devotes an entire section to poems on "Pond and Skiff."

7. Late summer and autumn are favorite times of the adolescent poet; three poems, for example, have the title "Herbst" ("Autumn," p. 38, p. 43, p. 48).

8. ES, p. 35; cf. Hans Bethge, ed., Deutsche Lyrik seit Liliencron (Leipzig, 1900), pp. 22-23, "Sicheres Glück" ("Sure Happiness").

9. Tideström, ES, p. 57.

10. Hans Benzmann, Moderne deutsche Lyrik (Leipzig, 1907, second edition), p. 163.

Chapter Three

1. Translated into English by Arthur G. Chater as Ida Brandt (New York and London, 1929).

2. Cf. Volker Klotz, "Jugendstil in der Lyrik," and Jost Hermand, "Lyrik des Jugendstils," in Jost Hermand, ed., Jugendstil (Darmstadt, 1971), pp. 358-367 and 402-412.

3. R. M. Rilke, Sämtliche Werke (Wiesbaden, 1954), I, 400 ("Herbst," "Autumn").

4. Cf. the Pan poems in Hermand's anthology, pp. 17-19, Patricia Merivale, Pan the Goat God: His Myth in Modern Times (Cambridge, 1969), and Henning Sehmsdorf, "Knut Hamsun's Pan: Myth and Symbol," Edda 74 (1974), 345-393, esp. 350-356.

5. Hjalmar Procopé--mentioned frequently by Edith Södergran in her letters to Hagar Olsson--writes in the title poem of Röda skyar (Red Clouds, Helsingfors, 1907) about "dead dreams, the land of my youth" and asks "Where am I--I hear faint bells ringing / Like a distant message over the evening wave"; in the same collection, "Pans död" ("Pan's Death") ends with "Sighing in wood and in crevice, / laments on the nocturnal sea." In the title poem of Gallergrinden, Gripenberg hears "distant soughing from a distant world," and says to himself: "Before the gate, which never creaks ajar / You may hearken to the muted song which from afar / Trembles with greetings from a world you'll never see." Likewise, in Finnish poetry's belated Neo-Romanticism, one finds the enchanted garden theme in Aino Kallas' (1878-1956) Suljettu puutarha (The Closed Garden, 1915). As Erik Therman correctedly observed in "Edith Södergran," Ord och Bild 45 (1936), 666: "Dikter caused a revolution with us (in Finland). But it was rather the revolt, forever recurring, of romanticism and mysticism, than of modernism...her aesthetic outlook was quite traditional in several respects."

6. Enckell, Edith Södergrans dikter 1907-1909, I, 158-160, mentions the relationship between the adolescent German verse and "the poem of the mature poet with long years of imprisonment in sanatoria behind her." See also Tideström's interpretation of "I" in Carl-Erik af Geijerstam et al., Lyrisk tidsspegel (Lund, 1971, second edition), pp. 60-63, which calls the poem "an entirely personal variant on a motif beloved of the folksongs and folktale: the young woman in a merman's power, who clearly remembers her home above the surface."

7. Herman Bang, Det hvide Hus (The White House, 1898) in Vaerker i Mindeudgave (Copenhagen, 1912), I, 231 and 222. Hilmer Gillqvist, in "Edith Södergran," Svensk Litteraturtidskrift 4 (1941), 32-35, finds a close resemblance between Edvard Munch's painting, Puberty and "To Eros."

8.   "Praeraffaelitische Frauengestalten," Fin-de-siècle, pp. 107-145, esp. p. 111, and Arianne Thomalla, Die femme fragile (Düsseldorf, 1972). Before scholarship gave a name to this literary and personal urge, Viveka Heyman had observed its presence in Edith Södergran, in "Vägen till landet som icke är," Själar, kvinnor mest (Stockholm, 1948), pp. 27-37: "she wishes to make the done undone. She will be both the (passionate one) she is and yet the innocent virgin who was happy and wise."

9.   Enckell, Esteticism, p. 73, says: "in Edith Södergran red variously symbolizes a desire for the fairytale's naive splendor, erotic heat, esthetic defiance of the everyday world, (and) the passion of the chosen prophet."

10. See Jost Hermand, "Undinen-Zauber: Zum Frauenbild des Jugendstils," in Hermand, Der Schein des schönen Lebens: Studien zur Jahrhundertwende (Frankfurt A.M., 1972), pp. 147-187, esp. pp. 151-154, for the importance of Böcklin in turn-of-the-century literature; Hans Hinterhäuser, "Zwiegestalt und Übertier," in Hinterhäuser, Fin-de-siècle, pp. 177-208, discusses the centaur and Böcklin's role in the figure's popularity. For Viveka Heyman (p. 30), the centaurs represent "wild male desire"; the amazons, however, could play with the centaurs in "virginal innocence."

11. Pierre Samuel, Amazones, guerrières et gaillardes (Grenoble, 1975), speaks of the peculiar "halterophilia" (excessive love of athletic achievement) which attaches to the figure in myth and literature.

12. It may be added that the quasi-virginal seductress is a favorite wish-dream of male authors in these years: see Knut Hamsun's "Iselin" in his novel Pan (1892) and Bertel Gripenberg's "Lindagull" in his poems, Rosenstaden (The Rose City, 1907). Both are imaginary princesses.

13. Enckell, Esteticism, pp. 97-99 and Jens K. Andersen, "Farvesymbolikken i Edith Södergrans debutsamling," Edda 73 (1973), 13-23, esp. 13-14.

14. Martin Allwood, The Collected Poems of Edith Södergran (Mullsjö, 1980), p. 24. In a German translation, Feindliche Sterne: Gesammlte Gedichte (Wiebaden / München, 1977), p. 13, Karl R. Kern translates the title as "Farbensehnsucht," which may mean either "The Colors' Longing" or "The Longing for Colors." Allwood's rendering is supported not only by the sense of the poem but by the passage in Also sprach Zarathustra about Zarathustra's longing for colors: "Deep yellow and hot red: thus my taste will have it--it mixes blood into all colors. However, he who whitewashes his house betrays to me a white-washed soul" (Nietzsche, Werke, ed. Karl Schlechta (Munich, 1954), II, 442). (Hereafter Werke.)

15. Tideström, ES, p. 99, p. 303, says that, according to a letter from Helena Södergran to Hagar Olsson, the poem was inspired by a painting (undesignated); Gunnar Ekelöf ("Den speglande brunnen," in

Samtid och framtid 1 (1944), reprinted in "Edith Södergran studier," SAH 75 (1967), 12-18), and Enckell, Esteticism, p. 70, both make the Tizian suggestion.

16. Hans Ruin tells how great a role the painting and the novella played for his father's generation; see Hans Ruin, "övertalning till kärlek" in his Hem till sommaren (Stockholm, 1964), pp. 141-155, translated by G. C. Schoolfield as "Persuasion to Love" in Swedo-Finnish Short Stories (New York and Boston), pp. 147-161.

17. "Eros' Secret" in Framtidens skugga (SD, p. 342); see Tideström, ES, p. 48: "a careful life in waiting and innocence or an erotic boldness which could entail death for her."

18. SAH, 15. Conversely, Björn Julén, analyzing the poem in his Tjugo diktanalyser från Södergran till Tranströmer (Stockholm, 1962), pp. 1-9, finds a Nietzschean tone in the poem's conclusion, a decision to find "death in red beauty."

19. ES, pp. 80-81.

20. The image of the ring appears again in the early poems, in "Livet" ("Life," SD, p. 121): "Life is the narrow ring which keeps us prisoner / the invisible circle we can never overstep," and in "Bruden" ("The Bride," SD, p. 139): "My circle is narrow and my thoughts' ring / goes round my finger" (a line repeated, with inversion, at the end of this poem about a bride's apprehensions). It should be added that, in one of the best of his poems, in Under stjärnor och lyktor (Beneath Stars and Lanterns, 1913), Hjalmar Procopé writes "There is a ring drawn tight around our souls, / And a law that states, uncompromising, / That none, no matter who, may enter the ring."

21. Translated by Martin Allwood, Keith Bosley, Frederic Fleisher, and Sheila Lafarge (see p. 156); it has also received cogent analysis by Tideström in Lyrisk tidsspegel, pp. 54-60, and by Lennart Breitholtz, in Gunnar Hansson, ed., Tjugotvå diktanalyser (Stockholm, 1968), pp. 95-103, reprinted in Breitholtz, Monsieur Bovary och andra essayer (Stockholm, 1969), pp. 191-200.

22. Breitholtz suggests that the crown alludes to Christ's crown of thorns, and finds an echo of John 19:30 ("And he bowed his head, and gave up his spirit") in the next lines.

23. Hans Ruin, "Finlandssvensk modernism," Svensk Litteraturtidskrift 9 (1947), 55, compares this poem to a painting by Munch, and says that both Södergran and Munch were "detail-haters on principle."

24. Sämtliche Werke I, 517-518. (First published in Neue Gedichte, 1907.)

25. Edith Södergran uses the word in this pejorative sense to Hagar Olsson (EB, p. 34): "Do you know that fellow (göken), and do you know what he has up his sleeve?"

26. Samuel Charters, We Women (Berkeley, 1977). Helge Åkerhielm, in "Drömmen om kvinnoriket," Tiden 34 (1942), 493-501, esp. 495, noted the resemblance between Södergran's thought and that of the Swedish novelist, Agnes von Krusenstierna (1894-1940), that "woman is a bearer of life's mystery and...exists in a mighty community from which men are excluded." Lise Loesch, "Eventyr og utopi--To sider af kvindebilledet hos Edith Södergran,"Edda 78 (1978), 293-303, gives a more complex feminist view.

27. See Tideström, ES, p. 121, on the Maeterlinckian model, and possible echoes, as well, of Runeberg's Idyll och epigram (Idylls and epigrams, 1838). The "three maidens," are a recurrent configuration in art and literature during the second half of the nineteenth century, from T. E. Brown's (1830-1897) "Tonight I saw three maidens on the beach" to Jan Toorop's (1858-1928) painting, Three Brides.

28. SD, pp. 144-145. Bertel Gripenberg, in "Orkidé" ("Orchid," in Dikter, 1903), describes the erotic flower whose odor comes from "the fever-fen's green mud," and which has a "slimily slick stalk"; Edith Södergran herself (in a German poem from 1908, ESD, p. 108) writes: "Out in the bog the wild orchids are abloom / Where, trembling, the foot into the green descends, / Upon whose poisoned breath the flower then / Drinks unto drunkenness and, exhausted, ends."

29. Esteticism, pp. 74-75. Harriet Löwenhjelm (1887-1918)--a Swedish poet and tubercular sometimes compared to Edith Södergran--uses this image in her sonnet, "Here are all wishes still": death waits in a hospital corridor, "pale and dark and quiet" (cf. Dikter (Stockholm, 1980), pp. 61-62). On the other hand, Ingala Frisell, in her interpretation, "Min själ," Lyrikvännen 8 (1961), 17, is convinced that the pale man is "the man from Terijoki."

30. "Diktaren som skapade sig själv," introduction to Edith Södergrans dikter (Stockholm, 1940), p. 27.

31. Werke, II, 1256-1259 ("Dionysos-Dithyramben") and II, 1138 (Ecce homo). See also Hermann J. Weigand, "Nietzsche's Dionysus-Ariadne Fixation," Germanic Review 48 (1973), 99-116.

32. See Wilhelm Widmann, "Verlassene Ariadne," Der Merker 8 (1917), 41-141; Lilit Friedmann, Die Gestaltungen des Ariadne-Stoffes von der Antike bis zur Neuzeit (Vienna, 1933), and Jost Hermand, "Undinen-Zauber," Der Schein des schönen Lebens: Studien zur Jahrhundertwende, p. 161 (with a reproduction of Hans Makart's painting, Triumph of Ariadne, from 1873).

33. There are signs that Edith Södergran used other details of the Ariadne myth in "At the Beach," where--like Ariadne--the speaker has taken refuge in a grotto or cave when Dionysus comes upon her: "What is it that hurts me so? / I hit myself so hard against a rock that I wanted to die, / because I stretched out my arm in vain / to a stranger I once had seen...."

34. Torsten Broström, "Digteren på trampolinerne," in his <u>Labyrinth</u> <u>og Arabesk</u> (Copenhagen, 1966), pp. 126–137, esp. 133–134, touches <u>en</u> <u>passant</u> on the Ariadne-myth in connection with "Our Sisters," but does not detect the development of the larger pattern in <u>Dikter</u>.

35. Tideström, <u>ES</u>, p. 101, p. 118, <u>Esteticism</u>, p. 200 (in connection with "God" and George's "Ich bin der Eine und bin Beide" ("I am the One and I am Both")); Tideström, p. 134, and Kjell Espmark, <u>Att över-</u> <u>sätta själen</u> (Stockholm, 1975), p. 192, also connect the use of the metaphoric catalogue with Konstantin Balmont (as do Lundström, p. 47, and Nag, p. 200 (see Chapter 1, Note 15)).

36. Frédéric Durand, "Les voies de l'expressionisme dans la poésie suédoise," <u>Etudes Germaniques</u> 10 (1955), 187–198, esp. 193, note 18, has detected the remarkable resemblances between "Vierge moderne" and the German expressionist Kurth Heynicke's (1891–   ) "Weib" ("Woman"). Yet Heynicke's poem cannot have been known to Södergran; it appeared in <u>Rings fallen Sterne</u> (<u>Stars Fall Roundabout</u>, 1917) a year after <u>Dikter</u>. (Elmer Diktonius subsequently translated "Weib" for his anthology of "new poetry," <u>Ungt hav</u> (Helsingfors, 1923), p. 111.)

37. Rilke, Sämtliche Werke, I, 269. (In <u>Das Stunden-Buch</u>, (<u>The</u> <u>Book of Hours</u>,) 1905.) In the <u>Geschichten vom lieben Gott</u> (<u>Stories</u> <u>of Dear God</u>, 1900–1901), Rilke has a child say: "Dear God can be everything."

38. Örjan Lindberger and Reidar Ekner, <u>Att läsa poesi: Metoder för</u> diktanalys (Stockholm), pp. 121–122, speak of the poem's "desperate power," and suggest that Gunnar Ekelöf may allude to it in his poem, "Helvetes-Brueghel" ("Hell Breughel").

39. Commented upon by Tideström, <u>ES</u>, pp. 96–98, Olof Enckell, <u>Estet-</u> <u>icism</u>, p. 75, p. 167, Ekelöf, <u>SAH</u>, 25–26, and Gunnar Svanfeldt, <u>Lyrisk tidsspegel</u>, pp. 64–68.

40. Tideström, <u>ES</u>, p. 96.

41. Elmer Diktonius' <u>Ingenting och andra novellistiska skisser</u> (Helsingfors, 1928), p. 12, reprinted in Diktonius, <u>Prosa</u>, ed. Olof Enckell (Stockholm, 1956), p. 64.

42. In his suggestive article on basic patterns in <u>Dikter</u>, Finn Stein Larsen says that "the urge to identification in Edith Södergran is extremely pliable": "Et grundmönster i Edith Södergrans förste digtning," <u>Edda</u> 58 (1958), 298–309, esp. 299.

Chapter Four

1. <u>Werke</u>, I, 99.

2. Introduction to <u>Min lyra</u>, p. 10.

3. In the line's mixture of physicality and spirituality, Tideström, ES, p. 129, sees an indication of an affinity between Edith Södergran and the German poet Else Lasker-Schüler (1876-1945). In EB, p. 115, she calls Lasker-Schüler "superlatively splendid."

4. Quoted in ES, pp. 146-147.

5. Esteticism, p. 100; Werke, II, 316-318.

6. Finn Stein Larsen, "Edith Södergran," in Sven Møller Kristensen, ed., Fremmede digtere i det 20. århundrede (Copenhagen, 1967), II, 169-183, esp. 176.

7. "Uti vår hage där växa blå bär" and Runeberg's "Flickan kom ifrån sin älsklings möte" ("The Girl Came From Her Lover's Meeting"), Samlade arbeten (Stockholm, 1941), I, 139.

8. Hans Bethge, Deutsche Lyrik seit Liliencron, p. 213. (Helena Södergran (EB, p. 201) told Hagar Olsson that she and her daughter did not own a collection of Mombert's poems, implying that they had to depend on their German anthologies.)

9. The line echoes a phrase repeated several times in Maeterlinck's La Princesse Maleine, where Maleine's beauty causes the men in the inn to fight with "big carving knives."

10. Elmer Diktonius, Arbetarbladet, July 9, 1924, reprinted in the journal Quosego 1 (1928), 21-23, and in Diktonius, Meningar, pp. 281-284; Hagar Olsson, "Ett diktaröde," Samtiden 40 (1929): 230-241.

11. ES, p. 158; Sten Selander, "Edith Södergran," Ord och Bild 38 (1929), 691-696, esp. 693.

12. "Edith Södergran," Ord och Bild 45 (1936), 658-666, esp. 662.

13. Triumf att finnas till, with sketches by Björn Landström (Stockholm, 1948), and Triumf att finnas till, with introduction by Jörn Donner (Stockholm, 1973).

14. Werke, II, 380.

15. Esteticism, p. 160.

16. Werke, II, 461.

17. Werke, II, 691; Enckell, Esteticism, pp. 113-114, lists many other Nietzschean elements in the poem.

18. Lyrisk tidsspegel, pp. 66-69.

19. Werke, II, 519.

20. EB, p. 72. In "Edith Södergran's 'Wallenstein-profil'," (in Carl F. Bayerschmidt and Erik Friis, eds., Scandinavian Studies Pre-

sented to Henry Goddard Leach (New York and Seattle, 1965), pp. 278-292), G. C. Schoolfield has attempted to follow the course of Edith Södergran's infatuation with Mannerheim, culminating in the hidden tribute (or criticism) of the "Wallenstein Profile" in Framtidens skugga (SD, p. 317).

21. Esteticism, pp. 79-81; Tua Forsström, in "Den heta villan," Författare om författare, pp. 122-123, is likewise critical of the decadent-esthetic attitude she believes Edith Södergran betrays in the poem. Yet the poet Werner Aspenström defends Edith Södergran's "tone" here, "which is virginally pure and innocent..." (Motsägelser (Stockholm, 1961), p. 42).

22. ES, pp. 165-166. The Hemmer story has been translated by G. C. Schoolfield in Swedo-Finnish Short Stories, pp. 161-174.

23. How puzzling Edith Södergran's allusions to current events could be, even for her contemporaries, is illustrated by the case of "Pansartåget" ("The Armored Train" (SD, 196)). She had heard that the United States government had refused to recognize Finland's independence, and to supply the new nation with grain, as long as German troops were within Finland's borders: "I had fifty cars of hopes loaded for your America. / Sent away, they returned empty." Hagar Olsson (EB, p. 230) confessed that she found the poem "quite strange and unclear," and advised her not to publish it, advice that was followed.

24. "The Translation of the Soul: A Principal Feature of Finland-Swedish Modernism," Scandinavica 15 (1976), 5-27, esp. 9-10, and Kjell Espmark, Själen i bild (Stockholm, 1977), pp. 76-78.

25. Werke, II 283. If Helena Södergran's statement about her daughter's limited Mombert reading is correct (see Chapter IV, Note 8), then the Nietzsche source is the more likely one.

26. SD, p. 166. Espmark takes the composite "kittelgräs" as meaning "tickle-grass" (from Swedish "kittla"). The word has been variously rendered by translators, Karl R. Kern (Feindliche Sterne, p. 55) using "Kitzelgrass" (again "tickle-grass"), but Regis Boyer (Poèmes complets (Paris, 1973), p. 100) has "l'herbe-à-chaudron" ("kettle grass") and Allwood (p. 138) "basin grass."

27. Walter Dickson, "En dikt av Edith Södergran," in his Hjärtfäste och hungertorn (Stockholm, 1953), pp. 22-28. Gunnar Hansson, "Material till en dikt: Läsupplevelser av Edith Södergrans 'Landskap i solnedgång'," in Gunilla and Staffan Bergsten, eds., Lyrik i tid och otid: Lyrikanalytiska studier tillägnade Gunnar Tideström (Lund: Gleerup, 1971), pp. 157-165, has reported on the strikingly disparate reactions of a group of readers to the poem--for example "a vision of judgement day," "old cradle-songs," and "the burning clouds lead one's thoughts in a sexual direction."

28. See Tideström's commentary in SD, p. 408.

29. Quoted in ES, p. 304.

30. Werke, II, 471.

31. Werke, I, 64, where Nietzsche quotes from the famous story, told in Plutarch's Moralia.

32. Werke, II, 519.

33. Bert Kanzog, "Der Gott des Jugendstils in Rilkes Stundenbuch," in Hermand, Jugendenstil, pp. 376-381, esp. 381.

34. Johannes Salminen, "Så har jag åter fot mot jord," in his Levande och död tradition (Helsingfors, 1963), pp. 118-134, esp. 119-120. In his convincing argument, Salminen is preceded by Olof Enckell in "Edith Södergran och den estetiska idealismen," Historiska och litteraturhistoriska studier 33 (1958), 82-99.

35. Klopstock, Sämtliche Werke (Leipzig, 1854), IV, 204-207.

36. See Enckell's analysis in Esteticism, pp. 108-110.

37. Werke, II, 555.

38. Esteticism, p. 115. Gunnar Ekelöf has suggested that Edith Södergran knew the "giant lyres" in the etchings and paintings of Max Klinger (1857-1920) (SAH, p. 16).

39. Note the androgynous nature of the poet, at once "a fair and damned brother of the angels" and "she."

40. Staffan Björck, "Att baka katedraler," in his Lyriska läsövningar: Trettio svenska dikter begrundade (Lund, 1961), pp. 104-108.

41. The novel was published in installments (1913-1914) in the journal, Sirin, of the publishing house of the same name, and issued in book form in 1916.

42. A poem from September, 1918, "Förvandling" ("Transformation," (SD, p. 244)), also has a display of dactyls: "Sjunga i helvetet så de fördömda, / Svarar dem himmelens eko ibland" ("If then, in hell, the damned sing in this fashion / Sometimes the echo of heaven replies"), and so forth.

43. Werke, I, 114.

Chapter Five

1. "Edith Södergran," in Ny generation (Helsingfors, 1925), p. 35, and "Edith Södergran--en bortgången finlandssvensk skaldinna," Clarté 2 (May, 1925), 15-17, esp. 16, reprinted in Ingmar Andersson, ed., Röda pennor: En Clarté-antologi (Stockholm, 1965), pp. 55-59.

2. Cf. EB, 22-26. The letter also contained "Pansartåget" ("The Armored Train") and "Gryningen" ("The Dawn")--both included by Tideström in his edition of Septemberlyran; the poem later called, in its full version, "Var bo gudarna?" ("Where Do the Gods Dwell?") is called "Fragment" here, and "Jorden blev förvandlad till en askhög" is called "På dödens marmorbädd" ("On Death's Marble Couch").

3. "Till de starka" ("To the Strong," SD, p. 234).

4. EB, p. 70, and SD, p. 411 (commentary).

5. Werke, II, 1152-1153.

6. Werke, II, 272-274.

7. "Edith Södergran," Nya Argus 16 (1923).

8. ES, p. 224.

9. The 'heart-poems,' in the order of the present discussion, are "Transformation," "Conjuration," "On foot I had to walk," "In the Fairies' Hammock," "Where Do the Gods Dwell?", "The Chalice of Suffering," and "The Tool's Lament." (See also, in Septemberlyran, the opening of "The Fairest God" (SD, p. 202): "My heart is the fairest in the world. / It is holy. / Whoever sees it must reflect its shine. / My heart is light as a bird.")

10. See Espmark's comment on the poem, in "The Translation of the Soul," Scandinavica 15 (1976), 5, and in Själen i bild, pp. 71-72: "This poem formulates an 'immoderate' emotional experience in concrete words."

11. The line, "Jag anar ren mig själv," has been variously rendered: Samuel Charters (We Women) writes "I already have a presentiment of myself," Allwood: "I already vaguely sense myself," and Keith Bosley (Books from Finland, 12 (1978), 10): "I can already glimpse myself." Mistaking the adverb "ren" ('already') for the adjective "ren" ('pure'), Regis Boyer has "Je m'imagine pure"!

12. In "De främmande länderna" ("The Foreign Lands," SD, p. 90) and "Sjuka dagar" ("Sick Days," SD, pp. 144-145).

13. Werke, II, 474.

14. Werke, II, 462. The sentence continues: "the advocate of the circle."

15. Werke, II, 404.

16. Maj-Britt Lindström offers an interpretation of this difficult poem in "Sången om oceanen," in P. O. Barck et al., Festskrift till Olof Enckell, pp. 203-213.

17. Rosenaltaret (Helsingfors, 1919), pp. 22-23, and EB, p. 24.

18. Werke, I, 30 and 33.

19. Samuel Charters, We Women, n.p.

20. The phrase shows her weakness for "stereotypes and verbal finery." See Walter Dickson, "Schablon och grannlåt hos Edith Södergran," Hjärtfäste och hungertorn, pp. 13-21, and Bo Hakon Jørgensen, "Visionernes dialektik i Edith Södergrans digtning," Kritik 6 (1972), 5-30, esp. 26: "she did not have a language to express the visionary experience...(this lack) kept her from fully understanding what it was she undertook."

21. Edith Södergran (Paris, 1970), p. 155.

22. Fedor Dostoyevsky, Crime and Punishment, tr. by David Magarschack (New York, 1951), p. 341.

23. "Så släpar man motsträvigt med sig en ung, fången barbar." Syntactically, the adverb "motsträvigt" ('reluctantly') seems to modify the verb, 'to pull along,' but the line's sense connects it with the barbarian's behavior. Allwood translates: "So one drags along a young, forced barbarian prisoner." Does Edith Södergran think of German "widerstrebend," a participle ('resisting') used both adverbially and adjectively?

24. ES, p. 149.

25. Werke, III 846 (Der Wille zur Macht).

26. Esteticism, p. 97 and 195.

27. Werke, II, 1159.

28. Tegnér, Samlade skrifter, utg. av Ewert Wrangel och Fredrik Böök (Stockholm, 1921), V, 204-206, ll. 21-22. A related image appears in her first published poem, "Hoppet" ("The Hope," printed in the youthmagazine of the Swedish People's Party, September, 1909): poetic inspiration is "for me, a quaking bridge/ high above life's raging stream." See Helen Svensson, "Två okända dikter av Edith Södergran," Horisont (Vasa) 25 (1978), 6:70-77.

29. See Mariam Faber, Angels of Daring (Stuttgart, 1979), esp. pp. 5-43, for the Nietzschean concept of the tightrope walker.

30. ES, p. 309.

Chapter Six

1. See Chapter III, note 30.

2. Werke, II, 526 ("You creators! You higher men!").

3. Werke, II, 545 ("How he rocks, the blessed, returning one, in his purple saddles!").

4. The word "tvingare" ("forcer") is not a normal word in Swedish. Edith Södergran coined it on the model of German "der Zwinger."

5. Sämtliche Werke, V, 390-392. Regis Boyer, "La structure de l'imaginaire chez Edith Södergran, génie baroque," Etudes Germaniques 26 (1971), 526-549, esp. 537, distinguishes an "inspiration sidérale" in her work.

6. "Säll" is one of Edith Södergran's favorite words, which she also likes to use with the privative prefix: cf. "osäll" (i.e. 'un-blissful') in EB, p. 103, in a description of her mood after the death of her cat.

7. ES, p. 244. In her letters, Edith Södergran—like Hagar Olsson—is often contemptous toward "stupid" Finland. Tua Forsström, Författare om författare, p. 125, remarks on their shared "elitism" and "delusions of grandeur."

8. Werke, II, 480.

9. Werke, II, 478. (See also p. 363, 384, for the same phrase.)

10. H. C. Andersen, Udvalgte Skrifter, ed., Vilhelm Andersen (Copenhagen, 1898), V, 378-385, esp. 384.

11. Esteticism, p. 165.

12. Werke, II, 461. The poem is a more lucid statement of the Nietzschean thoughts with which she had struggled in "Triumph of Existing" (see p. 67).

13. Lars Gustafsson, in "De gåtfulla partiklarna i kärnan," Strandhugg i svensk poesi (Stockholm, 1977), pp. 102-106 (translated by Robert T. Rovinsky as "The Enigmatic Particles in the Nucleus," Forays into Swedish Poetry (Austin and London, 1979), pp. 102-105) discusses Edith Södergran's concept of the will—"It is not death the poet desires"—in connection with the uncollected poem of 1919-1920, "Mitt liv, min död och mitt öde" ("My Life, My Death and My Fate" (SD, p. 285)).

14. Werke, II, 460.

15. In Hans Bethge, Deutsche Lyrik seit Liliencron, p. 211, there is a Mombert poem about a woman's ascent to, and sexual union with, the sun. "On a steep mountain ridge, stretched out mightily, a woman,/ Her soft white body a single, feeling eye (--) / The sun victorious above. The sun victorious, calmly clear. / She quivers, rears, twists! Upward! Shimmering in torment! / Golden streams..."

16. Samlade skrifter (Stockholm, 1954), pp. 97-101. The poem appeared in Fridas bok (Frida's Book, 1922).

17. Esteticism, pp. 152-153.

18. "Edith Södergranin runous," Valvoja-Aika 61 (1941) 420-434, esp. 429.

19. Sämtliche Werke, II, 435-438, esp. 436.

20. See Jens Peter Jacobsen, Niels Lyhne, tr. by Hanna Astrup Larsen (New York, 1967), pp. 42-44.

21. See SD, pp. 414-415 (Tideström's commentary).

22. Enckell, Esteticism, pp. 166-169, and Olof Lagercrantz, "Lekarnas lek," first printed in Dagens Nyheter, May 24, 1953, then revised, in Olof Lagercrantz, Svenska lyriker (Stockholm, 1961), pp. 43-50, and in Tretton lyriker och Fågeltruppen (Stockholm, 1973), pp. 105-110.

23. "Edith Södergran och döden," Dagens Nyheter, June 24, 1953, reprinted in Tidiga fanfarer (Helsingfors, 1953), pp. 199-205.

24. EB, p. 98 (Hagar Olsson's texte de liaison).

25. Werke, I, 48.

26. See Chapter I, p. 19, and EB, p. 52, p. 54.

27. ES, p. 250, Esteticism, pp. 170-172, EB, pp. 98-99.

28. Samlade Skrifter (Stockholm, 1917), XLV, 197. See also Edith Södergran's "Starka hyacinter" in Septemberlyran ("Strong Hyacinths" (SD, p. 167)): "I believe in strong hyacinths which drip primal juice."

29. Tidiga fanfarer, p. 202, EB, p. 99.

30. Gedichte, ed. Emil Staiger (Zürich, 1949), II, 114-120, esp. 119.

31. The phrase ("mitt stoft vill falla sönder") resembles the formulation in "Kärlek" (SD, p. 103): "mina skuldror var gjorda av stoft och smulade sig sönder" ("my shoulders were made of dust and crumbled asunder").

32. Werke, II, 533-536; ES, p. 263; Esteticism, p. 166.

33. "Jaguaren," first in Min dikt (My Poem, Stockholm, 1921), then, expanded, in Hårda sånger (Hard Songs, Helsingfors, 1922), reprinted in Dikter, ed. Olof Enckell (Stockholm, 1956), pp. 35-37.

34. Werke, II, 251, and II, 339.

35. Henri Barbusse (1874-1935), the French author and pacifist, and Hjalmar Branting (1860-1925), the Swedish Social Democrat, co-winner of the Nobel Peace Prize in 1921.

36. Esteticism, p. 174.

37. Enckell, Esteticism, p. 174; Enckell, Den unga Hagar Olsson
(Helsingfors, 1949), pp. 171-172; Tideström, ES, p. 257, Ekelöf,
SAH, 24-25.

38. "En romantisk skaldinna," Svensk nutidsdikt i Finland (Helsingfors, 1928), p. 167.

Chapter Seven

1. ES, pp. 281-282.

2. "Fremmedhedens overvindelse," in Indfaldsvinkler: 16 Fortolk-
ninger af nordisk Digtning tilegnet Oluf Friis (Copenhagen, 1964),
pp. 152-158.

3. As in "Jag" ("I"). See p. 38.

4. Det förklarade ögonblicket: Studier i västerländsk idyll från
Theokritos till Strindberg (Uppsala, 1977), p. 81.

5. Israel Kolmodin (1643-1709), Gabriel Lagus (1837-96).

6. Friedrich Hölderlin, Sämtliche Werke (Leipzig, 1940), p. 558.
Tideström, ES, p. 282, mentions Schiller's concept of "naiveté rewon"
in the same connection.

7. Hans Larsson, Spinoza (Stockholm, 1931), pp. 305-306; Esteticism,
p. 89; Modärn finlandssvensk lyrik, p. 7. The painting from 1885 is
reproduced in Onni Okkonen, A. Gallen-Kallela: Elämä ja taide
(Porvoo and Helsinki, 1949), p. 103.

8. Hans Ruin, Poesiens mystik (Stockholm, 1935, revised edition,
1978), pp. 229-230: "Here, she has reached the highest point--pre-
cisely this: to get us to experience that which she has not been
able to get us to understand."

9. "Edith Södergran--en bortgången finlandssvensk skaldinna,"
Clarté 2 (May, 1925), 17; reprinted in Ingmar Andersson, Röda pennor,
p. 59.

10. Edith Södergrans diktning 1907-1909; I: Inledning och kommentar, p. 234.

11. Ny generation, p. 38.

12. Tidiga fanfarer, p. 205, Svenska lyriker, p. 50.

13. "En romantisk skaldinna," Svensk nutidsdikt i Finland, p. 169.

14. Den unga Hagar Olsson, p. 174.

15. "Edith Södergran" in Sven Møller Kristensen, Fremmede digtere, II, 181.

16. See Göran Lundström, "Edith Södergrans förhållande till rysk lyrik," Poesi 3 (1950), 45. The poem is "Grjozovoe tsartvo" ("The Realm of Dreams") in Gromokipyashchii kubok' (Loud-Foaming Goblet, Moscow, 1915), p. 153.

17. SAH, 6.

18. ES, pp. 290-291.

19. The "child of man" is another detail which can lead in the direction of a religious interpretation: it is the mode of address employed for the prophet Ezekiel in the Old Testament ("människo-barn," "child of man," appears somewhat disguised in the King James version, as "son of man"); it is also the word used in the Swedish version of the passage from Job, quoted above in connection with the poem about the old woman and the cat, where "the son (child) of man is a worm." Entering Edith Södergran's vocabulary fairly late, the composite denoted the human being both in his impotence and in his quality of being elect: "The lightning does with the children of man as it will" ("Thou Mighty Eros"), "We wandering children of man" ("The Net"), "Child of man, hide your countenance before the incom-prehensible" ("The Star"); in her last phase, she uses it for the human being as, literally, a child, before the loss of its community with nature: "the crown which crowns a child of man in tender years" ("Oh Heavenly Clarity").

20. The language of the last poem is quite close to that in the deathbed letter written by the tubercular heroine of Knut Hamsun's Victoria (1898): "Last night I thought my final hour had come...it was as though I already heard eternity rushing toward me, far out... But Mama believes that it was perhaps only the river and the falls at home which I remembered."

Chapter Eight

1. Modern finlandssvensk litteratur (Stockholm, 1951), p. 28.

2. Holmqvist, p. 48; Thomas Warburton, Finlandssvensk litteratur 1898-1948 (Helsingfors, 1951), p. 218, calls her "the poetic awak-ener, who heralds and introduces a new epoch..."

3. See Leif Sjöberg, A Reader's Guide to Gunnar Ekelöf's A Mölna Elegy (New York, 1973), p. 38, pp. 46-47, p. 126, p. 136, pp. 143-144, p. 146, and the translation by Muriel Rukeyser and Leif Sjöberg, Comparative Criticism: A Yearbook 1 (1979), 215-269.

4. Fremmede digtere i det 20. århundrede, II, 169.

5. See Chapter Four, Note 21, for Aspenström's defense of Edith Södergran.

6. Finlands moderna litteratur, p. 197.

7. A translation of Carpelan's poem, by Pekka Virtanen, is included in Richard Dauenhauer and Philip Binham, Snow in May: An Anthology of Finnish Writing 1945-1972 (Cranbury, New Jersey, 1978), p. 186.

8. "40-talisme", Samtiden 56 (1947), 632-644, esp. 633.

9. See Kenneth Chapman, Tarjei Vesaas (TWAS, 100, New York, 1969), p. 101.

10. See also Halldis Moren Vesaas' essay on the poetry of the oil-cloth notebook, "Ei skrivebok med svarte permar," Syn og Segn 68 (1962), 167-172.

11. In his Fragmenter af en Dagbok (Fragments of a Diary, 1948, p. 66), la Cour writes: "The peaks of modern Scandinavian poetry (are) Fröding and Södergran, the great singers of sincerity."

12. Mogens Brøndsted, Nordens Litteratur efter 1860 (Copenhagen, Oslo, Lund, 1972), II, 269, speaks of his relationship to Edith Södergran's "life-ecstasy"; her formal influence on his work is also palpable.

13. His poem on Edith Södergran is at the conclusion of Bo Hakon Jørgensen's essay (see Chapter Five, note 20); a poem by Jens Lund Andersen, "Edith Södergran," may also be found in Bjørnvig's distinguished journal, Heretica 1 (1948), 209-211. In his essay on Paul la Cour, in Fredrik Nielsen and Ole Restrup, eds., Danske digtere i det 20. århundrede (Copenhagen, 1965-66), III, 138, Bjørnvig says: "In my opinion, absolute mastery of the short poem has been attained by one poet in the North, Edith Södergran."

14. Hans Magnus Enzensberger, Museum der modernen Poesie (Munich, 1964), contains five poems of Edith Södergran, three translated by Nelly Sachs, two by Enzensberger.

15. Poul Borum, Poetisk modernisme (Copenhagen, 1966), pp. 69-70 and 90.

16. Quoted in Sjöberg, A Reader's Guide to Gunnar Ekelöf's A Mölna Elegy, p. 47.

17. Anna Achmatova (1889-1966). Ekelöf's comparison is apt: both poets wrote about their erotic experiences frankly and unforgettably, both experienced the Russian Revolution at first hand. A comparison of Edith Södergran's work with that of another Russian contemporary, Marina Tsvetayeva (1892-1941), would also be illuminating.

Bibliography

Primary Sources

The standard edition of the poems is by Gunnar Tideström, Samlade dikter (Stockholm first edition, 1949, second edition, 1950), with a textual critical commentary. The Samlade dikter also include Brokiga iakttagelser of 1919 and the late aphorisms, "Tankar om naturen." Subsequently, the text--but not the commentary--of the Tideström edition has been reprinted by Wahlström & Widstrand (1958 and thereafter). The earlier "collected poems"--Edith Södergrans dikter (1940, third edition, 1946), a reprinting of the five poetry collections as they appeared during the poet's lifetime, Brokiga iakttagelser, and the text of the posthumous Landet som icke är--have been altogether superseded by Tideström's work.

The adolescent poetry has been edited by Olof Enckell, Edith Södergrans dikter 1907-1909, I: Inledning och kommentar; II: Texten (Helsingfors, 1961). The letters to Hagar Olsson, with textes-de-liaison by the surviving partner, have been printed as Ediths brev (Stockholm and Helsingfors, 1955). A complete edition of all extant letters from and to Edith Södergran, with scholarly commentary, is a desideratum.

Translations

Martin Allwood, in collaboration with Cate Ewing and Robert Lyng, has translated The Collected Poems of Edith Södergran (Mullsjö, 1980). The translation is generally dependable; however, it is incomplete, since it uses Edith Södergrans dikter of 1940/1946 as its basis (see the review by G. C. Schoolfield, World Literature Today 56 (Spring, 1982), 374-375). Stina Katchadourian offers excellent renderings of 31 early and late poems (with facing Swedish texts) in Love and Solitude: Selected Poems 1916-1923 (San Francisco: Fjord Press, 1981); it is discussed by G. C. Schoolfield in Scandinavian Review 70 (1982), 84-86. A new translation by David McDuff, Edith Södergran (London: Bloodaxe Books) has been announced for the summer of 1983.

See also:

Jaakko A. Ahokas, "I Saw a Tree . . . ," "Pain," "Hope," "A Decision," in Carol Cosman, Joan Keefe, and Kathleen Weaver, eds., The Penguin Book of Women Poets (Harmondsworth, 1979), pp. 229-231.

Malin Berman and Kenneth Gee, "My Artificial Flowers," "The Autumn Days," "Happiness," "Love," "Tantalus, Fill Your Cup," "Animal Hymn," "Lightning," "The Gipsy," Swedish Books 2 (March, 1980), 28-37.

Keith Bosley, "The Day Cools . . . ," "O My Peaks Tinged with the Sun's Fire," "The Moon's Secret," "The Reflecting Well," "I Had to Tramp through Solar Systems," "The Earth Was Transformed into an Ash-heap," "The Mystery," and "The Land That Is Not," Books from Finland 12 (1978), 8-11 (with an introductory essay by Gladys Hird).

Samuel Charters, We Women: Selected Poems of Edith Södergran (Berkeley, 1977). (See the review by G. C. Schoolfield, Scandinavian Studies 51 (1979), 319-323.)

Frederic Fleisher, "The Day Is Cooling," "The Last Blossom of Summer," "The Stars," "Love," "The Mirroring Well," "Three Sisters," "Loneliness," "Return Home," "There is no one in the world who has time. . . ," and "The Land That Is Not," in his Eight Swedish Poets (Stockholm, 1963), pp. 119-130.

Fritz König, "The Land That Is Not," "The Fair Daughter of the Forest," Micromegas 4 (1969), 12-13.

Sheila La Farge, "Northern Spring," "The Day Cools Down," American-Scandinavian Review 62 (1974), 38-39.

Rika Lesser, "Nothing," Swedish Books 2 (March, 1980), 26-27 (with an introductory note).

David McDuff, "I Saw a Tree," "I," "Violet Dusks," "The Bull," "Two Ways," "The King's Sorrow," and "To All Four Winds," Modern Poetry in Translation (Summer, 1973), 7-8.

Christer L. Mossberg, "Vierge Modern," and "I'll Bake Cathedrals," Folio: Papers on Language and Literature (1978), 127-128.

No full translation of the poems into Finland's majority language exists; however, Edith Södergran's work has attracted Finnish

translators who are,or were, distinguished poets in their own right.
Uuno Kailas (1901-1933) translated seventy-seven poems as Levottomia
unia (Restless Dreams, Helsinki, 1929); Aale Tynni (1913-   ) con-
tributed 35 poems to Nils-Börje Stormbom's Suomenruotsalaisen
lyriikan antologia Edith Södergranista Bo Carpelaniin (Anthology of
Finland's Swedish Lyric from Edith Södergran to Bo Carpelan, Helsinki, 1968); Pentti Saaritsa (1941-   ) presented 52 poems in his
selection, Tulevaisuuden varjo (The Shadow of the Future, Helsinki,
1972).

In French, the late Pierre Naert issued a generous selection in
1954, as Poèmes du pays qui n'est pas; it contains, in Naert's
phrase, "about seven-tenths" of the poems in Tideström's edition.
Regis Boyer brought out the Poèmes complets in 1973, also including
the aphorisms.

Edith Södergran was introduced to a German public fairly early,
with an article by Friedrich Ege, "Zwei Frühvollendete: Edith Södergran und Uuno Kailas--die Gestalter der modernen Dichtung Finnlands,"
Dichtung und Volkstum (Euphorion) 42 (1942), 54-76. At about the
same time, Södergran's work attracted the attention of a major poet,
Nelly Sachs (1891-1970), who had been brought to Sweden in 1940
through the intercession of Selma Lagerlöf; the fruit of Sachs'
enthusiasm was collected in her Schwedische Gedichte (Neuwied and
Berlin, 1965), where there are 27 poems by Edith Södergran--marred
by numerous howlers. A more accurate and a complete rendering is
that of Karl R. Kern, aided by Margareta Schlüter, Feindliche Sterne:
Gesammelte Gedichte (Wiesbaden and Munich, 1977). (See the review
by G. C. Schoolfield in Scandinavian Studies 51 (1979), 323-325.)

Translations into Danish (Samlede digte, by Peer Sibast, 1979)
and Russian (Vozvrashtsheniye domoj (Home-Coming), by Michael Dudin,
1980) exist; Jocelyne Fernandez, in her informative account of the
foreign reception of Edith Södergran, "Présence rimbaldienne d'une
Vierge moderne: Ou Edith Södergran et la critique étrangère," Scandinavica 15 (1976), 107-121, esp. 119, note 2, lists translations
(in book-form) into Greek and Slovakian.

Secondary Sources

Andersen, Jens K. "Farvesymbolikken i Edith Södergrans debutsamling," Edda 73 (1973), 13-23.

Björck, Staffan. "Att baka katedraler," in Björck, Lyriska läsövningar (Lund: Gleerup, 1961), pp. 104-108. (On "Förhoppning.")

Boyer, Regis. "Les structures de l'imaginaire chez Edith Södergran, génie baroque." Etudes Germaniques 26 (1971), 524-549.

Breitholtz, Lennart. "'Dagen svalnar'," in Gunnar Hansson, ed.,
Tjugotvå diktanalyser (Stockholm: Aldus, 1968), pp. 95-103,
reprinted in Breitholtz, Monsieur Bovary och andra essayer (Stockholm: Aldus, 1969), pp. 191-200.

Brostrøm, Torben. "Digteren på trampolinerne," <u>Vindrosen</u> 13
(1966), 4: 39-47, reprinted in Brostrøm, <u>Labyrint og Arabesk</u> (Copenhagen: Gyldendal, 1966), pp. 126-137.

Carpelan, Bo. "Edith Södergran" in Matti Kuusi et al., eds.,
<u>Suomen kirjallisuus</u> (Helsinki: Otava, 1970), VI, 203-226.

Dickson, Walter. "Schablon och grannlåt hos Edith Södergran"
and "En Södergran-dikt" in Dickson, <u>Hjärtfäste och hungertorn</u> (Stockholm: Tidens Förlag, 1953), pp. 13-21, 22-28. (On "Se i solned-
gången...")

Ekelöf, Gunnar. "Edith Södergran studier," <u>Svenska Akademiens
Handlingar</u> 75 (1967), 3-26. (Collective reprinting of Ekelöf's three
essays on Södergran.)

Enckell, Olof. <u>Esteticism och nietzscheanism i Edith Södergrans
lyrik</u> (Helsingfors: Svenska Litteratursällskapet i Finland, 1949).

Enckell, Olof. "Edith Södergran och den estetiska idealismen,"
<u>Historiska och litteraturhistoriska studier</u> 33 (1958), 82-99. (Edith
Södergran and Schiller.)

Enckell, Olof. <u>Edith Södergrans dikter 1907-1909, I: Inledning
och kommentar</u> (Helsingfors: Svenska Litteratursällskapet i Finland,
1961).

Espmark, Kjell. "The Translation of the Soul: A Principle Feature in Finland-Swedish Modernism." <u>Scandinavica</u> 15 (1976), 5-27.

Espmark, Kjell. <u>Själen i bild: En huvudlinje i modern svensk
poesi</u> (Stockholm: Norstedt, 1977), pp. 71-85.

Fages, Loup de. <u>Edith Södergran</u> (Paris: Debresse, 1970).

Fernandez, Jocelyne. "Présence rimbaldienne d'une Vierge
moderne: Ou Edith Södergran et la critique étrangère," <u>Scandinavica</u>
15 (1976), 105-121.

Forsström, Tua. "Den heta villan," in Merete Mazzarella et al.,
<u>Författare om författare</u> (Helsingfors: Söderström, 1980), pp. 120-
126.

Geijerstam, Carl-Erik Af. "Edith Södergran: 'O mina solbrandsfärgade toppar'." In Geijerstam et al., <u>Lyrisk tidsspegel</u> (Lund:
Gleerup, first edition, 1947, second edition, 1971), pp. 66-69.

Gustafsson, Lars. "The Enigmatic Particles in the Nucleus," in
Gustafsson, <u>Forays into Swedish Poetry</u>, tr. by Robert T. Rovinsky
(Austin and London: University of Texas Press, 1979), pp. 100-105.

Jørgensen, Bo Hakon. "Visionernes dialektik i Edith Södergrans
digtning," <u>Kritik</u> 6 (1972), 24, 5-30.

Julén, Björn. "Edith Södergran: 'Den speglande brunnen'," in Julén, Tjugo diktanalyser från Södergran till Tranströmer (Stockholm: Svenska Bokförlaget / Bonniers, 1963), 1-9.

Lagercrantz, Olof. "Lekarnas lek," in Lagercrantz, Svenska lyriker (Stockholm: Wahlström & Widstrand, 1961), pp. 41-50, reprinted in Tretton lyriker och Fågeltruppen (Stockholm: Wahlström & Widstrand, 1973), pp. 105-110.

Larsen, Finn Stein. "Et grundmønster i Edith Södergrans første digtning," Edda 58 (1958), 298-309. Basic situations in Edith Södergran's Dikter.

Larsen, Finn Stein. "Edith Södergran" in Sven Møller Kristensen, ed., Fremmede digtere i det 20. århundrede (Copenhagen: Gyldendal, 1967), II, 169-173.

Lindberger, Örjan and Reidar Ekner. Att läsa poesi: Metoder för analys (Stockholm: Svenska Bokförlaget / Bonniers, 1965, second edition), pp. 121-122. (On "Helvetet.")

Lindström, Maj-Britt. "Sången om oceanen--revolution och sublimation," in P. O. Barck et al., eds., Festskrift till Olof Enckell 12.3.1970 (Helsingfors: Svenska litteratursällskapet i Finland, 1970), pp. 203-213.

Loesch, Lise. "Eventyr og utopi: To sider av kvindebilledet hos Edith Södergran," Edda 72 (1972), 293-303.

Lundström, Göran. "Edith Södergrans förhållande till rysk poesi," Poesi 3 (1950), 43-53.

Nag, Martin. "Russiske impulser hos Edith Södergran," Ordet: Tidskrift for fri sprogutvikling 22 (1971), 196-212.

Salminen, Johannes. "Så har jag åter fot mot jord," in Salminen, Levande och död tradition (Helsingfors: Söderström, 1963), pp. 118-134.

Schoolfield, G. C. "Edith Södergran's 'Wallenstein-profil'," in Carl F. Bayerschmidt and Erik J. Friis, eds., Scandinavian Studies: Essays Presented to Henry Goddard Leach (New York and Seattle: American-Scandinavian Foundation and University of Washington Press, 1965), pp. 278-292.

Svanfeldt, Gunnar. "Edith Södergran: 'Ingenting'," in Carl-Erik af Geijerstam et al., Lyrisk tidsspegel (Lund: Gleerup, first edition, 1947, second edition, 1971), pp. 64-65.

Svensson, Helen. "Två okända dikter av Edith Södergran," Horisont (Vasa) 25 (1978), 6: 70-77.

Tideström, Gunnar. "Edith Södergran: Dagen svalnar...," "Jag," in Carl-Erik af Geijerstam, Lyrisk tidsspegel (Lund: Gleerup, first edition, 1947, second edition, 1971), pp. 55-60, pp. 61-63.

Tideström, Gunnar. Edith Södergran (Stockholm: Wahlström &
Widstrand, 1949).

Tottie, Thomas. "Edith Södergran och förlaget," Bonniers
Litterära Magasin 26 (1957), 238-248.

Werin, Algot. "Mitt liv var en het villa," in Werin, Vandring
kring en sjö (Lund: Gleerup, 1967), pp. 169-177.

Wrede, Johan. "Illusion-utopi-realism: Edith Södergran, Hagar
Olsson och Finland omkring 1920," Finsk tidskrift 195-196 (1974),
273-282.

Wrede, Johan. "Tidskriften Ultra," in P. O. Barck et al., eds.,
Festskrift till Olof Enckell 12.3.1970 (Helsingfors: Svenska Litteratursällskapet i Finland, 1970), pp. 145-165.

Wrede, Johan. "The Birth of Finland-Swedish Modernism," Scandinavica 15 (1976), 73-103.

Index

About the Author

GEORGE C. SCHOOLFIELD is Professor of German and Scandinavian Literature at Yale University. He has written *The Figure of the Musician in German Literature, The German Lyric of the Baroque, Rilke's Last Year, Swedo-Finnish Short Stories, Janus Secundus, The Woodcarver and Death, Soren Kierkegaard: The Myths and Their Origins,* and numerous articles.